The Fool and His Scepter

# The Fool and His Scepter

A Study in Clowns

and Jesters

and Their Audience

By William Willeford

Northwestern University Press       1969

William Willeford is a member of the Department of English of the
University of Washington and a psychotherapist in private practice.


The drawing on the title page and on the binding case is a free adaptation of
a device used as a watermark in Germany during the sixteenth century.

The picture of Danny Kaye in Plate 4 is from the film *The Merry Andrew,*
released by M-G-M in 1958, and is reproduced by permission of Danny Kaye
and Metro-Goldwyn-Mayer, Inc.

Stanzas from W. B. Yeats's poem "The Cap and Bells," from *The Collected
Poems of W. B. Yeats,* are reprinted with permission of Mr. M. B. Yeats,
Macmillan & Co., Ltd., London, and The Macmillan Company of New York.
Copyright 1906 by The Macmillan Company renewed 1934 by William Butler
Yeats.

# Acknowledgments

## Literary sources:

Permission to quote from the following works has been granted by the publishers: Mircea Eliade, *Images and Symbols,* copyright © 1961, The Harvill Press Ltd., London. Desidirius Erasmus, *The Praise of Folly,* trans. Hoyt Hopewell Hudson, copyright © 1941, Princeton University Press. Robert Payne, *The Great Charlie,* 1952, André Deutsch Limited, London; the American edition of this work, *The Great God Pan: A Biography of the Tramp Played by Charlie Chaplin,* was published by Hermitage House, 1952, permission granted by Bertha Klausner Agency, Inc. Herbert Weisinger, *Tragedy and the Paradox of the Fortunate Fall,* Michigan State University Press, 1953. Enid Welsford, *The Fool,* Faber & Faber, London, 1935, reissued in 1968, permission granted by Curtis Brown, Ltd.

## Illustrations:

PLATE 1. Photograph of Alberto Fratellini by Frank Horvat (Magnum), accompanying the article "Ce Soir les Clowns Ont Envie de Pleurer," by Dominique Lapierre, *Paris Match,* No. 623 / 27 (May, 1961). Reproduced by permission of Frank Horvat.

PLATE 2. Quinten Massys, "An Allegory of Folly," from the Julius S. Held Collection, New York. Reproduced by permission of Mr. Held.

PLATE 3. Jacob Jordaens, "Folly," engraved by Alexander Voet. Reproduced by permission of the Graphische Sammlung, Eidgenössische Technische Hochschule, Zürich.

PLATE 5. Alchemical *prima materia* as globe, illustration to Johann Daniel Mylius, *Philosophia reformata* (Frankfort, 1622), p. 96, Fig. 1. Photograph provided by courtesy of the Bollingen Foundation. This picture appears as Figure 163 in Carl G. Jung, *Psychology and Alchemy,* Volume XII of *The Collected Works of C. G. Jung* (Bollingen Series XX), 2d rev. ed., copyright © 1968 by Princeton University Press.

PLATE 6a. Domenico Locatelli as Trivelino. Engraving by Prudhon. Photo Hachette. Reproduced by permission of Librairie Hachette.

# Acknowledgments

PLATES 8 and 9. Marginal illustrations by Hans Holbein the Younger for Erasmus' *Praise of Folly*. Reproduced by permission of the Kupferstichkabinett Basel.

PLATE 11. Advertisement printed in the London *Observer*, November 29, 1964, p. 24.

PLATE 12. Austrian Tarot card. Reproduced by permission of the Kunsthistorisches Museum, Vienna.

PLATE 13. A. Watteau, "Italian Comedians," engraved and etched by Bernard Baron. Reproduced by permission of the Graphische Sammlung, Eidgenössische Technische Hochschule, Zürich.

PLATES 14 and 15. Title pages to a French history of Till Eulenspiegel printed by Simon Caluarin, *ca.* 1580, and to a Dutch history printed by Elzevir, 1703, used as illustrations in Helmut Wiemken (ed.), *Die Volksbücher von Till Ulenspiegel, Hans Clawert und den Schildbürgern* (Bremen: Carl Schünemann Verlag, 1962). Reproduced by permission of Mr. Wiemken.

PLATES 16 and 26. Illustrations from E. Gherardi, *Le Théâtre italien . . .* (Paris, 1717).

PLATE 17. The Rastelli troupe. Photograph copyright © Barnet Saidman and reproduced by permission of Mr. Saidman.

PLATE 18. Till Eulenspiegel doll, manufactured by Helen Diemer, Switzerand.

PLATE 19. Cartoon by Hans Haëm published in the *Nebelspalter* (weekly magazine), Rorschach, Switzerland, January 8, 1964, p. 28. Reproduced by permission of the *Nebelspalter*.

PLATE 20. Cartoon by Michael ffolkes, *Punch,* May 22, 1963, p. 739. Reproduced by permission of the Toronto Telegram News Service.

PLATE 22. Death as a jester, a drawing by Alfred Kubin, drawing No. XV in his book *Ein Totentanz: Die Blätter mit dem Tod,* published in 1965 by the Diogenes Verlag Zürich. First published by Bruno Cassirer, Berlin, in 1918 and 1925. Reproduced by permission of the Diogenes Verlag.

PLATE 23. Ink drawing by Hans Holbein the Younger. Reproduced by permission of the Kupferstichkabinett Basel.

PLATE 24. King with sprouting lance, Codex Monacensis Cat. 7383, from Kloster Hohenwart in Bavaria, first half of the twelfth century. Reproduced by permission of the Bayerische Staatsbibliothek München.

PLATE 25. Fools in nest, from Jean Bénigne Lucotte Du Tillot, *Mémoires pour servir à l'histoire de la Fête des Foux* (Lausanne and Geneva: Bousquet, 1751), Plate 4.

PLATE 27. Alchemical hermaphrodite on globed chaos, illustration to Herbrandt Jamsthaler, *Viatorium spagyricum. Das ist: Ein gebenedeyter spagyrischer Wegweiser* (Frankfort a.M., 1625), p. 75. Photograph provided by courtesy of the Bollingen Foundation. This picture appears as Figure 199 in Carl G. Jung, *Psychology and Alchemy,* Volume XII of *The Collected Works of C. G. Jung*

# Acknowledgments

(Bollingen Series XX), 2d rev. ed., copyright © 1968 by Princeton University Press.

PLATE 28. Jörg Schneider in a scene from Zürcher Ballade, 1966, photograph copyright © Hertha Ramme. Reproduced by permission of Foto Hertha Ramme, Zürich.

PLATE 29. Fool with naked woman, woodcut by unknown German master, photograph from Rudolph Z. Becker (ed.), *Holzschnitte alter deutscher Meister in den Original-Platten gesammelt* . . . (Gotha, 1808–16), Plate D 7.

PLATE 30. Fool and young mother, drawing by Urs Graf. Reproduced by permission of the Kupferstichkabinett Basel.

PLATE 31. Jacob Jordaens, "The Consequences of Wine," engraved by Paulus Pontius. Reproduced by permission of the Graphische Sammlung, Eidgenössische Technische Hochschule, Zürich.

PLATE 32. Voli Geiler and Walter Morath, photograph from Siegfried Melchinger and Willy Jäggi, *Harlekin: Bilderbuch der Spassmacher* (Basel: Basilius Presse, 1959), p. 138. Reproduced by permission of Basilius Presse AG Basel.

PLATE 33. Wheel of Fortune with kings, illustration from the title page of the *Carmina Burana,* Codex Monacensis Cat. 4660, fol. 1r. Reproduced by permission of the Bayerische Staatsbibliothek München.

PLATES 34 and 35. Illustrations to Sebastian Brant, *Das Narrenschiff,* printed by Johann Bergmann, Basel, 1494.

# Preface

It has been a great pleasure to read—indeed I may say to study—this fascinating book, in which Dr. Willeford examines "certain questions of 'why' which may still be profitably asked" about the nature of "the Fool and his Scepter" and the secret of his enduring popularity. Why are we so attracted to the clowns and jesters "who from widely diverse times and places reveal such striking similarities"? What is the significance of the "interactions between the fool actor and the audience of his show"? These questions are by no means simple, but recalling with respect "an earlier conception according to which folly is one of the supreme facts about human nature, perhaps even about the world," Dr. Willeford believes that they are well worth answering and sets out "to trace our relations, conscious and unconscious, to the kinds of experience upon which that conception was based." For this purpose he uses his expertise as a critic of literature and his training and experience as a psychotherapist to analyze data drawn from a field wide enough to include ritual clowning of primitive societies, "fool literature" and court jesters of the Middle Ages and Renaissance, Shakespearean tragedies, comic turns and vaudeville sketches drawn from the modern circus, stage, and screen. His book begins and ends with a meditation on the cock-cry of a dancing fool, who boarded a tram in Zurich, and his diagnoses of folly based on detailed examination of the sovereign fool in *Lear,* on the antics of Charlie Chaplin and Buster Keaton in the film *Limelight,* and of Valentin and Karlstadt in *The Bewitched Music Stands* are all in their different ways equally subtle and original. Through these and many other examples drawn from a great variety of sources, including numerous intriguing and very revealing pictorial illustrations, Dr. Willeford exhibits both the entertaining and the numinous character of the fool and his mysteriously ambiguous position on the

ix

borderline between good and evil, order and chaos, reality and illusion, existence and nothingness.

His conclusions may not in every case command assent. I find myself, for instance, in definite disagreement with his interpretation of the dialogue between Lear's fool and Kent in the stocks; I am not wholly convinced by his study of the "tragic dimension of Folly" in *Hamlet;* and I venture to think that at times he disregards the straightforward interpretation and human interest of a dramatic episode in his zeal to uncover its symbolical and psychological significance. I must confess, however, that on rereading the passages that have aroused these misgivings I have almost always found that they open up a fresh point of view and provide food for further meditation.

It has, I fear, proved impossible to give, in a short preface, anything but a most inadequate account of its rich contents; but I am grateful for this opportunity of recording my enjoyment of Dr. Willeford's enlightening and thought-provoking study of *The Fool and His Scepter.*

ENID WELSFORD

# Contents

# Illustrations

## Illustrations

# Introduction

The fools and instances of folly that I will discuss come from a variety of sources: records of folk festivals and court jesters, the fool literature of the late Middle Ages and early Renaissance, plays by Shakespeare and others, jokes, vaudeville and circus-clown skits, slapstick films, playing cards, paintings, and magazine cartoons. These have all been treated before in historical descriptions of fools and their kinds and in psychological studies of humor and laughter. In this study I will attempt to relate fools and instances of folly to a fundamental type, the fool of the title, and sketch the context of his folly and the functions it fulfills in art and life. This context includes the settings in which fools appear (for example, the circus or the court of a king) and the psychological sources of our response to fools (for example, hopes and fears and patterns of thought and decorum that they may play with). In describing fools and folly in this way I am concerned with certain questions of "why?" that may still be profitably asked. *Why is the fool, as bumpkin, merrymaker, trickster, scourge, and scapegoat, such an often recurring figure in the world and in our imaginative representations of it? Why do fools from widely diverse times and places reveal such striking similarities? Why are we, like people in many other times and places, fascinated by fools?* These are really questions about what fools are in their effect upon us, about the interactions between the fool actor and the audience of his show. I pose these questions out of respect for an earlier conception according to which folly is one of the supreme facts about human nature, perhaps even about the world. I wish to trace our relations, conscious and unconscious, to the kinds of experience upon which that conception was based.

We have all seen circus clowns threatening to drag a spectator off with them; this business goes back at least to the Middle Ages, when theatrical clown devils snatched at spectators as though to haul them into

Hell-Mouth (for example, in the Towneley play *The Judgment*). Such clowning is probably much older still, and it is very common outside of western Europe (for example, among the Pueblo Indians). We have all seen two circus clowns shaving a third with enormous razors and buckets of suds, a skit that has surely been presented in every modern circus. (One circus director grew so tired of it that he forbade it for a period of five years, only to have clowns then in his employ, the Fratellinis, flaunt his ruling and bring down the house.) Barbershop clowning appeared in the commedia dell'arte and in a number of English plays, as early as Richard Edward's *Damon and Pithias* (1563); it also occurs in Marston's *The Dutch Courtezan* (1603-4) and Ford's *The Fancies Chaste and Noble* (printed 1638), and it has been taken up by several film comedians, among them (with exquisite sadism) W. C. Fields. The temporal and spatial distribution of clownish threats to the audience and of the barber routine tells us nothing about why they are funny, but it tells us that they are relatively typical, in one way or another, of the bond between clowns and their audiences.

If we concern ourselves with the meaning of such clowning, with the reasons for its persistence or recurrence, with the way in which an individual clown takes it up, refines it, and makes it personal, and with its effects upon us, we are concerned with typical traits of fools and folly. The fool as a type—or more narrowly, this or that type of fool—is drawn from elements reiterated in what fools have said and done, in their dress and manner, and in their procedures in making a show of folly. The description of the type concentrates our attention upon correspondences, variations, and contrasts among these elements, and this concentration of attention should deepen our conscious relationship to folly. One main reason for considering the fool as a type is heuristic: as we study formal relations among different fool figures we notice phenomena that we would otherwise overlook and raise questions that we would otherwise not raise. Another main reason for considering the fool as a type is interpretative: some of the forms that thus emerge are, one may reasonably believe, attributes of folly as an abiding possibility of human experience. If we are aware of these attributes of folly, we are able to place particular instances of it in the context of wider human interests and concerns. In doing so, we will finally reach a point where we experience folly as a reality that cannot be captured in a description, as it belongs too much to the basic texture of our lives. We will have respected the refusal of Erasmus' Mother of Fools to "expound myself by definition, much less divide myself. For it is equally unlucky to circumscribe with a limit her whose nature extends so universally or to dissect her in whose worship every order of being is at one." [1]

We worship folly by seeing it in people and in the world and by willingly displaying it in ourselves. This complex enterprise, which implies the roles of audience and fool actor, is basically symbolic, as should become clear in the course of this study. I am here using the word "symbolic" in a sense that was earlier common but is now much less so. Goethe conveys this sense when he writes, "Symbolism transforms the phenomenon into idea and the idea into image; in the image the idea remains infinitely effective and unattainable and even when expressed in all languages remains inexpressible." [2] In other words, the symbol contains an element that is ahistorical and transcendent, and this is the source of its deepest effect on us. Regarded psychologically, the symbol expresses a basic and *a priori* mode of psychic functioning and of adaptation to the world. (The maladaptation of most fools is also a kind of adaptation.) Insofar as folly is symbolic it may be said, following C. G. Jung, to have an archetypal foundation. In his use of the term "archetype" Jung in turn follows various early writers, among them Irenaeus, who conjectured that "the creator of the world did not fashion these things directly from himself, but copied them from archetypes outside himself." [3] Applying this metaphor to the nature of the psyche, Jung writes that "what we mean by 'archetype' is in itself irrepresentable, but has effects which make visualizations of it possible, namely, the archetypal images and ideas." [4]

In trying to understand materials that are symbolic in this sense we must, I believe, alternate between two processes of understanding: that of abstraction and that of what is in German called *Einfühlung,* a form of imagination by which we feel our way into the object in its manifold relations to the world and let it become part of our inner life. [5] In forming a concept of something that has an archetypal effect we are drawing a distinction between what it is as a fact that may be known objectively and what it is as a content of subjective, personal experience. In doing this we are in some measure rendering it nonsymbolic, because we make a distinction between subject and object that is not present in our experience of the symbol. We cannot know what it is without being gripped by it, but we cannot form an unambiguous concept of the condition of being gripped or of the thing that grips us. Jung in many places describes the symbol under the aspect of the *coincidentia oppositorum,* the symbol forming a bridge between otherwise irreconcilable meanings. The psychic functions of abstraction and *Einfühlung* tend to be in one sense mutually exclusive, in another complementary, in the total workings of the psyche. Thus the ambiguous, even self-contradictory, nature of the symbol *as a content* has its counterpart in the ambiguity, and even self-contradiction, attendant upon our *understanding* of the symbol.

Empathic imagination (or *Einfühlung*) is, then, as necessary to an adequate understanding of symbolism as is intellectual judgment, since neither process can be reduced to the other. This necessity may be illustrated by an analogy from the realm of folly: we cannot describe a joke and its workings unless we get the point of it. If we do get the point of it, we were, while we laughed, inside the thing we wish to describe, and our description will have little meaning unless it conveys a lively awareness of that experience. Something that is deeply symbolic does not have a single point to get; rather, it presents us with facets behind which the effective core remains inaccessible. (No one succeeds in writing the last critical comment on *Hamlet,* and in every theatrical production of *King Lear* the Fool turns up in a different guise.)

To arrive at anything like an adequate understanding of a recurrent and powerful imaginative form, we must compare similar materials and analyze the psychic processes by which we (and others) relate to them and through them to the form. Similarity is, of course, not identity—the fool in a medieval play is not the same figure as a clown in a Pueblo Indian ceremony; and the psychological analysis of symbolism is limited by difficulties that I have already suggested. Nonetheless, the historical method characteristic of most of the good books that have been written about fools and folly also encounters difficulties and also has limits. These are well described by J. I. M. Stewart, writing of Shakespeare: "It is only too probable that what [the historical critic] would have us accept as a criterion [of a Shakespearean performance] is simply what he conjectures was felt, expected, taken for granted. And thus, at the best, he will stop short just where the dramatist himself must be supposed to begin." [6] From that beginning Shakespeare went on to make something that reached to the depths of his audience. The same depths are alive in us, and our principal connection with Shakespeare's fools and with many of the other fools to be met in the following pages is through them. I assume, then, that we may compare materials from different cultural and historical contexts, that we may find the similarities among them as impressive as the differences, and that we may be interested in the ways in which different but similar materials express basic psychic processes in different but similar ways. The nature of my own interest in fools and folly, and the focus of this book, may become clearer to the reader if I say that I am a student and teacher of literature and drama who has for several years worked as a psychotherapist in psychiatric clinics and in private practice. In a psychiatric clinic one becomes acquainted as a matter of life and death with irrational forces, their profundity, their contagiousness, and their power to create and destroy psychic and other structures (for example, the social structure of the family). There are moments when the atmosphere in a psychiatric clinic has much in common with the madhouses from which such clinics have developed. A madhouse contained people who were thought to be fools, as is suggested by the French *maison des fous* or "house of fools"; and modern psychologists are partly concerned with what was earlier known as folly.

The limited "explanation" of fools and folly to be found in these pages is thus primarily psychological rather than historical, anthropological, or sociological. Psychological and social phenomena are interrelated, and the psychological comments I make will often have a social implication.

Fools have their own characteristic kind of good luck, a providence that allows the clown to survive his pratfalls and the bumps on his head, the jester the rebukes and whippings of his master, and Lear's companion even the fury of Nature or the gods. The luck of fools also allows them to elude nonfools, and their elusiveness has often expressed itself in semianonymity. Some have been nameless, "only fools," and others have borne pseudonyms, as clowns do still in the circus, often less names than preforms or echoes of names in baby talk or idiotic gibberish. And whether they have had "real" names or not, fools have generally lacked the kind of fully established personal and social identities that can be made the subjects of biography or history. But despite the anonymity and pseudonymity of many fools and the ephemeral nature of much of what they have said and done, they have left many traces, and those traces have been recorded with a fullness that is in some ways surprising.

Erasmus' *Praise of Folly* (1511) is still the most satisfying account of what fools are. The essay is rich with the life of a complex historical moment, well described by Enid Welsford and others.[7] That moment and its breaking, the dissolution of what Enid Welsford calls the "medieval synthesis," were materials for Shakespeare, who made their darkness more explicit than Erasmus had. The turning is past; we live in part on the energies released in it, and the fool we know from Erasmus and Shakespeare has receded from us. Then costumed fools still rolled and tumbled in the street and reveled in their obscenities. The line dividing the make-believe world of the theater from "this great stage of fools" was fluid. Not long before, they had eaten sausages at the altar and had the strength, expressed partly in what amounted to a political show of numbers, to desecrate and delight in the desecration, within limits that they had helped to set in a volatile semicompromise with their nonfoolish brethren.[8] For both Erasmus and Shakespeare fools were still visibly there; the encounter between the fool and the spectator of drama or the reader of a book was immediate in the sense that the figure was not only recognizable but a part of daily life and of a living current of the imagination. Many potentialities of folly were actual at the same time and did not seem mutually exclusive; the fool could, for example, be meaningless and meaningful, worthless and valuable.[9]

If we imagine ourselves into that moment and look out from it at what has been written about fools before and after, we may see two main tendencies in the treatment they have been accorded. The first of them could be called the naïve view, summarized with the slogan "Ha, ha! Look at the silly fool!" In the earlier literature, roughly before Flögel (excluding the historical moment that gave rise to Erasmus), this naïve view predominated, alternating and sometimes fusing with the moralistic one which characterized Sebastian Brant's *Narrenschiff* (1494), that the fool is primarily an object lesson. The naïve view is vigorously and engagingly presented in *A Nest of Ninnies* (1609; reprinted London,

# Introduction

1842), by Robert Armin, the clown who succeeded William Kempe in Shakespeare's company. Armin tells stories about actual fools more or less contemporary with him, but despite touches that show him to have an eye for individual traits, his anecdotes are for the most part scarcely distinguishable from jokes in the jestbooks long current about characters who had become, or who had always been, legendary. In such jestbooks what would in real life be complex events are the gags and jokes of a clown's routine, the clown who enacts it being regarded as delightfully silly, as contemptible, or as both. This tendency is still extremely pronounced in books and articles by and about fool actors, including some of the most famous ones of recent times. (As a result, such writing is generally of very limited value as biography; at the same time it is dreary as entertainment, since it is just convincing enough as biography to make the jestbook style unconvincing.) It is true, as we shall see, that two-dimensionality belongs to the essence of the fool. But it is not the whole of that essence: the surface of folly sometimes breaks open to reveal surprising depths, and these are as much a part of what the fool finally is as are his shallowness and triviality.

The second main tendency, which characterizes most recent studies of fools and folly, principally Enid Welsford's *The Fool* and Robert H. Goldsmith's *Wise Fools in Shakespeare,* is an attempt to reach through what is taken to be the clownish surface of the fool to the meaning behind it. But almost invariably, despite the receptivity of many of these writers toward their subject, the meaning that is found oversimplifies the figure and abstracts it in a way that causes it to lose its vivid presence and, with it, some of the depth of that meaning. The oversimplification emerges with special clarity in what has been written about fools who may be thought to have wisdom or sanctity. It amounts to an inversion of Sebastian Brant's moralism, replacing his judgment "bad" with "good" and justifying approval of the fool by an appeal to right reason, morality, and religious tradition. This tendency provides a way of understanding the fool's meaning but impairs the mode of seeing him by which we gain access to his life. In the following pages that life will be of primary importance; I do not assume that it can be reduced to the neat form of paradox or that it necessarily belongs to the ironic expression of wise truth.

## Introduction

The first part of this study is about the materials of folly, the ways in which they are made into a certain kind of spectacle—what I will call "the fool show"—and the ways in which the audience is implicated in that spectacle. In the second part I will discuss the magical powers of many fools and their relations to disorder and order, even to chaos and cosmos. In the third part I will treat the role of folly in the kingdom conceived as a realm with certain symbolic properties, and the relations of the fool to the king (and other important figures), especially in the formal drama.

# Part One  The Fool and His Show

This mime of mortal life, in which we are apportioned roles we misinterpret. . . .

(Seneca, *Moral Epistles*)

If a person were to try stripping the disguises from actors while they play a scene upon the stage, showing to the audience their real looks and the faces they were born with, would not such a one spoil the whole play? And would not the spectators think he deserved to be driven out of the theater with brickbats, as a drunken disturber? . . . Now what else is the whole life of mortals but a sort of comedy, in which the various actors, disguised by various costumes and masks, walk on and play each one his part, until the manager waves them off the stage? Moreover, this manager frequently bids the same actor go back in a different costume, so that he who has but lately played the king in scarlet now acts the flunkey in patched clothes. Thus all things are presented by shadows; yet this play is put on in no other way.

(Erasmus, *The Praise of Folly*)

# 1 The Fool as an Apparition

Not long ago a man boarded a tram in Zurich, took out a harmonica, and began gleefully playing it while dancing up and down. Now and then he stopped, stuck his head out of the window, jeered at a passer-by, and crowed like a cock at dawn. The passengers, wheeling around, roared with laughter. The conductor, neither demanding a fare from him nor putting him off, ostentatiously pretended that he did not see him, as though the cock-man had been there all along, part of the normal uneventfulness of things. Continuing to cavort without paying his fare, the cock-man grinned at the conductor, both of them now fools upon what had suddenly become a stage, then included us in his gaze and crowed again. His cry burst through our laughter, as though he recognized himself in us and was overjoyed. His brief show brought us in touch with a world spanning continents and centuries. It is peopled by actors similar to him, and its form is expressed in events similar to those that made up our interaction with him. The passengers on the tram did not need to reflect in order to know who and what he was. But if they had done so, they might have recalled the companies of cock-crested fools who still appear in the *Fastnacht* processions. And there is in their everyday language a metaphor which would have accommodated him, though less specifically, to their understanding: *Er hat einen Vogel,* literally, "he has a bird"—he is a bit mad. There have been cock-men who have caused surprise and laughter at least from the time of the antique drama; they include the coxcombed jesters of the Middle Ages and the bizarre cock-criers who crowed the hours in the English court long after the disappearance of the official jester—in fact, well into the eighteenth century.[1]

In being part cock this man on the tram thus calls to mind many

3

parallels and antecedents: Lear's coxcombed jester has links to them that are as real as his links to the King, to the other characters of the play, or to us. And in being flamboyantly eccentric and in displaying his folly as though it were a treasure which everyone should admire, the man on the tram revealed his kinship with an even broader domain of people whom others have recognized as fools and who have at least not protested that recognition. When one thinks of these figures, one may have the impression of a chaotic rush of movement, of jokes and tricks, just as one may when one tries to remember the clowns in the circus last year. Yet when a fool suddenly stands before us as the cock-man did on the tram, it may seem as though he has been there a long time and has at last triumphed over our attempts not to see him. (See Plate 1.)

He comes and goes like an apparition glimpsed for a moment. Thus Lear's Fool wanders off the stage in the middle of the tragedy in which he has appeared, saying only, "And I'll go to bed at noon" (III. vi. 85).[2] We may ask why he leaves and where he goes; we could also ask where these other fools went or where they came from. There have been many works of imagination with the theme of "Ubi sunt . . . ?" in which we follow the great ones of the earth as they yield to the common fate of death; we look at the point where they left us and try to find in dust and ashes a trace of their light. We do not ponder about fools in this way. Nonetheless, there are many stories and legends about a topsy-turvy world, a fool's paradise or limbo. The cock could be taken as the emblem or even the genius of that realm of fools, the cock being lecherous, vain, and stupid. (According to legend, the cock calls the day into being. Symbolically the day is the time of consciousness; in the same way that the cock expresses the coming dawn, the fool often expresses an incipient consciousness still in the darkness of the unconscious.) Thus the cock's cry on the Zurich tram seemed the perfect device for calling us to see the man as a fool. (See Plates 2 and 3.)

We see fools again and again in variations of a single form: the figure, whatever the details of his appearance and actions, whose folly we recognize in an act of spontaneous judgment and who, even if he does nothing at all, commands attention. Some fools have powers that are seemingly exhausted in their tricks and jokes; others share magical and religious functions with priests and medicine men who have a direct

4

# The Fool as an Apparition

PLATE I. The fool as clown (Alberto Fratellini). Stumbled upon in some no-man's-land, he does not mirror our surprise at seeing him; he seems to feel that we have been admiring him all along. He strikes us as more mysterious and yet more real than he would tramping around the circus arena. Stupid, blobby, and baby-like as his face is to us, it expresses both the radiant calm of some archaic sculpture and the menace of Harlequin masks. He resembles many things—a crude stone, a duck, a doll made by an idiot—and he resembles us. He is an object, he is fascinating; yet to what extent and in what ways is he a person? What are we to make of his resemblance to us? This is one way of translating the riddle that the fool represents and dissolves in his show.

PLATE 2. Quinten Massys, "An Allegory of Folly" (*ca.* 1510–20).
According to Julius Held, "the basic idea of the picture can be
expressed in the words 'Fools will talk.' While the right hand
of Folly makes the traditional gesture of silence accompanied by
the wise maxim MONDEKEN TOE (Keep your mouth shut), the
cock of the fool's cap (coxcomb) cackles merrily, presumably
giving away all the secrets" (Erica Tietze-Conrat, *Dwarfs and
Jesters in Art* [London: Phaidon, 1957], p. 94). Yet in keeping
with the fundamental nature of folly, the idea of the picture
is even more complex: the cock, speaking its own (and not our)
language, does not simply blab out secrets that should be kept.
The cock cries out of another level of being. That level is
magical, and the magical dimension of folly (to be discussed in
Part II) is further implied in the bare-buttocked man protruding
from the fool's staff: this indecency is rooted in a kind of fertility
magic which also serves to ward off such malign influences as the
Evil Eye. The fool, silenced, crows as a cock, and rational
understanding is for a moment violated by a life it had excluded.
Compare the cock-headed fools at the bottom of Plate 3 and the
bare-buttocked baby below the fool at the right of Plate 31.

PLATE 3. Jacob Jordaens, "Folly" (engraved by Alexander Voet). The feather in the fool's hood calls to mind the frequent connection between fools and birds, as do details in the ornamental border.

responsibility for the well-being of society. In either case, their effects depend upon the attention they gain from us.

The fool often presents himself uninvited to our attention, like the cock-man on the tram or the clowns who have performed until recently (and perhaps still do) in the company of trained bears, acrobats, sword-swallowers, fire-eaters, and people who stick knives through their arms and legs on the sidewalks of European cities. Or he may be sought out by his audience, as when the king called for the jester he had already in another act of decision come to retain, or as when people now pay to see the clowns of the circus, as they did earlier to be amused by the inmates of the hospital of St. Mary of Bethlehem (or Bedlam) in London. He belongs to his audience and it to him in a form of entertainment that is essentially ephemeral, whatever meaning and value it may have. He is sufficiently a part of the normal world that he repeatedly appears in it; he is alien enough that he disappears again and is forgotten, when the momentary fool show—for example, this spectacle on a Zurich tram—comes to an end. The bond between us and someone so ridiculous and indecorous, even obscenely grotesque, may in the naïve view be slender and casual, but considering his recurrence in a limited variety of forms, that bond also seems indissoluble.

Some Basic Characteristics of the Fool

Several important and recurrent traits of fools are implied by the words we use as generic *names* for foolish people. We leave the abstraction of dictionary definitions and come closer to the fool figures to be met in actual experience if we consider the *physical deformity,* the *dress,* and the *psychic aberration* of many fools. The fool's physical and mental abnormality impairs the functioning of his *will;* the resulting difficulties are central to the spectacle presented by fool actors.

It is true, as William Empson writes in his essay, "The Praise of Folly," that ". . . the group of ideas in question is very ancient and widespread, and clearly did not depend on having a single word to express it." [1] Nor did the ideas depend on having a single language to express them, though the words used for the purpose often lose their precise shading in translation. Still, we gain a good general idea of what folly is if we look at the chief English words used to *name* a person's implication in it. The most common of these is "fool"; according to the *Oxford English Dictionary* it is most frequently used in these senses:

1. One deficient in judgment or sense, one who acts or behaves stupidly, a silly person, a simpleton. (In Biblical use applied to vicious or impious persons.)
2. One who professionally counterfeits folly for the entertainment of others, a jester, a clown.
3. One who is deficient in, or destitute of reason or intellect; a weak-minded or idiotic person.

In his essay, Empson offers a more differentiated definition, which assigns different but overlapping sets of meanings to the word as used by Erasmus and Shakespeare. "Fool" could, as Empson notes, mean

9

"Everyman in the presence of God," as it did primarily for Erasmus. It could also mean madman (more or less interchangeably with imbecile and clown or jester), as it did for Shakespeare, although the religious meaning sometimes sounds in the plays.

The fool is, in short, a silly or idiotic or mad person, or one who is made by circumstances (or the actions of others) to appear a fool in that sense, or a person who imitates for nonfools the foolishness of being innately silly or made to look so. In the time of Elizabeth I a distinction came to be expressed between the "natural" and the "artificial" fool, the latter being the person who "professionally counterfeits folly"; either could serve as a jester or clown.

The feeling that "to appear a fool," to be duped, is unpleasant is probably as widespread as fools and folly, and the Biblical sense of fools as "vicious or impious persons" seems a moralistic application of the same feeling to the person who allows himself to be made a fool of. This implies that normal behavior is not foolish and that foolishness can and should be avoided. A contrary feeling toward fools is implied in the fact that "fool" could, in earlier times, be a term of endearment. (Similar ambiguities of feeling may be seen in the historical development of the words "silly," which once meant blessed, and "fond," which once meant foolish.) The fool actor, then, stands somewhere between the reality, possibly horrible, of idiocy or madness and its character as a show, something to be entertained by and, if taken seriously, loved rather than despised.

The most usual derivation of the word is from Latin *follis,* "a pair of bellows, a windbag." A fool is like a pair of bellows in that his words are only air, empty of meaning. The plural of the Latin *follis* is *folles,* which means "puffed cheeks," whence, according to Skeat, "the term was easily transferred to a jester." [2] Taking these derivations together, one might say that a fool looks and acts silly in various ways, such as grimacing, and that what he says is empty of meaning. This is so despite the fact that wind, which "bloweth where it listeth" (John 3:8), is one of the most archaic representations of spirit. And "buffoon" is closely cognate with the Italian *buffare,* "to puff." The fool has the freedom and unpredictability of spirit, but in his show it seems to issue into mere air, a commotion of spirit with neither focus nor direction. The fool's wind scatters things and meanings

yet in the confusion reveals glimpses of a counterpole to spirit: nature
with the purposes and intelligence of instinct, which, like spirit, cannot be
accommodated to rational understanding.

Thus one lexicographer, Ernest Weekley, carries further the derivation
of "fool" from the Latin *follis,* which he defines as "bellows, windbag, but
probably here in the specific sense of *scrotum;* cf. It. *coglione,* 'a noddie, a
foole, a patch, a dolt, a meacock' (Florio), lit. testicle; also L. *gerro,* fool,
from a Sicilian name for pudendum." [3] One could also compare the
obscene oath "ballocks!" or "balls!"—testicles—meaning "nonsense!" or
"silly pretension!" Weekley's derivation is in keeping with the
exaggerated sexuality of many clowns and fools throughout history and
with a commonly accepted idea of the origin of the European clown; as
Thelma Niklaus summarizes the notion, "It seems probable that all
mimes, clowns, drolls, and mummers known to Europe were engendered
by the Satyr of Greek Old Comedy, a form of entertainment derived from
the phallic ritual and ceremonies of Dionysos." [4] The dialogue between
clowns derived from this source creates the beginnings of the native
drama in Italy. These clowns took part in the celebration of nuptials or
harvest home. "The clown's coarse and salacious patter, concerned wholly
with fertility, propagation, and phallephoric humour, became known as
Fescennine verse, a name derived either from [*fascinum*] the male organ
of generation, regarded as a symbol of fertility and magic in all folklore;
or from the town of *Fescennium,* where harvest-home may always have
been celebrated with such clowning." [5] And the word "folly" for the fool's
behavior had from an early date (1303 according to the *O.E.D.*) the
meaning "lewdness." The Authorized Version of the Bible sometimes
employs the word in this sense, retained from Coverdale's translation, as
in Genesis 34:7: ". . . he had wrought folly in Israel in lying with Jacob's
daughter." This characteristic of the fool is emphasized, too, in the fact
that the Renaissance figure of the Arlecchino wore a phallus, as had the
Roman mimes and, a thousand years before Arlecchino, the Greek
*Phallophores.* Attached to the bauble of the European court jester was
often a bladder formed into a clear representation of a phallus. [6] (See Plate
7.) Paul Radin describes the Trickster of Winnebago Indian myth, a
knavish fool, as a "stupid phallus." [7] The drum of the Koyemci clowns
among the Zuñi is supposed to contain the wings of butterflies that can

make girls sexually crazy. This property of the fool and of his bauble is the basis of a simile in which Mercutio, in *Romeo and Juliet,* describes Romeo's infatuation for Rosaline: "this drivelling love is like a great natural, that runs lolling up and down to hide his bauble in a hole" (II. iv. 88–89). In keeping with the vulgar saying, "A fool's bauble is a lady's play-fellow," Fanny Hill's friend Louisa seduces an idiot, the sight of his genitals causing Fanny to remark, "Nature had done so much for him in those parts, that she perhaps held herself acquitted in doing so little for his head." [8] And the "cock" with which fools are often identical is also a figure of the phallus, as in the mad Ophelia's, "Young men will do't, if they come to't; / By Cock, they are to blame" (*Hamlet,* IV. v. 57–58).

Whereas a fool is "deficient in judgment or sense" altogether, a clown, according to the derivation of his name, lacks "judgment or sense" specifically with regard to social decorum. A clown was originally "a farm worker, hence a boor, hence—boors seeming funny to townsmen—a funny fellow, a buffoon, a jester." [9] According to the *O.E.D.,* cognate words in related languages (such as Dutch) convey such ideas as clod, wooden mall, log, block, stump. "So far as concerns the sense-development, then, it is clear that we have here a word meaning originally 'clod, clot, lump,' which, like these words themselves . . . has been applied in various langs. to a clumsy boor, a lout." An idiot may seem funny because of a deficient understanding of the world in general, including, for example, its natural laws; a country fellow, who understands those laws adequately, may seem funny because he fails to understand how people should act according to certain social forms. Since man's views of himself, nature, and society are interrelated and tend ultimately to converge, the words "fool" and "clown" quite early became more or less synonymous. In Shakespeare's time they were sometimes used interchangeably, as at the close of Hamlet's speech to the Players (III. ii). More recently, however, a "clown" has come to have the more specialized meaning of the clown of the modern circus. (The original circus "Clown" was a white-faced descendant of Pierrot of the commedia dell'arte and appeared in the circus in the eighteenth century. [10] Since then the term has expanded to include the "Auguste," the "Joey," and the other circus entertainers now generally called clowns. [11])

In other words, some of the earlier differentiations of the fool type, among them the fool figures of the commedia dell'arte, lost their claim to attention, though traces of them survived. These vestiges became associated with the lumpish circus clown and in popular usage assumed his name. There are historical parallels to this process. Thus M. Willson Disher writes, "Clowns maintain their distinctive characteristics despite, not because of tradition. All Greek and Roman comedies, the medieval religious plays, the Commedia dell'arte and the English Harlequinade certainly possess definite types in common. Yet these are the very types that are manifestly not borrowed but spontaneously created afresh." [12] Once created, they develop in complex ways. "And at each metamorphosis the world has to hatch another [clown] from a clod." [13]

The amoral and asocial character of many fools is conveyed by the word "idiot," which is ultimately derived from the Greek *idiotes*, a "private person." The idiot is widely thought to be the primary model of the symbolic fool, who seems to have originated somewhere outside society and its normal laws and duties and to continue to belong to the "outside" from which he came. The fool is often a "private person" who gives symbolic expression to the problems of human individuality in its relation both to rational norms and to what exceeds them. "Jester," on the other hand, can be any kind of merrymaker but is usually one maintained in a prince's court or nobleman's household; he is thus a domesticated form of the fool who in other forms is lawless. "Jest" comes from the French *geste,* as in *chanson de geste* or song of exploits. According to Weekley, *"To break a jest* was suggested by *breaking a lance.* Cf. to *crack a joke."* [14] This word which now names something comic or farcical and very brief, a witticism, was earlier applied to a mocking tale, still earlier to a specifically mock-heroic one, and before that to an extended serious presentation of heroism. The etymology thus implies something of the relations that we will be considering between the fool and the hero and between both and the king.

The fool has antecedents and relatives among a wide range of people who in various ways violate the human image and who come to a *modus vivendi* with society by making a show of that violation. If we look to the remote predecessors of the modern circus, which is one of the last refuges of the professional fool, we encounter the entertainers who wandered the

European Continent after the fall of the Roman Empire, among them cripples, the blind, paralytics, amputees, prostitutes, and quack doctors.[15] Components derived from these sources of *physical deformity*, even freakishness, psychic aberration, and criminality are, in varying proportions, present in the figure of the fool. According to Enid Welsford, the court fool, for example, "causes amusement not merely by absurd gluttony, merry gossip, or knavish tricks, but by mental deficiencies or physical deformities which deprive him both of rights and responsibilities and put him in the paradoxical position of virtual outlawry combined with utter dependence on the support of the social group to which he belongs." [16]

In many times and places dwarfs and hunchbacks have served as jesters, the dwarf being defective in physical size in a way that corresponds to the idiot's insufficiency of intelligence, the hunchback being deformed in a way that corresponds to the psychic aberration of the madman. The earliest jester of whom we have any knowledge was, in fact, a dwarf at the court of the Egyptian Pharaoh Pepi (or Papi) I. There were dwarf jesters in China in the earliest days, and in both areas of high civilization in pre-Columbian America dwarfs and hunchbacks served as court jesters. Cripples and freaks were sold in Roman markets, and dwarfs ran about naked in the salons of Roman ladies. This aristocratic appreciation of human monstrosities flourished as late as 1566, when thirty-four dwarfs, almost all deformed, served at the banquet given by Cardinal Vitelli in Rome. In the courts of Christian Europe dwarfs and other freaks served as jesters, as they had earlier. The first court dwarf in England was Xit, in the reign of Edward VI, and the last was Copperin, dwarf of the Princess (Augusta) of Wales, mother of George III. Artificial dwarfing and other kinds of monster-making had been learned by the Greeks and Romans from the Orient; and in Greece, according to Erica Tietze-Conrat, children were locked in special chests which made them into dwarfs able to pursue a profitable career. Such pursuits continued in Europe till fairly recently. The first wife of Joachim Frederic, Elector of Brandenburg, and Catherine de Médicis are both said to have tried to breed dwarfs in the hope of securing dwarf offspring; and the *Miscellanea Curiosa Medica Physica,* published in Leipzig in 1670, offers a recipe for dwarfing by anointing the backbone of the victim with the grease of moles, bats, and dormice.[17]

Familiar, permissive, and even privileged treatment of physical grotesques might at first sight seem to contradict the belief, also widespread, that they embody some kind of evil influence. The two attitudes fuse in the attribution of magical power to such creatures. Frazer describes the practice of deliberately courting vituperation to gain good luck and offers examples from Greece, Rome, Esthonia, the Carpathians, Berlin, and many parts of India.[18] Perhaps this custom, as well as others according to which physical grotesques are granted exceptional powers and privileges are, in part, as Enid Welsford suggests, forms

> of that universal human instinct, the dread of what the Greeks called the sin of "hubris" or presumption. The malign power of the Evil Eye is not only found in concentrated form in some human beings, it exists in a vague, undefined way suffused throughout the universe. . . . To praise oneself or be praised by others is a sure way of attracting this queer, cosmic jealousy, and conversely the surest way to evade its unwelcome attention is to depreciate oneself or be mocked by other people.[19]

Such deformities, including the exaggerated phallus, recur throughout the world of clowns and fools, and the Evil Eye is related to the ability of fools to reduce the world around them to chaos. However, it would seem one-sided to find the reason for the fool's existence simply in a human preoccupation with this negative magic and attempts to counteract it. The use of physical freaks as jesters is surely in part the expression of an ambivalence that also results in the relegation of such people to the margins of human society: grotesques have both positive and negative powers; they are hideously attractive; they should be approached and avoided, abused and placated. The grotesque jester, like other kinds of fools, is a mascot who maintains a relationship between the ordered world and the chaos excluded by it. This, as we shall see, is a complex function, and the ways in which the fool fulfills it are complex.

The misshapenness of dwarfs, hunchbacks, and other grotesques is reflected in the *dress* of the fool, which characteristically contains chaotic and disproportionate elements but sometimes brings them together within a balanced and harmonious pattern. One can view the most usual costumes of the fool as ranging from lumpishness (in keeping with the origin of the word "clown") and incongruity to balanced form. The lumpishness is familiar from many circus clowns (among them Alberto Fratellini as shown in Plate 1). Charlie Chaplin's baggy trousers and shapeless shoes have antecedents in the dress of some Elizabethan clowns.[20] This lumpishness suggests chaos registered by consciousness as a mere, crude fact: the audience is confronted with something relatively shapeless, yet material—there, with a human presence. The motley of medieval jesters, figures in the *Fastnacht* processions, and many circus clowns implies a rudimentary differentiation of the primal lump, the guise that chaos assumes when attention is paid to it: it consists of particolored bits and pieces. Such dress for fools is also found outside Europe, for example in Arabia, where clairvoyant madmen are reported to have worn long loose coats composed of patches of cloth of various colors and to have carried staffs with shreds of cloth of different colors attached to them.[21] The principle of motley also finds immaterial expression in the fool show, for example in the Feast of Fools at Sens, in which the prescribed vespers were replaced by a medley of all the vespers throughout the year—clown patches of religious text.[22] And there is a fictional adaptation of motley to the electronic age in Donald Barthelme's story "The Dolt," about a writer whose eight-foot-tall son wears a serape woven out of two hundred transistor radios, each of which is tuned to a different station.[23]

Between these two ways in which chaos may be worn as a disguise, as a lump or as scattered pieces, lie various costumes in which the fact of disproportion is emphasized—for example, between the too-large trousers and shoes of Charlie and his too-small jacket, between the slovenliness and fastidiousness of his costume as a whole; similar discrepancies recur in many circus-clown costumes. The element of disproportion is common to lumpishness—disproportionate in relation to what it should be—and to motley—in which the clearly discernible elements of the dress are disproportionate with relation to any organized whole they might make. It is clear that the fool's motley, as it emerges from his lumpishness, contains the possibility of development into a harmonious formal pattern.

16

PLATE 4. The film comedian Danny Kaye in a scene from the M-G-M release *The Merry Andrew* (1958).

## Characteristics of the Fool

Thus the costume of Harlequin, which consisted at first of irregular patches, had developed by the middle of the seventeenth century into a symmetrical pattern of blue, red, and green triangles, which in the eighteenth became in turn lozenges.[24] (See Plates 4–7.) However, such a development of the relatively chaotic into simple order is, if the formal perfection becomes paramount, at the expense of the fool's being a fool: divorced from chaos he may become, for example, a ballet dancer. In his show the fool expresses both the emergence of form or meaning out of chaos and their reversion *to* it; this reversion has also taken place in the history of fool dress. As Disher observes, whenever the costume of the clown-fool develops too far from the crude dress of the country bumpkin, when that dress

> is elaborated out of recognition, the conscious mirth-maker finds inspiration anew in the unconscious mirth-maker [the lout or boor, the "clown" in the original sense of the word]. When Harlequin's patches had become a pattern of coloured lozenges, the clown of the English Harlequinade was invented as a tatterdemalion. After his rags had become frills, the black-faced scarecrow, called Jim Crow, appeared. When nigger minstrels wore white collars and red-and-white striped trousers, the comedian was born with a red nose (not because the medieval devil and Elizabethan Jew had red noses) and with patched trousers (not for any other reason than that patches were funny in in everyday life). Before Grock gave a sort of regularity to the costume, Auguste of the cirque wore old, ill-fitting garments.[25]

The fool reverts to the chaotic lump when he has turned his back on it too long. But *our* having turned our backs to it too long is the precondition of his appearance. The fool turns us around. Ben Jonson catches this capacity of the fool when he describes Carlo Buffone, a character in *Every Man out of his Humour,* as "A publick, scurrilous, and prophane Jester; that (more swift than Circe) with absurd similies will transform any Person into deformity."

Animal elements are frequently found in the dress of the fool: Harlequin often wore a soft cape with a hare's or rabbit's scut,[26] and the medieval jester usually wore asses' ears or a coxcomb or both. Enid Welsford remarks that there is

PLATE 5. An alchemical representation of the *prima materia* from
which the highest value—wisdom or the spiritual gold—is to be obtained.
The roundness of the two figures in Plates 4 and 5 is expressive of totality,
but this totality belongs to chaos and to the unconscious; the operations of
consciousness break it down. Nonetheless, it is a necessary preform of the
totality that is the goal of the alchemical work.

considerable variety in fool-clothes and we hear of fox-tails, cockscombs,
calf-skins, long petticoats and feathers as suitable wear for lunatics. It
has been pointed out that the fool thus adorned is not unlike the
animal-mummers who so often play a part in traditional games of various
countries and are usually supposed to be connected with religious ritual.
Dr. Chambers suggests that not only the calf-skin and fox-tail but also
the traditional eared hood and coxcomb may be conventionalized
survivals of the old sacrificial *exuviae*.[27]

It is not certain how fools were dressed on the Elizabethan stage,
although we have evidence of kinds of fool dress current at the time.

# The Fool and His Show

PLATE 6a. Domenico Locatelli (1613–71) as Trivelino, a form of Harlequin. The costume of the fool actor often expresses (even more immediately than do his words, gestures, and actions) qualities characteristic of the fool's inner life. Locatelli's costume suggests, for example, kinds of stupidity common in Harlequin and in many other fools: weak logic and a poor grasp of formal pattern in the outer world. Beyond this, his costume suggests the disorder that is an important part of the experience of nonfools and that is one of the links between them and the fool actor.

PLATE 6b. Detail of the costume of Locatelli as Trivelino, or Harlequin.

PLATE 7. Detail of a modern variant of Pierrot, the pattern of this costume being derived from Harlequin figures. (The costume may be seen in full in Plate 32.) Plates 6b and 7 illustrate the chaotic patches and the geometric patterns that are interrelated in the development of fool costumes and that are often brought together in one costume. When geometric pattern is emphasized in the fool's costume, it represents the order *of* or *in chaos*. The rush of Harlequin's movement, focused for instants in stylized attitudes, was part of the life of his costume. Its geometric order was glimpsed in a welter of distortion and emerged clearly only in what were known to be fleeting moments of rest. It was thus like the impersonal truth that the fool may blurt out as part of his nonsensical folly. In any case, the orderliness of the fool's costume stands in grotesque contrast to the incoherence of his sayings and deeds. (The "Great Stone Face" of Buster Keaton is in similar contrast to the excitation expressed in his bodily movements.) If this orderliness is asserted to the exclusion of its contrary, the fool ceases to be a fool.

## The Fool and His Show

These costumes were lumpish, motley, or in other ways indicated that the fool was disproportionate. The differences between these ways of presenting chaos are in the deepest sense unimportant because they imply one another, and that implication is enacted in the fool's jokes and tricks. A good account of Shakespeare's fools by Francis Douce, published in 1807, presents a description of how Lear's Fool (in kinship with his contemporary brethren) might have appeared; Douce's picture was, in any case, of a figure with roots in then current tradition and in the essentials of what we know about fools in general and of their relation to chaos. According to Douce, the Elizabethan fool's

> coat was motley or parti-coloured, and attached to the body by a girdle, with bells at the skirts and elbows, though not always. The breeches and hose close, and sometimes each leg of a different colour. A hood resembling a monk's cowl, which, at a very early period, it was certainly designed to imitate, covered the head entirely, and fell down over the breast and shoulders. It was sometimes decorated with asses' ears, or else terminated in the neck and head of a cock. . . . It often had the comb or crest only of the animal, whence the term *cockscomb* or *coxcomb* was afterwards used to denote any silly upstart. This fool usually carried in his hand an official scepter or bauble, which was a short stick ornamented at the end with the figure of a fool's head, or sometimes that of a doll or puppet. To this instrument there was frequently annexed an inflated skin or bladder, with which the fool belaboured those who offended him, or with whom he was inclined to make sport; this was often used by itself, in lieu, as it should seem, of a bauble. The form of it varied, and in some instances was obscene in the highest degree.[28]

Among the toys fools love most are bells, which were often, from earlier than Shakespeare, a part of their dress. (They may be seen in several of the illustrations to this study.) Despite the sometimes fanciful conjectures about them, the source of the medieval jester's bells is unknown.[29] Yet they accord with his essential self-division: they are at the end of his ass's ears, the ass often being, in the fool show, the counterpart of the human being. These stylized ears were usually two in number (although sometimes they were doubles of the two, four, or, less often, three); and occasionally the bells were scattered elsewhere upon the fool's costume.

22

## Characteristics of the Fool

The customary two bells would distract from the normal sense of what the fool hears and, like the cock's crow, present signs from another level of being. The bells could tinkle together, when the fool moved decisively; when he moved more gently or when the wind touched the bells they could tinkle independently, with the attention of the fool divided between the tinkling and the details and sense of whatever else he heard. It belongs to the nature of his show that his patches more often than not seem light, though they may weigh heavily upon him, and the tinkling of his bells seems a sign of freedom, though they may deafen him to the world he wants with part of his being to understand.

Most of the people we recognize as fools experience the world and act within it in ways that indicate a fundamental abnormality, real or pretended, of psychic functioning. The specific *psychic aberrations* implied by the behavior of fools range through most of the table of contents of a psychiatric textbook. Kinds of psychic abnormality clearly distinguished from one another in the psychiatric classification are treated in the symbolism of folly as though they were more or less interchangeable. Signs of mental deficiency and, for example, of schizophrenia are mixed at random as materials of the fool show. This reduction of stupidity and madness to a common element is still current among nonfools: I think of someone who expressed surprise that another person required psychiatric treatment although the other person had "always seemed intelligent."

The scientifically differentiated symptoms, syndromes, and illnesses that now provide the means of describing various kinds of psychopathology have in many times and places been conceived as expressions of something diffuse but unitary. Folly is one name for it. In this view, one is, for example, schizophrenic because one does not perceive, understand, and act in accordance with things as they really are, and this failure is seen as the result of the same deficiency of intelligence that is to be encountered in simple stupidity or idiocy. (This view has the justification that psychic difficulties often make intelligent people behave, for practical purposes, as though they were stupid.) But folly in the sense of what makes people stupid or mad has also been considered as not a nothing but a something. Various phenomena of psychic aberration have been thought to be also

23

more or less interchangeable evidences of a positive power. This power is analogous to the Evil Eye and perhaps even partly identical with it in essence. Thus, according to Enid Welsford,

> Ill-defined feelings concerned with mascots and the power of the Evil Eye were probably partly responsible for the vogue of the dwarf-fool in the Graeco-Roman world, and may have influenced the attitude to buffoons in India; the behavior of the festival-fool in Europe also suggests that he was acting on somewhat similar impulses. On the other hand the general behavior of the masquers and revellers at festival seasons suggests that at such times there was an epidemic of divine or demonic inspiration, and that folly was regarded by them not as a fault but as a desirable symptom of the infection—an attitude to mental disease which is as widespread as the horror of the Evil Eye.[30]

Erasmus, too, is inclined to lump together as "madness" all forms of psychic aberration, and he wishes to use this madness as a conceit in his ironic praise of folly. But he is aware that madness, far from being merely a joke, is often horrible; and he acts upon this awareness by dividing madness into two classes. The first class is "one the revenging Furies send secretly from hell whenever, with their snaky locks unbound, they put into the hearts of mortal men lust for war, or insatiable thirst for wealth, shameful and illicit love, parricide, incest, sacrilege, or any other bane of the sort; or when they hound the guilty and stricken soul with fiends or with torch-bearing goblins." [31] This kind of madness is demonic, and by making a separate class of it Erasmus pretends to isolate the dangers of madness as a whole. (His description of demonic madness is, at the same time, a satiric picture of normality; he thus implies that normality, too, should be avoided, and pushes us a step toward welcoming abnormality.) The second class "is far different from this. It comes, you see, from me [Folly]; and of all things is most to be desired. It is present whenever an amiable dotage of the mind at once frees the spirit from carking cares and anoints it with a complex delight." [32] This kind of madness is folly, and a blessing, and by making a separate class of it Erasmus prepares to make this blessing available to us.

Having reduced madness to a blessing, Folly still finds herself uncertain "whether every deviation of the senses or the faculties ought to be called by the name of madness."[33] Perhaps sensing that her magical conception of psychopathology renders the question unanswerable, she shifts her attention from madness to folly and resumes talking about the two as simply equivalent. It is, of course, madness if someone

> thinks he is listening to a fine orchestra whenever he hears an ass braying; or if some beggar, born to low station, believes himself to be Croesus, King of the Lydians. And yet this kind of madness, assuming, as is usually the case, that it tends to give pleasure, can bring a delight above the common both to those who are seized by it and to those who look on but are not mad in the same way. This variety of madness is much more widespread than people generally realize. Thus one madman laughs at another, turn about, and they minister to each other's mutual pleasure. You will often see it happen that the madder man laughs more uproariously at the one who is not so mad.
>
> The fact is that the more ways a man is deluded, the happier he is, if Folly is any judge. Only let him remain in that kind of madness which is peculiarly my own, and which is so widespread that I do not know whether out of the whole world of mortals it is possible to find one is wise at all times of day, and who is not subject to some extravagance.[34]

Erasmus' notion of madness as folly, and as a blessing, is crucial to his whole enterprise of ironic praise. The notion entails a rhetorical trick that complements that by which he has banished the dangers of madness: having convinced us of the blessing of madness, he plays with the various senses in which this blessing may be understood. Sometimes, for example, he regards such madness, satirically, as equivalent to vanity and self-delusion; and at other times he regards it as analogous to a transformation of consciousness that would allow us to see things more truly. And, quite generally, he is at pains to keep us from knowing for certain in what sense he is, at a given moment, praising folly. As a result of these pains, and despite the subtle logic of his ironies, we feel that in the *Praise of Folly* madness is a unitary and contagious force, as it was in folk belief.

Erasmus' description of madness, or folly, as analogous to a transformation of consciousness in the interest of truth draws upon an ancient tradition, which is also based upon a magical conception of psychopathology. This tradition, in which the fool is thought to be akin to the shaman, is discussed by Enid Welsford in a chapter on "The Fool as Poet and Clairvoyant." Some fools have, in fact, been clairvoyant or mediumistic: their divine or demonic inspiration is a special instance of the fool's speaking the truth, of his being a disguised form of the sage. But even more characteristic of fools and folly than this is precisely the fact that his truth-telling is *not* necessarily central, that it is more or less interchangeable with expressions of stupidity, madness, or freakishness. This amounts to a confusion between what has value (truth of whatever kind) and what has none (nonsense); it is this *confusion* that is central—the fact that diamonds and dull stones are treated as interchangeable, both of them either supremely valuable or worthless, depending upon the momentary state of the fool's mind.

What the "too little" of idiocy and the "too much" of madness have in common with such truth-telling and with physical deformation is that they are the result, we may feel, of the fool's having touched the abyss and having been possessed by something within it.

As we have seen, physical monstrosities regarded in a certain way fall within the province of fools. The passive, sluglike Fat Lady of the circus sideshow cannot make herself be less hideous than she is, and this is surely part of what makes her thrilling. More commonly, though, and more centrally to the fool as a type, fools are active. Whether active or passive, fools are caught in problems of *will*. In his show the fool actor wants to be a fool, or he wants not to be a fool but cannot help being one; or else he is indifferent to his folly, in which case he contradicts what we think he should want to be. He usually does not want what we consciously want; if he does, he is usually not physically and mentally equipped to go about getting it as we would; if he is, he usually comes into conflict with the wills, nonfoolish and foolish, of other people and even apparently of things.

The fool is often clumsy as well as stupid. He is lacking, that is to say, in his ability to perceive, understand, or act in accordance with the order of things as it appears to others. His perception, understanding, and actions are thus relatively uncoordinated, even chaotic. What he says and does seems symptomatic of an inadequacy or aberration. He has difficulties with physical objects, with social forms, and with the rules that govern both. These difficulties and his failure to master them result in what strikes us as a ridiculous loss of dignity. Often, however, he does not feel the pain and embarrassment that such oddity and failure would cause in us—he may even be proud of them; in any case, his notions of what constitutes accomplishment are different from ours. His inability or unwillingness to perceive, understand, and act in accordance with the normal order of things leads him to transgress bounds of many kinds. In this transgression he triumphs and is defeated. When he triumphs, he often does so in spite of the normal order and in spite of his stupidity, his clumsiness, and his peculiar ideas of what to do and how to do it.

The fool is, in the somehow onomatopoetic pair of terms coined by the psychoanalyst Michael Balint, a "philobat,"

> a person who finds pleasure in existing or moving about in what are to him friendly open spaces; who is not so much interested in leaving a place or arriving at another, as in the thrills and pleasures he experiences during his journey. These thrills are proportionate to his satisfaction in his skills, physical and mental, which enable him to make the journey. His pleasures therefore are partly in himself, in his own competence and power, and partly in the achievement which allows him to feel at one with objectless space.[35]

The fool is, at the same time, an "ocnophil," "a person whose pleasure is found not in journeying from one place to another but in being in one place close to an object which he needs and values."[36] Since he is both, he is neither; he expresses, relieves, and ridicules the anxieties of others in the face of objective reality. One may think of the clown Linon clinging in fright to the platform from which he should begin tightrope-walking, then walking the tightrope in a virtuoso way.

From the point of view of Jung's psychological types, the fool is often, though by no means always, predominantly introverted, with intuition and feeling as his main functions for dealing with reality. However, in his actions his inferior extraverted sensation and thinking are emphasized—but in such a way that a contamination is apparent between his customarily exercised attitude and functions, which are really inferior, and those of his psychic background, which are really superior. The inferiority of his sensation may be seen in the clumsiness and virtuosity, already mentioned, of the circus clown. The inferiority of his thinking is apparent in his frequent inability to discover and act logically upon the rules relevant to simple mechanical problems as well as by his occasional hyperlogicality in situations in which logic does not apply. The feeling of the fool may be seen in the Pierrot of the commedia dell'arte and his descendant, the "sad clown" of the circus. Intuition is what allows the circus clown or film comedian to survive the results of his weak sensation. Thus the eccentric funnyman Red Skelton has what he calls "extra-sensitive perception"; after many years of dangerous pratfalling he can still say, "I've got the sixth sense, but I don't have the other five."

This classification breaks down, as others do, if the fool is intensely imagined as bearing the point of a joke. In the moment that point is reached, soon after to explode, it escapes any of our ways of dealing with it. Habitual ways of understanding do not work properly in him. The point of the joke often expresses this fact and momentarily impairs these ways of understanding in us. Thus, for example, his perception and judgment of a thing interfere with each other so as to create a confusion in which we, too, are caught up. The actualities of the fool's person and of his life (for example, his physical appearance, dress, and social position) tend to be inferior or inappropriate. But his interests are generally not in actualities but in possibilities, and he is much more open to them than we are. Thus, for example, when he is witty, the stream of his jokes stays slightly ahead of our ability to react to them.

The fool usually survives both his clumsiness and stupidity, or even madness, and the adversity that searches him out; yet his final survival seems a triumph not so much of the human will as of something else.[37] The functioning of the fool's will is, as we have seen, often an expression of his derangement. Very often in human dealings with the supernatural, the breaking-down of form is taken to imply possession by a higher power; something of this view continues to live in our attitude toward fool actors. It was certainly very much alive in Erasmus. The principle on which this view is based may be seen in the ancient and widespread phenomenon of glossolalia, "speaking in tongues," saying things understood neither by oneself nor by others. If one speaks in tongues, one's personal will is impotent; from this loss of power the presence of a superior power is inferred. What one says then may be partly translated into normal speech; a sense may emerge from it. But we have no right to assume that the "point" of glossolalia lies more in this translation than in the shattering of our customary forms of discourse. Glossolalia is, in turn, no closer to meaning in the usual sense than silence is. Thus van der Leeuw writes, "Deep emotional agitation produces *silence* also; *favete linguis,* 'keep silence,' which was originally magically intended and supposed to overcome the power of some unpropitious word, became through 'transposition' the positive expression of the inexpressible, the language of the unutterable." [38] We may sense this silence in that of the innumerable fools and clowns who are mute mimes (among them, recently, Grock in most of his tricks and Harpo of the Marx Brothers). Many other fools babble as though speaking in tongues. These two ways of expressing folly, through silence and babbling, are shown in the picture of Folly by Quinten Massys. (See Plate 2.) Foolish babbling also often suggests drunkenness or is the result of it, wine being essential to saturnalia. Drunkenness is license, but it is also possession. Thus people chosen to be sacrificial victims in Rhodes and Mexico were made drunk to show their transcendence of the profane condition and their connection with the gods.

What Erasmus finds desirable is an aberration of sense and understanding sufficient to effect a qualitative difference from the normal human condition, a difference like that between a dwarf or other grotesque and a normal person. This change, which opens the way to new relations between subject and object, occurs through the constellation of an archetype, that of folly. The symptoms of mental deficiency or illness are expressive of its operation, since it results in a basic reorientation of customary modes of sense and judgment. For Erasmus, as throughout the whole world of folly, what are for us symptoms, syndromes, and disease entities are symbolic of the diffuse but unitary, potentially healing power of folly. That power also counteracts the forces behind events which do not present an overt threat to our normal ways of experiencing the world but which are signs, for those who can read them, that the prevailing order of the world has lost vitality or meaning or both.

## 3 The Fool and Mimesis

When the cock-man appeared on the Zurich tram, he released energies that belong to the bond between us and the fool; folly was for a moment mirrored in action. The cock-man's show can be understood as a special instance of the mimesis, or imitation, by which our identities are formed and, as part of the same process, by which they are mirrored in drama. There is, however, something problematic about the fool's identity; we assume the problem ourselves if we grant that our identities include an unpredictable bond with the fool. The problem is also present in the fool's relation to the process of mimesis. King Lear broke partly under the weight of the problem, as the substantial and ordered world became for him "this great stage of fools." His metaphor contains echoes of two interrelated ideas that recur throughout the nondramatic literature of fools and folly that had passed its flowering but was still current in Shakespeare's time. They are playful conceits; yet they are pregnant with the darkness that engulfed Lear.

The first of these recurrent ideas is summarized in two mottoes reiterated in that nondramatic fool literature: *stultorum plena sunt omnia,* "all places are filled with fools," and *stultorum infinitus est numerus,* "the number of fools is infinite." [1] Taken together these assertions describe part of the dilemma that Lear must explore. Fools and folly are a natural fact, but the fact is, the mottoes imply, omnipresent. Any fool we see is demarcated from what we assume to be a nonfoolish background; otherwise he would be like the philosophers' black cat at midnight. We see this fool here only by disregarding that fool or those fools there, including the fools that we also are. Our blindness to them means that our perception of this fool is an illusion. By seeing this fool as one, and thus penetrating the illusion that he is not a fool, we come no

30

closer to the reality of what he is than we do by not seeing him as one in the first place, and we are no further from our own folly.

The second of these ideas, in a sense at odds with the first, is that a fool recognizably participates in a typical form and that our recognition of him as a fool is immediate and total. The notion that there are fools everywhere is a way of describing our awareness that anyone might at any moment make a fool of himself: a power lurks in us and may manifest itself in a foolish way of looking at others or of being seen by them. This possibility is the threat and promise of folly as a show. In that show a fool is seen as a fool.

But if that power is in all of us, it belongs to our essential human nature. Instead of regarding a person's foolishness as an accident by which he falls out of the role proper to him, we might view it as an expression of what he essentially is, and we might view his nonfoolish role, however willfully he upholds it, as an aberration. In fact, fools lure us for moments into this second way of looking at folly and nonfolly; Lear sustained the fool's vision to its depths. In his madness Lear was partly the witness and partly the bearer of what could be called a burlesque revelation. That revelation is of the typical figure of the fool and of the characteristic life within him and around him. In seeing that figure at all, we are involved in his way of seeing. And that involvement is the basis of our connection with the fool when he appears.

The fool literature in which these mottoes about the omnipresence of fools were current reached its culmination in Desiderius Erasmus' *Praise of Folly* (1511), which was read in Shakespeare's England.[2] Erasmus made use of an ancient rhetorical trick: he took conventional images of fools, principally those of the babbling idiot and ass-eared jester, and casuistically superimposed them upon people normally thought to be nonfools. Even the king might babble and wear ass's ears. These images are convenient, semitransparent masks; wearing them, nonfools become foolish. Yet Erasmus slily sidesteps the question he pretends to raise: "What is a fool?"—or with a different emphasis, "Who is the fool?" The foolish trappings, such as ass's ears, tell us little about what a fool is: they are hints of a totality that includes both him and us. We may ourselves suddenly be wearing the ass's ears in the sight of others; and no matter who wears them, the heart of that totality remains hidden and full of its own power. Thus the multiplication of examples that constituted the stock-in-trade of the fool literature inherited and brought to its height by Erasmus always threatened to get out of hand, and this was part of the fun. The mock sermons about folly played with the possibility that the reader, too, might suddenly have to see himself as a fool. And the procedure excited both fears and hopes, as folly could at different times, or even at once, be damnation and blessing.

When we recognize someone as a fool, he becomes for us semidramatic, momentarily an actor, but in a special and elusive sense. Since he becomes for us the center of a show, the stage with an actor upon it provides a metaphor for the way in which the fool stands out against a background. The fool may, in fact, appear upon a stage, but if he does so he partly dissolves the nonfoolish conventions governing it, just as he partly dissolves the distinction between fools and nonfools, between himself and us. These distinctions can be only partly dissolved, or can be completely dissolved for only moments at a time; if they were thoroughly dissolved, we would be too foolish to find anything exceptional about the fact that the fool is a fool. Our attention would no longer focus upon him. Yet the fact of folly within ourselves is as essential to our participation in the fool show as is the appearance of someone we recognize as a fool. Among the instances of folly enumerated by the Mother of Fools in Erasmus' oration is that of the Greek who sat a whole day in an empty theater laughing, shouting, and clapping his hands and who, when cured of his delusion, hoped for a speedy relapse into it.[3] In the tricks he plays upon us, the fool proves us to have been deluded in our assumption that we are merely members of the audience, nonfools, watching a fool upon the stage. The figure we see before us may, in other words, be at least as much a product of the blissful Greek's way of seeing as it is an object simply there. If the figure is illusion, he may reduce the real world to that, too. But the fool on the stage strikes us as radiant with a life that transcends his stylized attributes and often inconsequential jokes. The radiance flickers. It is the light of folly, by which we see the fool interacting with folly and nonfolly, linking them and transforming them into each other.

One of Holbein's marginal illustrations to the *Praise of Folly* can be taken as a succinct representation of the way the fool is born as a phenomenon. In a psychological sense this representation may be regarded as prior to the apparition of the cock-man. I assume that we relate to the fool actor partly through the mechanism of "projection," by which we see in him our own foolish tendencies; here the subjective need for such an object is asserting itself. The drawing is of a reveler, a jester, or a fool actor who is for the moment a nonfool in that his cowled hood with its ass's ears is hanging down his back, revealing his whole head, while he gazes reflectively into the mirror. Perhaps, in Erasmus' metaphor of the comedy of human life in which we all wear different disguises, the man is backstage, where the fool role has just been assigned to him, and is wondering how to play it. As he studies himself, his image appears to stick out its tongue. (See Plate 8.) The man is the involuntary victim of the experience we invite when we look at ourselves in the wavy mirrors of the funhouse. Yet nothing in the drawing suggests that his mirror is any different from the one in which he has always looked at himself or that what happens as he looks now can be explained with respect to a reasonable cause. What should be his nonfoolish image gains its own capricious life, as though something weird and lawless within it had suddenly risen to the surface. What confronts him is the semblance of himself alive with folly; the nonfool is suddenly a fool. The Holbein drawing suggests the line separating and joining nonfool and fool as that line is present in the nonfool; the same line is present in the fool, and it is present in various ways in our relations to fools. This line fluctuates; sometimes it is not discernible at all, and sometimes it is a line of self-division that does not correspond to the division between nonfool and fool. The line is implicit in certain forms of duality that run through the range of clowns and fools.

The medieval court jester often expressed this duality by carrying a bauble, capped with an emblematic replica of his head. A picture of the uses of the bauble can be deduced from early references to it, from the devices of clowns and other entertainers, among them the ventriloquist with his dummy, from the behavior of children with dolls and other toys, and from certain phenomena of psychopathology. With it the jester carried on conversations for himself and the bauble and sometimes the whole company to hear. He also used it to beat others and to play a variety of unexpected tricks, some aggressive, some obscene, upon them.

# The Fool and His Show

His jokes and tricks with his bauble assumed and furthered a kind of make-believe which brought about many confusions of the normal order. Things were no longer what they seemed. The bauble, an object suddenly alive and human, could start an argument with the fool. Between them they could satirize a third person, even the king, with the fool defending him while the bauble persuasively argued that he was a fool. The fool could also address the bauble as though it were that person and treat it with respect, although the reduction of that person to a bauble had already made a fool of him. These confusions called in question the nature of objects, people, and the world, but the confusions were in fun; thus the world remained what it was, despite its seeming absurdity; reality and seeming were held together by the fool. This loss of normal relations between things also annulled the fool's responsibility for his tricks and allowed him to revenge himself playfully upon others for their lack of clear moral obligation toward him. (See Plates 9–13.)

The self-division of the fool as the source of foolish happenings is also implied in the figure of the rogue-fool Till Eulenspiegel. His name suggests the mirroring of the owl (*Eule*), symbolic of wisdom, in the glass (*Spiegel*) of reflection. In that mirroring the source of knowledge (the owl) and our means of experiencing it (the mirror) are linked by the fool, who makes knowledge and meaningful action difficult, if not impossible. This implication of Till Eulenspiegel's name is pictured in the title pages of early books about him. He is shown holding the owl in one hand, the mirror that reflects the owl in the other. Between them, he looks into the mirror, but it is not clear whether he sees the owl or himself in it. Or else he stands back from the mirroring and mischievously smirks, holding a bauble in his hand. (See Plates 14 and 15.) The fool often appropriates or replaces the image of someone else; his victim may be either another fool or a nonfool. A variation of this theme is presented in a skit about a broken mirror by the Clown Pipo (Pipo Sosman) and the Auguste Rhum (Enrico Sprocani). The Auguste breaks the mirror that the Clown wants to use as he dresses for a performance; the Auguste tries to evade punishment by standing behind the glassless mirror and aping every movement of the Clown, so that the Clown believes he is studying his own reflection.[4] The same device occurs in *Duck Soup* (1933), in which Harpo Marx confronts his brother Groucho in a dark house and

PLATE 8. One of Holbein's illustrations to Erasmus' *Praise of Folly,*
showing a fool looking at himself in the mirror (a motif that
Holbein took over from the illustrations to Brant's *Narrenschiff*).
The thoughtful expression of the man suggests that he is attempting
to learn something about who or what he is; as he does so, his image
seems to stick out its tongue at him. This caprice of the image accords
with the fact that an unexpected and incomprehensible turn of events
is often required to goad a person to serious self-reflection. Moreover,
the man's image appears to be hooded, presumably with the ass-eared
cowl hanging from his shoulders. Seneca had written, "When I want
to look at a fool I have only to look in the mirror," and Erasmus
referred to his *Praise of Folly* as a mirror in which he, too, had found
himself revealed (Desidirius Erasmus, *Opus Epistolarum,* ed.
P. S. Allen [Oxford: Clarendon Press, 1910], II, 94–95).

PLATE 9. Another of Holbein's illustrations to the *Praise of Folly,* showing a fool addressing or playing with his bauble. Since the bauble is a replica of the fool, this picture has been interpreted as an example of the vanity that impedes self-knowledge. But it is also an example of the playful fantasy that is a necessary part of one's adaptation to the world. (About this plate and the preceding one see F. Saxl, "Holbein's Illustrations to the *Praise of Folly* by Erasmus," *Burlington Magazine,* LXXXIII [November, 1943], 276.)

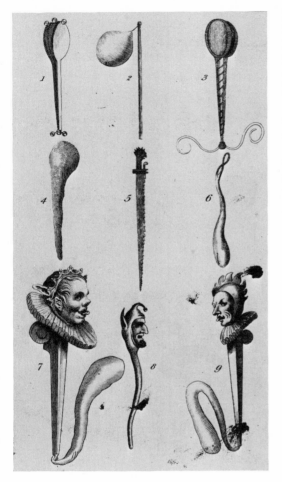

PLATE 10. Jesters' baubles. Figures 7 and 9 represent a late development of the bauble from the more primitive club; in them the human image is reduced to the fool's head and the exaggerated phallus. The ass's ears (of 7 and 8) and the cockscomb (of 9) link the figures to animals famous for their sexuality as well as their silliness. The figures represent the intelligence of the phallus—a counterpart, on the level of instinct, to the reason of the head; or they represent reason drawn into the sphere of the instinctual element and overwhelmed by it. The figures are sticking their tongues out insultingly, like the image in the mirror in Holbein's drawing (Plate 8). Thus these baubles may be seen as a symbolic form of the power behind or within the encounter between fool and nonfool in which the customary lines between folly and nonfolly are blurred or broken.

PLATE 11. The vaudeville comedy team is here pictured in a way that suggests the self-division common among fools, as when a jester carries a bauble representing a double of himself.

apes his movements to make him believe that he sees his own reflection in a mirror. Only a fool would think of imitating the two-dimensional reflection of another person, and only another fool would be deceived by the imitation: together they constitute the fool nature in which the distinction between reality and reflection is broken down.

The same interplay between the fool and himself (reflecting that between folly and our means of understanding it and interacting with it) may be seen in the device of the fool pair, familiar from countless forms of comic entertainment, most simply that of knockabout farce; it is present in a more differentiated form in many pairs of fictional characters whose destinies are interrelated, among them Lear and his Fool, Don Quixote and Sancho Panza, Don Giovanni and Leporello, Tom Sawyer and Huckleberry Finn. On the more primitive level of clowns, one of the

PLATE 12. Tarot card, Austria, 1453–57, inscribed "Female joker. Looking at her grinning idiot's face in the mirror." (Actually, *she* is grinning; her reflection is stupidly straight-faced.) Here, too, as in Plates 8, 19, and 20, there is something "wrong" with the reflected image: the face in her mirror is too small, and the mirror is directed toward the viewer, not toward her. The image has something of the bauble's character of being semiautonomous with respect to the fool and of reflecting the audience as well as him (or, in this picture, her).

39

PLATE 13. Jean Antoine Watteau, "Italian Comedians" (etched and engraved by Bernard Baron). The figure seated to the lower right holds a bauble-like staff as tall as he is.

pair is usually the knave or wit, the other the dupe or butt, the two often exchanging roles back and forth in a flood of surprises, involving confusions of identity, of sense and nonsense, of mundane reality and hints of unexpected and inexhaustible powers within it. Neither of the characters has a claim to existence without the other, and their interchangeability is often suggested in foolish names that mirror each

40

PLATES 14 and 15. Title pages to histories of Till Eulenspiegel (Plate 14, edition of Simon Caluarin, Paris, *ca.* 1580; Plate 15, Elzevir edition, Amsterdam, 1703). The fool's mischief extends from crude pranks with objects, as when he steals or destroys, to subtle caprices in our reflection upon ourselves and upon the world.

41

other, such as Dario and Bario, Brick (an early partner of the famous clown) and Grock, Dick and Doff (the German names for the film comedians Laurel and Hardy). (See Plates 16 and 17.) In the same vein an English Harlequin pantomime bore the title *Harlequin Fat and Harlequin Bat.* There is an echo of clown pairs who have such names in the Tweedledum and Tweedledee encountered by Alice and in the Shem and Shaun of Joyce's *Finnegans Wake.* Some fool pairs are explicitly twins. The two Dromios, twin comic servants of twin masters in *The Comedy of Errors,* are derived from Plautus and may be regarded as a development from the more primitive clown doubles. Such figures recall distantly and in burlesque form the mythological "Primordial Pair," the sometimes complementary, sometimes hostile opposites that according to various religious traditions are present in the background of things.[5]

Often when we recognize someone as a fool, we do so partly because we sense that he is somehow double, even if he is alone, without his image or alter ego (in the visible form of his bauble or of his partner in folly or in the invisible form, for example, of the cock who crowed out of the man on the Zurich tram). There have been many clown skits in which the clown's right hand literally does not know what his left is doing. This self-division is often expressed in the immediate physical appearance of the fool, for example, in costumes the right and left halves of which make a pattern of contrasts. (See Plate 18.) In and around the fool things combine in ways that violate our sense of propriety; we expect this to happen and to happen in unexpected ways. Sometimes when the fool thinks that he has overcome the difference between him and us, he has only succeeded in falling deeper into his own folly and may be rewarded with a glimpse of how wrong he has been. (See Plate 19.) Nonetheless, in important ways he is a person like us, and he shares some or even many of our assumptions about what a human being is and should be and do. Under the influence of projection we exaggerate the difference between nonfool and fool and the extent to which we are neatly here and he there at a distance. At the same time we relax our guard against being fools ourselves. The self-division that we sense in the fool is made, partly by means of projection, to correspond to the division between fool and nonfool. The relations between them are reconstituted at a distance from

PLATE 16. A scene from a seventeenth-century play about confusions caused by doubles of Harlequin.

PLATE 17. The Rastelli troupe, including clown doubles (Alfredo and Oreste Rastelli). The contrast between the white clown (Antonio Poletto) and the black clown ("Chocolate") illustrates the tendency of fools to serve the principle of wholeness by bringing together extremes and even opposites. This principle is further suggested by the fact that the figures are the interrelated elements of a fourfold pattern, or quaternity, which is itself symbolic of wholeness.

us, this giving us the feeling that the fool's show will adequately contain any dangers that the fool holds for the nonfool. He carries on for us the war against folly, but he does so from a different vantage point and with different prospects of success and failure. Whatever equivalent he has of our intelligence struggles and plays with, on the one hand, his foolishness and, on the other, the normal human image.

All of this is implied in the metaphor of the fool as it was explored by Erasmus: if I recognize someone as a fool, I assume that I am a nonfool; in thinking that I am a nonfool, whereas I am at least potentially a fool, I become a fool in fact. As Empson writes,

44

# The Fool and Mimesis

Plate 18. A contemporary "Till Eulenspiegel" doll (made by Helen Diemer, Switzerland). It shows a symmetrical mirroring of contrasting elements, here black and white, seen frequently in costumes of court jesters and of figures in carnival processions and in the commedia dell'arte. These elements are interrelated in a way that suggests the quaternity, symbolic of wholeness, in Plate 17.

it is a major activity of the Fool to make a fool of other people, so that this word gives a particularly strong case for . . . the return of the meaning of the word upon the speaker. Everyman displays by contrast the folly of the wise, and the clown jeers at his betters; the contradictions that appear in the doctrine were felt to be a gain, not an obstruction, because they brought out this feeling of mutuality: "I call you a fool of one sort speaking as myself a fool of another sort." Indeed on the theory of Socrates, that the fool is he who does not know that he is a fool, any direct use of the word inherently recoils and it can never help being mutual.[6]

However, this mutuality is not limited to the use of the word or to the Socratic theory. It belongs to the fool show in a deeper sense and to the

45

PLATE 19.  A contemporary cartoon showing the obverse
of what is represented in Holbein's drawing of the nonfool
looking in the mirror and finding that his image plays
foolish tricks on him (Plate 8). Here a clown looks in the
mirror and sees himself as normal. A curious distortion
has occurred either in the mirror or in his own mind.
(Perhaps he even thinks that he and his image are two
separate figures looking at each other through a window.)
The question thus stated—Who is the fool?—was the
basic rhetorical trick of the late medieval fool literature
and is at least implicit in virtually every presentation of
fools.

illusion characteristic of that show. And even when the fool loudly and convincingly proclaims that we are fools, too, what the fool is partly remains the fool's secret, though he may pretend to disclose it.

The fool is the image of ourselves, but he is this in a quite special sense. The jokes and tricks of his show are his equivalent of our action; it is informed with his equivalent of our knowledge. These equivalents may suffice for him—indeed, they must—but that does not mean they would for us. It may be true that our action and knowledge rest on beliefs which we assume to be more adequate than they are. Nonetheless, we know and act for a purpose, which belongs to our natures as much as the fool's apparent purposelessness does to his. That purpose may be expressed as the realization of the human image: to find and affirm our individual destinies within the frame of society and of nature. The difficulties we inevitably have in achieving that purpose are expressed, for example, in Hamlet's soliloquies about the nature of man. Since the fool may interfere with that purpose, and since he seems incapable of being transformed into a nonfool, we must banish him or find an accommodation to him, a *modus vivendi* that allows him and us a measure of freedom and yet of interaction.

Holbein's drawing of the man confronting his reflection with its stuck-out tongue suggests images that describe two of our profoundest means of seeing what man is and what each of us is. These two ways of seeing are complementary, and the fool stands at the edge of each. The first is dramatic. Its nature is summed up in the mirror imagined by Hamlet in his speech to the players: ". . . the purpose of playing, whose end, both at the first and now, was and is to hold, as 'twere, the mirror up to nature; to show virtue her own feature, scorn her own image, and the very age and body of the time his form and pressure" (III. ii. 21–26). The second is concerned with our relation to whatever lies beyond our forms of action and understanding. Its nature may also be imagined as that of a mirror; St. Paul describes it in a simile: "When I was a child, I spake as a child, I understood as a child, I thought as a child: but when I became a man, I put away childish things. For now we see through a glass, darkly; but then face to face: now I know in part; but then shall I know even as also I am known" (I Cor. 13:11–12).

47

These metaphors for ways of seeing things complexly are based on the common mirror into which we look to find the simple images of ourselves. More complex ways of seeing are necessary because those simple images break down; we may be startled by an extraneous element of ourselves, as Holbein's little man was by the stuck-out tongue. The reflections provided by drama and religion should leave us with less by which to be startled. Because they are complex, these ways of seeing often make some allowance for the fact of fools and folly, even if that fact is at first trimmed and tucked into parentheses. Still, we may spontaneously see others as fools and be seen as fools by them, and both they and we may be fooled in our assumptions about things. And the fool who characteristically violates the distinction we make between nonfools and fools may end by appropriating the fragments of the nonfoolish image.

The fool may appear on the stage as a clown, performing in a loose relationship, or perhaps none at all, to the dramatic action. Or he may, with a sacrifice of his freedom, become a comic character, whose behavior, though foolish, is consonant with the larger form of that action. The fool also appears at the edges of our religious understanding. He does so in that we discover ourselves fools in our ignorance and sin (the most common sense of the word "fool" in the Old Testament). Or he may do so as someone to be emulated because he has a pure and unwavering relation to the mystery of "eternal things." We are told that we should become "fools for Christ's sake": "For the wisdom of this world is foolishness with God" and "the foolishness of God is wiser than men" (I Cor. 4:10, 3:19, 1:25). "Fool" has often been used to mean "heretic" for people who were presumed, for example by Adelung in his *Geschichte der menschlichen Narrheit* (1785), to be cranks, charlatans, madmen, and victims of ignorance and superstition. But some of the same people might also, and just as well, be considered "fools in Christ." Religious fools in the second sense, in an ambiguous relation to the first, have been an undercurrent within European Christianity. Elsewhere in the world, primarily in the Eastern Orthodox Church, in Islam, and in some religious traditions of the Far East, such figures have sometimes been even more highly venerated.

However, though the fool appears in these modes of representation and is part of their characteristic life, he does not really belong to them and is ultimately excluded from them. When the clown begins to ruin the dramatic performance, his lines must be written out for him; he must be made into a comic character. At the close of his remarks to the Players, Hamlet takes up the problem of keeping the clown in his place within the written piece:

> And let those that play your clowns speak no more than is set down for them; for there be of them that will themselves laugh, to set on some quantity of barren spectators to laugh too, though in the meantime some necessary question of the play be then to be considered. That's villainous, and shows a most pitiful ambition in the fool that uses it.

(III. ii. 36–43)

And when the comic character turns out to have too much of the power of the fool, he must be banned altogether, as Falstaff was from Shakespeare's history plays. Thus toward the end of the seventeenth century Harlequin, having become a clown in the commedia dell'arte, was removed from the dramatic action to appear in *scènes détachées,* inserted into plays of the most various kinds.[7] Ultimately, the drama, as a presentation of meaningful action, belongs not to the fool but to the actor. And though we are enjoined to be "fools in Christ," the kingdom of Heaven belongs not to the fool but to the child. The fool is neither the player nor the audience in Hamlet's sense but both and something else. The fool is neither child nor man in St. Paul's sense but both and something else.

Yet is is doubtful whether either of these mirrors can be more than momentarily free of the fool's image, and there is an important sense in which he may be imagined as ultimately holding them, just as he may hold the simple mirror in which we may someday be mocked by a stuck-out tongue that does not belong to ourselves. The action in Hamlet's mirror of the stage usually takes place, if it is convincing, at the expense of a distinction between the actor and his role and between it and ourselves. The artificial action of drama, based on illusion, on our being fooled, may allow us to "See better" (as King Lear is told to do—I. i. 157) than we can without the dramatic mirror. However, even though we may arrive at a more adequate vision by being fooled in this way, that vision may blind us to an even more adequate one. The same is true of our relation to the religious mirror. Struck by St. Paul's simile, we may feel that we are seeing reality face to face when we have really only lost sight of the shifting interplay between the darkness of ignorance and the clarity of vision that St. Paul implies to be part of our experience in the world.

Yet even when our folly becomes dangerously swollen with pride, it contains the possibility that the fool will illumine our darkness in a spontaneous show. It is the possibility that his show, replacing the light by which we usually understand and act, will free us from the dead forms of what we foolishly thought was life. If the fool's show accomplishes this, it does so less often by increasing our understanding than by freeing us from its demands. This is not the grace of seeing "face to face" and of knowing "even as I am known," any more than dramatic action is real life. It is rather a kind of play, neither that of an actor nor that of a child but both and neither, in which our final ignorance of our natures is brought to expression.

When we are caught up in the fool show, we are not aware of the mutuality between the fool and the nonfool. Despite our commitment to the mimetic purpose and to the forms (among them those of dramatic action) into which the fool intrudes, we are usually content to see him the way he wants to be seen, even if he ends by playing a trick upon us. He mirrors us in his own way. This is well illustrated by the encounter between Touchstone and the melancholy Jaques in *As You Like It*. At one point Jaques appears transformed in merriment and exclaims "A fool, a fool! I met a fool i' th' forest, / A motley fool" (II. vii. 12–13). Touchstone had mirrored Jaques's dour philosophizing. Jaques says:

> And then he drew a dial from his poke,
> And, looking on it with lack-lustre eye,
> Says very wisely 'It is ten o'clock;
> Thus we may see' quoth he 'how the world wags;
> 'Tis but an hour ago since it was nine;
> And after one hour more 'twill be eleven;
> And so, from hour to hour, we ripe and ripe,

## The Fool and Mimesis

And then, from hour to hour, we rot and rot;
And thereby hangs a tale'.

(ll. 20–28)

Jaques is beside—or rather, before—himself. In mirroring him, the fool
*is* he, and he is the fool: "My lungs began to crow like chanticleer . . ."
(l. 30). Jaques is possessed, as were the passengers by the cock-man on the
Zurich tram. He has been delivered over to the space and time of the fool
show: "And I did laugh sans intermission / An hour by his dial"
(ll. 32–33). Regaining himself, he falls into his own folly anew: "O that I
were a fool! / I am ambitious for a motley coat" (ll. 42–43). This is
foolish, because he is already a fool, and in a figurative sense he already
wears a motley coat. All he lacks is a mirror, and that, too, he has had
without knowing it. The fool's duality has reasserted itself; the audience
of the play is presented with doubles of a figure compounded of
Touchstone and Jaques.

Jaques may serve as a prototype of the nonfool in the sense that when
we see a fool we do so in ignorance of the fool within ourselves. This
ignorance is more specifically the blind spot that keeps us from knowing
in advance the point of the fool's trick or joke; it also keeps us from being
aware of the larger fool show into which the trick or joke will dissolve,
eluding our understanding. But that point momentarily illumines our
blindness. It sometimes does so with intelligent purpose, a suggestion of
meaning. The circus clown or comedian, for example, actively and
consciously structures his presentation around the points of his tricks and
jokes. And when we "get the point," it strikes us as intelligent enough to
seem unintelligent; it impinges upon meaning at least enough to be felt as
a violation of meaning. The point of a joke may lie in a hidden meaning,
and this, as it comes to light, may be what strikes us as funny. But the
point may also lie in the fact that the joke issues into nonsense with only a
few strips and tatters of sense or that it seems to have a sense that one
cannot get at; one gets stuck in one's inability to deal with it
meaningfully at all. There have been innumerable attempts to account for
jokes and their effects. Without debating theories of humor, one can
imagine that most jokes play upon the notion of the fool and the
mutuality implicit in it.

51

# The Fool and His Show

The mutuality between fool and nonfool may often be felt in the self-division of the single fool, especially when he creates irreducible ambiguities between meaning and meaninglessness. An example of this is provided by a circus-clown joke—First Clown: "I'm the father of seven sons!" Second Clown: "I'm the son of seven fathers!" The second clown's answer sounds at first like a meaningful statement the sense of which eludes us (the fool's main interest, and the interest he awakens in us, usually being in possibilities). The sense continues to elude us until we realize that it is illusory (the fool's relation to actualities, and the actualities he presents to us, often being inferior). It is as though the clowns had conspired with the fool within ourselves; our expectations and our attempts at understanding are thwarted, the energies invested in them are taken up by our sense of identity with the clowns, and we are for the moment as silly as they are. In general, however, we soon come to terms with the trick that the fool plays on us, either by seeing a meaningful point in it or by giving it up as nonsense. The moment of being startled by something expressive of folly is like the moment in which the man in Holbein's drawing sees his image in the mirror sticking his tongue out at him. The moment of laughter at the foolish thing is like that in which, we may imagine, the man in Holbein's drawing looks again, finds his image normal, and is released from the role of the fool. However, one is not always released in this way. The lunatic asylum of earlier times and, for that matter, the metaphorical ship of fools have much in common with the situation of *Huis Clos* or "No Exit" portrayed by Sartre. (See Plate 20.) The fool's mirror may be threat or promise or neither; it may be all of these at the same time.

The duality of the fool and the division between the fool and the nonfool (with its corollary, the mirroring of meaning and meaninglessness) are both reflected in the role of the fool actor. Writing about the masks common to nonfoolish actors and clowns, Disher points out that the word "mask" comes from an Arabic word, *maskharat,* for clown. "Sooted cheeks in Ancient Rome, red noses for devils in the Middle Ages, masks in the Commedia dell'arte, bismuth and rouge in the English Harlequinade, flour in old French farces, and burnt cork in the nigger-minstrel shows"—clowns and fools usually wear some kind of

52

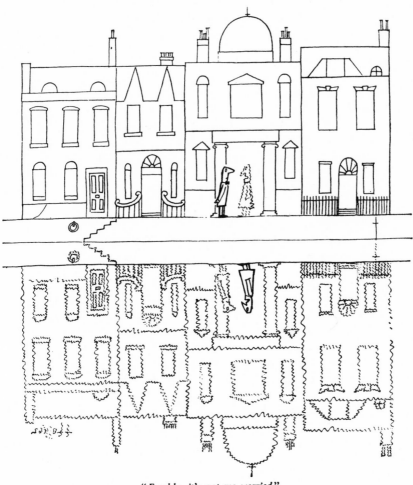

*"Frankly, it's got me worried."*

PLATE 20. Another contemporary cartoon, suggestive of the way in which folly, having possessed a person, may refuse to release him and allow him again to discriminate in anything like a normal way between reality and illusion—and between a "right" reflection of reality and a "wrong" one. The figure in the cartoon knows something is "wrong" with his situation, though he cannot tell what. This accords with our reaction to many jokes and with much of psychopathology (as when a person is obsessed with peculiar ideas while knowing that he is possessed and knowing that they are peculiar).

mask, though a natural deformity often takes its place, as did the flattened nose of the jester Tarlton in Shakespeare's time. However, the mask of the clown or fool serves a different function from that of the comic or tragic actor.

> Unlike the actor's disguise, which made him into another being, it served merely as a disfigurement. . . . Instead of representing a comic character [the Roman sooty mime at the time of the New Comedy] had to be himself in spite of his disguise. His familiar manner made his everyday reality known to the audience; his fantastic face made him a creature of the imagination. He was thus in himself a standing joke.[8]

And "being neither wholly real nor unreal," he was the personification of his role in a different way than an actor is of his.[9]

This ambiguity between the fool and his disguise was frequently as characteristic of his personal life as it was of his performance. Often there was no distinction between the two. Enid Welsford remarks that fools and buffoons

> were regarded as funny in themselves, their pranks were played in real life, and they moved in comparatively small though varied social circles: the court, the market town, the village tavern. Even the theatrical clowns acted in an atmosphere of small talk, discussion and personal gossip, and did not belong wholly to the drama: for whereas Burbage ceased to be Hamlet when the play was over, Tarlton was Tarlton both on and off the stage; Martinelli [an actor of the commedia dell'arte] entitled himself Arlequin even in legal documents; and both Martinelli and Dominique acted as jesters to French and Italian princes.[10]

The kind of disguise described by Disher, which partly creates an illusion and partly violates it, may be seen clearly in the reversal of sexes characteristic of saturnalian revels. "Dramatic disguise," he writes, ". . . is for the players to become the men and women whose clothes and titles they assume. Saturnalian performances [such as the Feast of Fools], on the contrary, rely on the absence of illusion—on the incongruity of the man being the opposite of what he half appears to be."[11] Jokes involving the reversal of sex and the failure of the illusion by which that reversal is maintained may become the material of drama, for example in *As You Like It* and in Hofmannsthal's *Der Rosenkavalier*. Then such jokes are

54

not made simply for the sake of the breakdown they effect between reality and illusion; they serve a dramatic purpose. A fool actor, however, aware of the freedom of saturnalian folly may violate stage conventions in a way that partly serves dramatic purpose and partly serves his folly as something that transcends the theater. Enid Welsford writes, "As a dramatic character [the fool] usually stands apart from the main action of the play, having a tendency not to focus but to dissolve events." [12] The fool as clown may spoil the play; the fool in a broader sense may dissolve action altogether. Thus Enid Welsford speaks even more generally of "one of the perennial functions of the fool, the power of melting the solidity of the world." [13]

During the storm upon the heath Lear's Fool, in keeping with the fool's function of dissolving both reality and the imaginative imitation of it, drops his role as the personal jester of a king who is real in the make-believe of the theater; the Fool falls out of time. He begins a flood of gnomic doggerel with the announcement, "This prophecy Merlin shall make, for I live before his time" (III. ii. 95). S. L. Bethell writes about it:

> If the passage be genuine, it is interesting to find Shakespeare employing direct address at the height of his powers. The convention can be acceptable only to an audience conscious simultaneously of play-world and real world. The Fool is recognized as stepping out of the story for a moment: he addresses the audience in character as the Fool, but not in any direct reference to the story. This half-and-half adjustment is rendered possible by the fact that the audience will recognise him (*a*) as actor belonging to their own (real) world, and (*b*) as character, belonging to the play-world. . . . The Fool's prophecy concerned matters common to the Lear story and contemporary life, occupying a no-man's-land between the play-world and the real world.[14]

This use of the Fool serves a purpose noted by Bethell: it is "as if Shakespeare wanted to underline the relevance of the *Lear* world to contemporary affairs." [15] The passage is not, however, merely a dramatic device to engage the audience. The timeless confusion of the Fool's utterance expresses one of the deepest elements of the play, of the plot, in Aristotle's definition, as the "soul of the action." The Fool, that is to say, also brings us into touch with a level of being on which the reality, not only of the dramatic action but of the kingdom it imaginatively reflects, becomes a play of illusion in a mirror.

The fool actor can in this way call reality into question, or even dissolve it, because of the queer nature of the reality he has for us as a person. (As we have seen, his role as a fool actor tends again and again to collapse, with the result that he simply presents what he is in a way more immediate than that of formal drama.) As a person he is sometimes *too much there,* the clod who gets in the way of nonfools as he asserts himself, coarsely indifferent to the conventions of either reality or the imitation of it. He is also sometimes too *little* there. He is often "not all there" with respect to intelligence or sanity, as when Lear's Fool sings of his "little tiny wit" and how he "Must make content with his fortunes fit . . ." (III. ii. 74 and 76). But this inadequacy goes deeper, to the center of what the fool is as a person; we see this, for example, when the dog familiar of the Devil in *The Witch of Edmonton* (by Rowley, Dekker, Ford, and others, probably first performed in 1623) finally dismisses the clown, Cuddy Banks, with the words, "Hence, silly fool! / I scorn to prey on such an atom soul" (V. ii). These extremes of "too much" and "too little" are not mutually exclusive; the fool who is one characteristically becomes the other for moments at a time. Either may serve as the basic element of a presentation that also draws the other into it.

The great fool figures of the silent films, among them Buster Keaton, Charlie Chaplin, and Harry Langdon, carried their personalities over from film to film, as did W. C. Fields and the Marx Brothers of the talkies. Keaton invariably wears his flat hat and deadpan look and Chaplin his baggy pants, bowler, and mustache through may films, which present a variety of circumstances in which the comedians assert their unchanging personalities. The films often imply the problem, "How might the comic figure be cajoled, deceived, or beaten into surrendering himself to some alteration of character?" Possible solutions are considered, and each is rejected in turn. There is, of course, a nonfoolish variant of this persistence of a set character through various stories. This is in the serial adventures of figures in the picaresque tradition, for example, heroes of comic strips and detective fiction. The circumstances in which they find themselves are to be taken seriously; they are at least dimly frightening to us as we participate in the story through the figure. But when Ben Turpin of the silent films hurtles across a snow-covered landscape in a sled drawn by yapping huskies, his panic seems to be inspired only in part by the circumstances; it seems inspired just as much by the fact that he is unalterably Ben Turpin and that his attempts to fit in anywhere are so preposterous that they must sooner or later lead to panic, whether he is trying to survive the cold or to look at home in a harem of Amazon women. He has some success in dealing with such problems, but finally he is what he is, and there is for him no way out of it.

We are not surprised if, say, a figure in a cartoon film divides and becomes two. Nor, strangely enough, are we surprised if one of the highly individual fools I have been talking about does this. The sharply etched and self-assertive Groucho Marx makes jokes playing upon the divisibility of other people. Thus in *Animal Crackers* (1930) he drives his stupid brother Chico to remark, "He thinks I look alike," this earning Groucho's retort, "Well, if you do, it's a tough break for both of you." But in another scene from the same film Groucho himself divides, and the two Grouchos interact before us on the screen. (In *The Playhouse* [1921] as many as nine Buster Keatons dance together.) Upon reflection, we might feel that Groucho's self-division violates the realistic conventions that allow him to become so much a person to us. Yet his brash character is partly expressed in his grease-paint mustache and his glassless spectacles; these may be regarded as remnants of two-dimensionality or as the beginnings of a reversion to it, and they are constantly before our eyes.

Taking folly for a moment in the very narrow sense of "that which makes us laugh," we can see that, if the fool were less thoroughly himself, it would be less funny than it is that he is a half-person; if he were less deficient as a person, it would be less funny that he is, or so insistently pretends to be, someone, even more of someone than a nonfool is. These ambiguities belong to the nature of the semidramatic fool role; they emerge with great clarity in the fool's characteristic relationship to the device of disguise within a dramatic action.

In the theater of many times and places, and in many of the very greatest plays, one character disguises himself as another, this disguise and the revelation of the original character from behind it being essential to the action. (Shakespeare not only made extensive use of the device: it is essential to his vision of what the stage and the world are.) It is generally necessary to the effect that the audience recognize the original character in the disguise he has put on. We are fascinated by the interplay among the disguise and the character and behavior demanded by it, the adaptation to the disguise and the residue of the still apparent original character. In a variant of this procedure, sometimes to be seen in the brief actions that make up a program of cabaret skits, one character plays several roles. Alec Guinness does this in his film *Kind Hearts and Coronets* (English title, *Noblesse Oblige*) (1950), a sustained action in which there are traces of the complex interplay between character and disguise to be found in more substantial pieces of drama. The difference between this comic use of disguise and the fool's characteristic use of it becomes apparent if we compare the Guinness film with another, *The Family Jewels* (1965), by Jerry Lewis, one of the modern comedians in whom the poetry of the silent-film masters is for the most part reduced to loud banality, but a fool actor nonetheless, in contrast to the more reflective Guinness. In the film Lewis plays several roles, in each of which he is simply himself; it is precisely his almost complete lack of adaptation to the roles he assumes that is the point of the undertaking. In Lewis' playing of various parts we see the self-division of the fool (the fool actor dispersed in several roles), the maladaptation of the fool to the role, and his stubborn assertion of his essential character.

This conflict between role-playing and foolish self-assertion is epitomized in the appearance in the commedia dell'arte of Harlequin as Diana, goddess of the chase. His black satyr's face is partly ringed below with the crescent moon and above with curls and plumes; he wears a woman's elaborate dress and carries a bow. (See Plate 21.) The effect is less that of a dramatic character assuming a disguise than that of the kind of trick photograph in which a bald-headed man sticks his head up above a screen on which the body of a woman is painted. The same effect was achieved by the great Munich beer-hall comedian Karl Valentin when he appeared as Lorelei, as an aviator, or as one of various military types from various centuries that he liked to impersonate, all the while looking very much himself.

In these pieces Ben Turpin, Jerry Lewis, Harlequin, and Karl Valentin remain obviously themselves; they do this at the expense of what would

PLATE 21. Engraving by Jean Mariette (1660–1742) of Harlequin dressed as Diana, Goddess of the Chase. The picture illustrates various traits that recur in the fool show: discrepancy between the fool actor and the nonfoolish role, burlesque of the sacred, transvestitism and ambiguity of sex, confusion of the crude (Harlequin's face) and the fine (Diana's dress), of dark and light.

be credibility if they were not working within the conventions of both the fool show and the formal drama. Groucho Marx divides; Lewis and Valentin are dispersed in several figures, each of which represents a potential dramatic or real identity botched rather than actualized by the fool. All of these fool actors are individuals and types at the same time, as are many purely dramatic figures. But these fools also represent a permanence in the midst of flux that is very different from the dramatic development of character and even negates it.

However, a fool performance may be based not on the individuality of the fool, on his being "too much there," but on his being "too little there," on his ability to disperse himself and on his two-dimensionality. Stith Thompson has observed this quality of being "too little there" among fools in folk tales:

> The essential nature of the ego . . . has troubled the thinking of fools. Sometimes a man may not know himself because in his sleep his beard has been cut off or his garments have been changed, or he has been smeared with tars and feathers. . . . Or he may be sitting with other fools and they get their legs mixed up, so that they cannot tell whose is whose. . . . One fool concludes that a member of their party is drowned because he fails to count himself. . . . The difficulty is sometimes solved by the whole group sticking their noses into the sand, and then counting the holes.[16]

The jokes of the fool actor may also play upon the fact that he ignores the necessity of being a substantial person and is content, or even wants, to be something else. This is shown in another circus-clown joke (related to the Marxes' "He thinks I look alike!")—First Clown: "I wish I were two puppies!" Second Clown: "Why?" First Clown: "So I could play together!"

An example of the fool's ability to move from two-to three-dimensionality is provided by a commedia dell'arte play. In it there is a scene in which old Pantalon is deceived by various characters at the instigation of his daughter. He has promised that if she will marry the Captain, Pantalon will have a picture of Cupid painted to go over their marriage bed. The painter, Mazetin, begins to work on a blank canvas, behind which the fool Harlequin stands dressed as Cupid, with wings and bow and arrows. Instead of painting on the canvas, Mazetin makes cuts in it with a knife. Harlequin's head appears, then his limbs; at last he steps out of the picture, a three-dimensional burlesque of a painting of Cupid—and in this role is as obviously and grotesquely himself as he is when dressed up as Diana.[17]

This foolish shifting of dimensions is also illustrated by another scene from the Marx Brothers' *Duck Soup*. Groucho (as Rufus T. Firefly) asks the dumb Harpo who he is; in answer Harpo rolls up his sleeve to show a tattooed likeness of his own head. He demonstrates the duality of which I have been speaking, the equivalence between himself as two- and himself as three-dimensional and his unawareness of the need for a social identity, such as that expressed in a name. Groucho then asks him where he lives and is shown, on Harpo's chest, a tattooed image of a doghouse; by means of trick photography a live, three-dimensional dog is made to come barking out of the doghouse. A natural continuation of the joke, if this were possible, would be for the cinematic dog to become a real one and then vanish in thin air.

Beginning from the fool's divisibility and two-dimensionality it is also possible for his jokes to play with the possibility that he might not be anything at all or that he might reduce others to that condition, too. This is illustrated by a circus-clown skit in which one clown teases another with the specious argument that, since the second clown is not in Hamburg and not in Dresden, he must be somewhere else and that, if he is somewhere else, he is not here and cannot respond to the slap the first clown has just given him, especially since the first clown is anyway not here either. The second clown here plays the role of the reasonable nonfool as a dupe and hence a fool; the audience senses its kinship with the second clown and thus feels the threat with which the first clown backs up his slap, that the fool can be nothing and also reduce the nonfool to nothing.

The slap of the first clown abruptly reminds the second clown of reality. It may happen, though, that the fool suggests the possibility of nothingness without drawing the nonfool up short and punishing him for entertaining the suggestion. Nothingness is then no longer simply part of a foolish game; it is a threat to the nonfool, who may regard it as a game but is anyway careful not to enter into it. Such a threat is presented, slightly veiled, in *Twelfth Night,* when Viola remarks to Feste, "I warrant thou art a merry fellow and car'st for nothing" and is answered, "Not so, sir; I do care for something; but in my conscience, sir, I do not care for you. If that be to care for nothing, sir, I would it would make you invisible" (III. i. 24–28). Lear's Fool, too, has a profound link to "nothing," a matter to which I will return in Part III.

Thus the fool in his connection with nothingness may jar us into an awareness of how far away we are from reality, how much we are like the Fool of one of the conventional Tarot packs who, lost in his dreams, is about to step over a precipice. In the same connection the fool may seem a threat both to reality and to our ways of seeing it complexly. But the fool in his link with "nothing" may also transform both reality and these ways of seeing it. I have already considered a number of such transformations, involving in various ways the fool and his double, such as his bauble or his clown partner. One could even say that the nothingness with which I am now concerned separates the elements of the pair. I have shown that these transformations touch on problems of meaning and meaninglessness and of reality and illusion—for example, in the relations of disguise to dramatic action. I have also shown that the foolish duality may be expressed in the self-division of the single fool and the mirroring of elements within him. This nothingness also belongs to his inner life; his connection with it brings about within himself, too, transformations of the kind that I have considered.

An example of such a transformation as part of the fool's inner life is provided by a gag by Hanswurst, a reincarnation of Harlequin in the eighteenth-century Viennese theater. The gag explores a state of consciousness in which "I" and something that might or might not be "I" but is separated from it by a kind of "nothing" are hopelessly confused and in which life goes on in accordance with intentions that Hanswurst's "I" has trouble in understanding. Hanswurst lies down to sleep, dreams that he is dreaming, and in this second dream dreams again that he is dreaming; in this dream-within-a-dream-within-a-dream he dreams that he has awakened, goes to sleep again, and dreams that he is awake and must force himself to sleep so that he can dream; he dreams that he again goes to sleep and is in his sleep so angry about not dreaming that he awakens and lies the rest of the night without dreaming in a kind of sleeping wakefulness that is at the same time a dream. Karl Valentin falls into the same problem when he dreams that he is a duck and awakens just as he is about to seize a worm. He reasons that it would have been unpleasant for him, Valentin, to have eaten it. He then loses himself in speculation about how it would be possible to know whether or not the duck could dream, and, if it could, what the relation of the duck's dream to his would be.[18]

Although presented on a stage by fool actors with theatrical presence, the jokes are extraneous to drama of a kind that relies on a sustained plot. Nonetheless, the make-believe of a play or other formal dramatic entertainment requires the spectator partly to lose himself in the performance like Hanswurst and Valentin in their waking dreams. The specifically dramatic form of reality-in-illusion can itself, in turn, be made the theme of dramatic action, as it is by Shakespeare in many places and by Pirandello, with the autonomous clown barred from the stage or subordinated to the plot.

There is, however, a moment in Shakespeare in which a fool caught in a problem similar to those of Hanswurst and Valentin is brought into an explicit, but enigmatic, relation to plotted dramatic action. In the Induction to *The Taming of the Shrew* Christopher Sly, the tinker, rouses from sleep, having become, unawares, the butt of a fool's joke played upon him by a Lord. The Lord, shocked into an awareness of death by the tinker's prostrate drunken form, has had him transported to his house, dressed as a Lord—thus making him the double of the Lord, who disappears—and presented with a page disguised as his Lady. The attendants of the newly created Lord devote themselves to persuading him that he has recovered his wits after fifteen years out of them. Unlike the macabre Valentin, whose intellectual acumen is kept sharp by his fascinated revulsion at the thought of eating the duck's worm, Sly yields lasciviously and simple-mindedly to the confusion between reality and dream, between himself and someone he is not:

> Am I a lord and have I such a lady?
> Or do I dream? Or have I dream'd till now?
> I do not sleep: I see, I hear, I speak;
> I smell sweet savours, and I feel soft things.
> Upon my life, I am a lord indeed,

63

## The Fool and His Show

And not a tinker, nor Christopher Sly.
Well, bring our lady hither to our sight;
And once again, a pot o' th' smallest ale.

(Induction, ii. 66–73)

The sight of the Lady from whom he has been parted for fifteen years
inflames him; she refuses further intimacy with the warning that it would
put him back into the dream of being Christopher Sly. From the point of
view of dramaturgy this admonition serves to keep him from discovering
that the Lady is really a page and that his blissful expectations are a joke.
Frightened by the prospect of being again the ragged pauper he really is,
Sly allows his attention to be diverted from his lady to an entertainment
provided by itinerant players. Thus the joke, instead of coming to its
farcical point, expands to include the play within the play that is the main
action of the piece. The point of the joke on the tinker, who does not
appear again, is diffused in the illusory action of the play proper; in
accepting the play world as real, the audience is partly brought to Sly's
benighted condition.

Thus the fool's relation to "nothing" often partly nullifies him; he
presents himself "as though" he were a person, and we take him as one in
the same way. He is *as though the same as himself* and *as though the
same as an actor.* The same imagination, his and ours, that can make him
nothing, or that partly keeps him from being something, can sometimes
make him into anything that he wants to be, even if in becoming it he
mixes and dissolves levels of reality and illusion. In some respects he may
be regarded as the prototype of the dramatic actor, and his show may be
regarded as the prototype of drama—though from the dramatic point of
view these prototypes remain on the level of possibilities, actualized in
drama only at the expense of the fool as clown and of folly as nonsense.
But even more, he and his show embody a prototype of the imagination,
shared by actor and audience, that is essential to drama. This is
understood by Duke Theseus in *A Midsummer Night's Dream,* as he
shows in his response to the play put on by the clowns. His Master of
the Revels, Philostrate, has warned him that the dramatic production of
the clowns "is nothing, nothing in the world" (V. i. 78), but he insists
that it be performed. Such thoughts as that expressed in his famous lines

64

about the power of the poet to give shape to the unknown and name and place to "airy nothing" (ll. 12–17) enable the Duke to see in the "nothing" of this foolish play a value to which Philostrate is blind. Theseus knows that the problems of the clowns with mimesis reflect, in a ridiculous but remarkably exact way, those of the poet or the ruler, or of any other nonfool, intent upon knowing and expressing certain elusive but important qualities of experience.

There are kinds of experience in which general structure is less important than what William Blake called "Minute Particulars" and in which the main polarities (for example, those of subject and object, pleasure and pain, form and substance, time and timelessness) lose their importance and with it their power to coordinate experience according to discursive reason. A convenient way of describing these kinds of experience is by saying that they are governed by the "I-Thou" relationship described by Martin Buber. In this relationship the subjectivity that I thought was my own is known also to belong to the object, which thus comes alive and becomes an opening to a much deeper subjectivity than that which I thought was exclusively mine. This condition is attributed to mystics; then again it is maintained that mystics have withdrawn from the primitive life force essential to it. Children, lovers, poets, and madmen are often supposed to live in it, and there is presumably no one who does not know it in one form or another. Many names have been given to our relationship to it, the most common in modern Western thought being imagination—when that word is used to describe a radical reconstitution of experience in the interests of immediacy, totality, and a kind of meaning that is otherwise lacking. This condition is essential to the experience of symbolism discussed in the Introduction.

In one sense there is a mutual antagonism between such experience and the formal drama, with its interest in such matters as social relationships. In another sense the essence of great drama is thought to reside partly in the fact that it draws upon such experience. When drama is deeply effective, it often brings us to a kind of "seeing" that makes us aware of the relativity of things and that makes us accept the world as based on a kind of "seeming," though one that does not make the wonder and the horror of the world less real. In this view reality is finally made out of what Prospero called "the baseless fabric of this vision" (*The Tempest*, IV. i. 151).

The "baseless fabric of this vision" has much in common with the fool's "nothing"; they may even partly be the same. But they are also partly different. It is one thing to sense the limits of meaning, at least the meaning available to a certain person in a certain situation, and even perhaps to sense something beyond those limits. Many of Shakespeare's great characters finally come to moments in which they do this. It is another thing to be, as many fools are, incapable of grasping that meaning, to be impervious to experience. Of course, *seeing through* illusions and even *through* the conventionalized structures that make understanding possible may be expressed as *not seeing at all*. The latter may, in fact, be a symptom or even a precondition of the former—as in the familiar figure of the wise man as blind seer. Though *seeing through* and *not seeing at all* are very different things, and though they may be brought together in the wise man, they may also be brought together in the fool, who is ambiguous, noncommittal, reluctant, or overly direct about what he knows, if he knows anything. If the fool comes to life, he tends to retain these qualities and to stay on the periphery of whatever action is important. He stands in front of the "I-Thou" experience of which I have been speaking; it shines around him, and, broken and altered, it comes through him. But he is not the central agent who has borne the action this close to a kind of experience that might simply undo it. The fool show has its own kinds of actuality, and these enter again and again into complex relations with those of drama. He is both old and innocent enough to see that the two realms must be brought together.

The fool we see in his special relation to dramatic convention is recognizable as a person, and he interacts with each of us, the part-fools who watch him. He is a fool only in that interaction. This is not merely to say, as one could about the hero of a drama, that he mirrors something that exists within ourselves, at least as a possibility. Rather, the fool is in a unique way both the actor and the thing he enacts. He plays roles, foolish and nonfoolish, but his doing so is at every moment a direct expression of his person and of his foolish nature.

66

# Part Two   The Pattern of Folly

. . . I consider that I am most piously worshipped when men—and they all do it—take me to their souls, manifest me in their actions, and represent me in their lives.

(Erasmus, *The Praise of Folly*)

The Womb of nature and perhaps her Grave,
Of neither Sea, nor Shore, nor Air, nor Fire,
But all these in thir pregnant causes mixt
Confus'dly, and which thus must ever fight,
Unless th' Almighty Maker them ordain
His dark materials to create more Worlds. . . .

(Milton, *Paradise Lost*)

# 4 The Permanence of the Fool

The comment of Lear's Fool, "This prophecy Merlin shall make, for I live
before his time" (III. ii. 95), not only shows him to belong both inside
and outside the dramatic action; it also expresses a relationship to time
that is common among fools. Thus the ritual clown dancer taking part in
the Navajo Night Chant continues to dance after the other dancers have
retreated, pretends to realize that he has fallen out of the time governing
the ceremony, and hurries after them.[1] And the medieval Feast of Fools
was directly descended from the Kalends and Saturnalia of ancient Rome,
which were very probably survivals from an even more ancient intercalary
period inserted into the calendar to fill the gap between solar and lunar
years; Saturnalian folly was thus celebrated in a period lying outside the
normal course of events. This timelessness is also suggested by the fool in
a French mystery play, *Saint Didier,* who is not only invisible to the
serious characters but is not even contemporary with them and thus may
remark to the audience, "This must have happened very long ago."[2]
Closer to us, the Marx Brothers sometimes give the fleeting impression
that in their presence time can move backwards. Thus in the battle
directed by Groucho at the close of *Duck Soup* he and the figures around
him appear in uniforms that keep changing to suggest progressively
earlier wars.

The fool's relative independence of time is, as we shall see, matched by
his relative independence of space and of various kinds of law and order.
These different kinds of anomalousness are in the larger view interrelated.
They may combine in this or that bit of what we sense to be very
ephemeral fool business. However, when we regard the fool's strange
relationship to time separately, we may sense the curious permanence that
he often has for himself and sometimes has for us.

Much of the fool show is occupied with what might be called

69

impossible possibilities—with what, on the one hand, *might be* but, on the other, *is not* because, for one reason or another, it *cannot be*. These reasons derive from the nature of the world or from his nature as a fool. Such a possibility may be illusory, at odds with reality, one that only a fool would think of, as when the clown wishes he were two puppies. Or else, such a possibility may be genuine enough, one that only a fool would turn into an impossibility, as when a clown steps on one foot with the other so that he cannot climb a ladder. Often the fool is not defeated by the apparent impossibility but triumphs over it. When Baron Munchausen lifts himself up by the hair of his own head, he is a fool in this sense.

In his concern with possibilities and what can be made of them the fool's procedures of thought and action have much in common with those of nonfools at certain times. Fantasy is hardly ever at rest within us; it is virtually impossible for us to devote long periods of time to tasks requiring concentration without having it interrupted by extraneous lines of thought and images. It is even quite conceivable that in our unconscious life an equivalent of what we consciously experience as fantasy is never still at all—and that Hanswurst and Valentin with their dreams within dreams reflect a basic fact about human nature. But not all dreams are "idle dreams," and fantasy may be highly relevant to the conscious task. Fantasy may proceed in such a way that it is detached but not divorced from a practical interest in its products, as we ask ourselves whether or not they might be given form, whether they are realizable, and, if so, whether or not they are worth realizing. The fantasies that arise from within us always have value for us, even if they are daydreams and even if that value is negative; but when our interest in them takes a practical turn, when we bring hope to them, we enter an area between reality and fantasy and may find that we share it with the fool. His play with the possibilities revealed by fantasy is less bound to the structure of what *is* than is the nonfool's play with them. And the fool (such as Baron Munchausen pulling himself up by his hair) may have powers that we lack and that will enable him to triumph over the impossibilities created by his fantasy in its divergence from reality or in its conflict with it.

The fool lives in a no-man's-land in several senses, one of which is his connection with the area of consciousness into which hunches, intuitions, and interesting but not quite meaningful images and ideas emerge. He often seizes them before we are aware of them and plays with them trickily and jokingly, enjoying being ahead of us. This process is reflected in the structure of almost any clown routine. In it the clown is ahead of us in the sense that the points of his gags surprise us, even when he seems more stupid and less adapted to reality than we. He is also ahead of us in his capacity for triumphing over what would be for us failures that bring movement to a halt. And he is ahead of us, further, in that his routine requires a planning of artistic means and an anticipation of the audience's reactions. This quality of being ahead of us in time is part of what gives him his permanence. His special status as a fool deprives him of a dimension that we feel ourselves to have; yet the deliberate element of his show, when the fool is an actor, gives him another.

The fool is thus relatively independent of our time and of the modes of conscious thought and action dependent upon it; he has what strikes us as permanence in the sense that he seemingly has an intimate connection with the future from which meaning and nonsense, often combined or annulling each other, are disclosed to us. We are unlike those fools who are blissful in their folly, since our relation to the future is in important respects a matter of nonfoolish value, of a coordinated and sustained attempt to conform to an ideal of what we should be, whether the ideal is relatively more individual or relatively more social in origin and character. This ideal may for convenience be called the human image, especially since this expression readily suggests the mimetic rendering of reality, Hamlet's mirror of the stage. Such ideals reach into the future in which we may encounter the fool, for example, in our own foolish failure to live up to them.

However, the fool's permanence is also derived from an element, complementary to that of his connection with the future, from which new contents enter consciousness and in which we are called upon to realize the human image. This element is expressed in the fact that traits belonging to our developmental *past*, both individual and social or cultural, are often present in the fool now. We feel that they do not belong to the human image, and we are left to make what we can of the fact that in one sense or another he reflects us. But on the other hand, in him these traits seem an opening into a past to which we have closed ourselves by becoming what we are, and sometimes that opening may strike us as a sign of freedom and even of superiority. The individual developmental past can be seen in the infantile physical appearance of many fools in the illustrations to this study. One may also think of some film comedians not shown in these photographs, among them Harry Langdon and Harpo Marx. Remnants of our collective past are suggested by the feathers and scraps of animal fur common in fool costumes. This aspect of the fool's relation to our past is less obvious than is his foolish infantility; in connection with this aspect such words as "archaic," "primitive," "mana," "magic," and "taboo" suggest themselves, and these require comment (which they will be given in the next chapter).

The fool who nonsensically plays in the present with what *might be* may at the same time remind us of a past that precedes all of us, fools and nonfools alike, and that remains important to us. This is illustrated by the Koyemci clowns among the Zuñi. They are said to be silly, yet they are wise, like the high priests and even the gods. Though like simpletons and crazy people they are startled to new thoughts by every flitting thing, they are sages and oracles, interpreting the ancient dance dramas and, in other ways, too, making a connection between present members of the tribe and their primeval ancestors.[3]

# 5   The Fool as Primitive and Magical

In using the behavior of a Navajo clown to illustrate a point that I also illustrate by the behavior of medieval theatrical fools and modern film comedians, I mean to imply that the latter are in some sense primitive and that primitive clowns in some sense take part in the fool show that I have been describing. Various features of folly may be described as "primitive," "archaic," and "magical," as entailing "mana" and "taboo." When these words are left unqualified, they cast as much shadow as light; thus I wish to explain my use of them, though this demands a brief digression from the fool.

The pioneer depth psychologists drew upon the work of anthropologists contemporary with them. Since the borrowing took place at a relatively early period in anthropology, before certain valuable contributions of ethnographic material and certain important refinements of methods and concepts were made, most words drawn from those sources have a life in psychological literature that they no longer have outside it. Some of these words were used to express genuine insights into the nature of psychic processes; others were used more speculatively. In either case, they are fossils of anthropological thought, implying correspondences between personal and cultural life that lie in the realm of more or less promising or already disproved hypothesis.

Two such words, "totem" and "taboo," already had long histories of changing meanings before Freud wrote his book about them. The concepts associated with them have been criticized in great detail, "totem" especially by Claude Lévi-Strauss and "taboo" especially by Franz Steiner; their analyses leave Freud's anthropological assumptions in shreds. It has been argued in defense of Freud that he was not describing the actual development of human society but presenting an analogical model of the way in which certain psychic conflicts develop. Whatever merits this

73

argument may have as a defense of Freud, it means abandoning one of
the links he tried to make between the present psychic situation of the
individual and the cultural past of the group. On the whole, Jung was, I
believe, more fortunate and more judicious in his borrowings from
anthropological sources (primarily from Lucien Lévy-Bruhl) than was
Freud in his (primarily from William Robertson Smith and James G.
Frazer). But Lévy-Bruhl hardly provides a model of empirical
procedures; his psychology of "primitives" is often factually very
inaccurate and theoretically one-sided. The kinds of phenomena with
which Lévy-Bruhl was concerned do exist in great plenty, however, and
Jung was justified in incorporating them into a larger view of psychic
processes. But Lévy-Bruhl was often unclear about the functional
importance of specific beliefs and kinds of behavior in the complex whole
of the culture in which they are found, and Jung, in turn, describes
primitive psychology as being more of a piece, and more of a piece of a
certain kind, than most contemporary anthropologists would grant that
they are.[1]

Nonetheless, such expressions as "totem," "taboo," "magic," "mana,"
"primitive," "archaic," *"représentations collectives,"* and *"participation
mentale"* were used by Freud, Jung, and others to record important
insights into the nature of psychic processes. We are nowadays cautious
about many psychological statements that employ these words. Not only
are we aware that some of the information upon which those statements
were based was faulty; we also find the ethnocentrism and the often facile
evolutionism that colored them very hard to accept. (In keeping with our
own attitudes, if anyone were to devise a practical and convincing way of
doing completely without such value-toned words as "primitive," he
would leave a mark on anthropological writing. In sometimes reverting to
the term "savage," Lévi-Strauss plays ironically upon the problems of
what to call "primitive" peoples and how to define the similarities and
differences between them and us; but they remain problems.)

Interest has faded from questions that would require larger schemes of
cultural development to answer them. Moreover, there has been a
tendency in more recent anthropology to find structures in what had
seemed blurred and complexity in what had seemed unity. Thus magic,
for example, has a different character now, when interest is centered in the

cultural and social functions of certain specific magical activities, than it
had when interest centered on the ways in which such activities were
typical of a stage in the development of culture. It would seem, then, that
when we encounter anthropological borrowings in depth-psychological
theory, we must bring to them a measure of skepticism born of our
distance from earlier anthropological assumptions and of our awareness
that we are dealing with hypotheses; we must also bring to them a
measure of resignation, introducing qualifications where we can and
hoping that sooner or later the psychological use of these materials will be
clarified in a way that gives us a new point of reference. (A similar
mental adjustment must be made by anyone who for any reason reads
earlier anthropological literature in the hope of gaining something from
the wealth of material available, even in garbled form, to earlier writers
and no longer available to us at all.) The despair of this counsel is
mitigated—or heightened—if we consider the motives behind the earlier
assumptions, the validity of many insights based on them, and the fact
that many of the old problems have kept their importance despite
attempts to dissolve them by improvements in information, method, and
conceptualization.

The chief motive behind the adoption by depth psychologists of words
and concepts from anthropology lies in the suggestiveness of the analogies
to be seen in the behavior of primitives, children, the mentally ill, and
normal people under exceptional circumstances. It is clear to us now that
such analogies yield readily to oversimplification. Yet they cannot, I
believe, be ignored if we wish to arrive at a deeper understanding of
either psychological or cultural facts and especially of areas in which
collective and individual psychology are inseparable and even one. I
believe that earlier anthropologists were right in assuming that there are
such areas and were justified in being interested in them. These
anthropologists raised questions about psychological development in a
cultural sense, or cultural development in a psychological
sense—questions about processes that extend over generations and that are
embodied by individuals acting as members of groups. The current
emphasis on the psychology of the individual and the nuclear family
reflects the altered circumstances of our lives as well as changes in
philosophical and scientific viewpoint; still, the phenomena of mass

psychosis, for example, show that these processes of more collective psychology are very much alive even now, no matter what our viewpoint. Moreover, the search for "roots" that is a dominant theme of our literature shows that despite our uprootedness, or rather because of it, the past from which we and our forefathers came is often of great psychological value. Our nostalgia for what we vaguely imagine to be primitive can be brought under the same heading. This nostalgia is often romantic, but it is also often a matter of bitter psychological desperation, as we feel when we read Conrad's story about a journey into "The Heart of Darkness."

The work of Frazer, Lévy-Bruhl, and others described certain magical processes of thought, largely governed by the principles of similarity (that like produces like, that an effect resembles its cause, that like things are identical), of contact or contagion (that things once in contact remain in contact), of *pars pro toto* (that a part of a person or thing *is* for magical purposes that thing), of magical affinity (that injury to one member of a group, for example, is an injury to the other members), and of magical cause and effect (that events may be influenced by supernatural and irrational factors and comprise sequences different from those based on natural and rational cause and effect). Magic was seen to be coercive, even if it took a reactive form (as when a person tried to defend himself against magic produced by someone else). In a generalized way, and partly on the analogy of the behavior of nonprimitive people, magic was thought by some writers to represent a kind of emotional thinking, though specific magical acts are often carried out dispassionately and even mechanically. Also in a generalized way, magic was thought to represent a kind of faulty science, a failure of rational and empirical procedures. These anthropological observations were congruent with the attempts of the precursors of depth psychology to expand the picture of mental processes given by early associationist psychology, with its emphasis upon consciousness. It was realized, for example, that associations can accord with what Wilhelm Jerusalem called "fundamental apperception," which causes one to regard the world "animistically" and "anthropomorphically": then objects seem to possess human qualities of life, will, intelligence, and soul.[2] Each of these various views of magic has substance, whether or not any of them can accommodate all magical phenomena. The resulting picture is still convincing. But quite apart from inaccuracies of description in specific cases, this picture requires qualification, especially if we are concerned with the analogies that made the psychologists turn to anthropology.

These necessary qualifications are provided by the assumption, made more or less explicitly by most depth psychologists, that magical processes of thought, based on "fundamental apperception," are operative in everyone. They may be especially striking in the behavior of a person performing a magic rite in accordance with the conscious beliefs of his culture, in the behavior of a psychotic person who has devised a magical rite in accordance with beliefs that no one else shares, or in the behavior of a child in certain moments of play. But we must realize that the magical processes of thought expressed in this behavior have very different functions in the psychic economy of the different individuals and that these functions are also those of the psychic economy as a whole, which includes the strength and complexity of its consciousness and consists of both personal and cultural factors. We must also realize that in being struck by the behavior of these individuals we may well be in the position of the nonfool looking at the the fool and not seeing the folly within himself: we may have no idea of the extent to which our whole orientation is saturated with the magical attitude, though this is visible to others, for example, in our prejudices. By now we should have learned from anthropology that primitive people have often achieved a highly differentiated cultural and psychological accommodation between magic and nonmagical modes of thought. And we should have learned from the terrible history of our own century thus far that consciousness is not simply empirical and rational and the unconscious not simply magical. Great masses of people have recently been killed rationally and largely unconsciously for rational and largely unconscious purposes. And looking back a few centuries, we may conclude that Shakespeare in his conscious openness to magical thought processes has more in common with a Neolithic primitive than with a modern factory worker, without being for this reason less conscious than the latter.

If magical processes of thought are active in everyone, and if the unconscious is largely, though by no means completely, governed by them, our difficulty in understanding primitive people in whom they are everywhere apparent strongly reflects our attitude to the unconscious. An adequately yielding yet resistant attitude toward it is extremely difficult to achieve, and whatever attitude one has toward it is usually colored by emotion. Thus the primitives described by earlier anthropologists may often have seemed bloodthirsty, immoral, and superstitious partly because the anthropologists were impressed by how *unlike* them the primitives were. Over the decades, and as part of a reaction against earlier value judgments, primitives have got progressively better marks for deportment and intellectual achievement. One of the most influential modern anthropologists, Lévi-Strauss, has carried this process to its current height in being impressed by how *like* primitives are to the experts in ethnology, linguistics, taxonomy, and communications theory to be employed in the understanding of primitives. The importance of the depth-psychological view of these matters, with its motley anthropological heritage, may emerge more clearly if we glance critically at certain details of Lévi-Strauss's thought.

Lévi-Strauss demonstrates effectively and with impressive evidence that for cultural life to be possible a line must be drawn between nature and human culture; this line must then be complemented by others that place man *in* nature and give him an orientation in it. This radical division between nature and culture is in his view an irreducible fact of the human condition, and the classification of man and the world based on it is primarily motivated by the requirements of rational thought and of adaptation to outer reality. I would object that his position ignores the requirements of emotion and of adaptation to inner reality; it ignores the ways in which inner demands may make directed thinking impossible; in effect, it denies the reality of the psyche, organized as it so largely is (in the depth-psychological view) by inner determinants. Lévi-Strauss's description of this split and the permutations of language and culture based on it is partly an empirical analysis of phenomena; it is at the same time the expression of an archetype. A radical alteration of the human creature at the outset of its experience as man is the subject of many myths, including the Biblical story of the Fall, and of many works of art and literature. In some of these, interests in taxonomic classification are apparent; in many they are not. These nonscientific versions of the symbolic fact of man's radical alteration are by and large more adequate to the human reality known to depth psychologists than is Lévi-Strauss's description, because they admit affective and emotional factors of cause and effect—they admit the reality of the psyche and of the unconscious—in the process of transformation that made man human and that is still at work in him. Nonetheless, Lévi-Strauss's work is invaluable in calling attention to complexities of structure in the life of primitive peoples. In an important sense primitive psychology is a matter of "we" more than of "I," of Aztecs willing to have their hearts cut out for the common good; thus we may continue to regard Lévy-Bruhl's *participation mystique* as a characteristic of primitive mentality, but we can no longer see it as incompatible with great rational and empirical subtlety. These complexities were often invisible owing to the projections made by earlier anthropologists and depth psychologists upon their material. The value of Lévi-Strauss's emphasis is not lessened by the fact that it, too, unavoidably includes his projections. But our awareness of *this* fact also reminds us of the value of the writers who have sought to bring depth psychology and anthropology together.

In one sense the modern Western nostalgia for "the primitive" is an expression of our cultural and psychological situation; in another it is extremely ancient. The notion of being completely *in* the world and not separated by the human condition with its burden of culture is as archetypal as is the notion of being radically divided from the world. This condition of being *in* the natural world—and out of culture—is often conceived as primitive, and the fool is one of the recurrent figures in which it is expressed.

There is in northern Europe a conventional picture of the primitive man *in* nature; it is the figure of the "wild man" to be seen occasionally on inn signs and in family coats of arms and those of guilds. It is also associated with the cities of Basle, Lucerne, and, in another form, Constance. The "wild man" is most generally a vegetation demon, though sometimes he also controls wild animals; he shares characteristics with other mythical and legendary figures represented in masks, emblems, dances, and ceremonies. But the significance he once had has largely been lost, and he has become for us a remnant of the archaic *Naturvölker*, "peoples *of* nature," as primitive peoples are still commonly called in German. He and his kindred spirits may well have had something of the same psychological significance for people centuries ago, though people then would have conceived that significance differently than we do. In our eyes the "wild man" as an archaic remnant stands alone, free of the structures of language, thought, belief, and social organization characteristic of primitive peoples. In our imagination we have liberated the "wild man" from responsibility for those structures, and through the projection that gives him an imaginative life for us he liberates us from our social and cultural responsibilities. Under the influence of the psychic factor approximated by this figure a person might take part in the Swiss and southern German *Fastnacht* celebrations that have a direct link to medieval and even premedieval traditions of folly. The person might wear a grotesque costume and join in the making of *Guggenmusik,* a cacophonous music played with battered and out-of-key horns and drums and cymbals, some of the drumming perhaps being done on old pots and pans. This music sounds "primitive" and "archaic" in that it strikes us as cruder than the kinds of music we usually play and hear; it represents to us an earlier and inferior stage of these. But *Guggenmusik* is sometimes extremely eerie; it stops being a joke and makes us feel what we might be in the presence of spirits; it is "primitive" and "archaic" in this sense, too. In the course of the celebration, emotions, including sexual and aggressive ones, may be less inhibited than they are usually; they may even take orgiastic forms.

The general messiness and loudness of feeling and the inferiority of thought that results—the "naturalness," as we may take it to be—does not necessarily reflect with any accuracy the life of the *Naturvölker,* who are generally more concerned with the serious business of living than with saturnalian play. (Such play may, of course, serve serious vital purposes on levels deeper than those of which the revelers are aware.) The loudness and messiness of the reveling are symptomatic of what Pierre Janet, one of the most important immediate precursors of depth psychology, called *abaissement du niveau mentale*—a lowering of the level of consciousness that allows unconscious contents and modes of behavior to usurp the place of conscious ones. However such a lessening of consciousness is effected, it may result in either an inferiority or a superiority of psychic functioning. Thus the reveler may become an obnoxious bore, or he may turn out to be extremely witty. Someone in a state of intense emotion may gawk tongue-tied, or he may act cleverly and efficiently. (At the close of Buster Keaton's film *Battling Butler* [1926], for example, the hopelessly mild Keaton at last becomes angry and methodically beats up an ugly boxing champion.) And in dreams about what could roughly be called the world of the "wild man" the emphasis may be upon threatening gloom, or it may be upon bits of intelligent structure; such dreams may even record, in careful detail, patterns of behavior and adaptation characteristic of primitive and archaic peoples.

The primitiveness of fools is usually much closer to that of the "wild man," as an imaginary remnant of a state in which man and nature were one, than it is to the primitiveness of primitive peoples. However, though the primitiveness of fools may mean inferiority of psychic functioning, it may mean superiority; in either case, it rests on processes of thought that are magical, and their emergence attests to the dissociability of the psyche. The role assumed by fools, and their behavior in accordance with it, often suggests the operation of mana, conceived as relatively neutral psychic energy set free by dissociation and available for the formation of part-personalities. This role also often implies taboos of various kinds, for example, that surrounding the fool as he performs antinatural or anticultural acts. These are all qualities of nonfoolish as well as foolish experience; they are attributes of nonfools as well as fools. But in the fool show they usually appear in a different light than they do outside it. For example, if they are serious outside the fool show, they are ridiculous in it; if they are ineffective outside it, they are effective in it; if they are of apparently secondary importance outside it, they are of primary importance in it. The primitiveness and magic of fools is, like other qualities frequently characteristic of them, relative to the attitudes and behavior of nonfools with whom the fools stand in a dynamic relation. Fools most usually emerge as primitive and magical in contrast with nonfools who think they are, or who at least pretend to be, rational and realistic. The judgments "rational" and "realistic" are, of course, as relative as the judgment "foolish," but "foolish" remains in contrast to them. Thus there are clowns in societies in which magical ceremonies are important; when such clowns perform magic, it contrasts with the more "rational" magic of priests and magicians who are not clowns—"rational" here meaning in accordance with the structure of values that are thought to be essential to the continuing life of the society and of the individuals in it. According to a commonplace and convincing theory, clowns release psychological tensions resulting from the laborious process of maintaining culture. But that release may also be a transcendence of culture and the forms of consciousness sustained by it. Such transcendence for limited moments may be necessary to the maintenance of culture and those forms of consciousness. But such transcendence may also serve deeper necessities that are among the wellsprings of culture: "fundamental apperception" is in some measure necessary to the symbolic imagination that reveals valuable unconscious factors. These factors demand attention, even when there seems no way to make them a part of a nonfoolish adaptation to the world.

Institutionalized clowning reached especially impressive heights of differentiation and importance in Central and North America. In the Plains many individuals were called, usually as a result of dreams or visions, to engage in ritual "contrary behavior," including reverse speech and the widespread trick of plunging their hands into boiling water to take out meat, then splashing the water on their backs while complaining that it is cold. Sometimes this behavior was carried out solemnly, with the spectators enjoined not to laugh; more generally it took the form of clowning. In the Pueblos, "contrary behavior" was an important element of ceremonial clowning and was often sexual and scatological in character, as in sexual jokes, exhibitionism, transvestitism, and mock sexual intercourse and in eating and drinking excrement and urine. In the various tribal and larger cultural areas of North America clowning had magical functions of fertility, shamanism, curing, war, and policing. Where institutionalized clowning did develop, it did so in various ways to fulfill various cultural and psychological functions. Only to a limited extent do these various kinds of clowning represent patterns that extend, with little change of function and meaning, beyond the limits of specific tribal cultures. In many areas of North America it did not develop, as it did not in many areas in the rest of the world. Where it did develop outside North America, as in Africa and Polynesia, it had a very different character. In a developmental sense, then, one can speak only in a qualified way of a single thing, "clowning," that has developed in all these ways and that in some places has not developed at all. That qualified sense is nonetheless important to an understanding of the larger fool show. It is important partly because a great many specific elements of the clowning that did develop among primitive societies echo those of clowning in the history of the Western world. It is also important because clowning in these societies reveals something of the nature of the mimetic enterprise of clowning wherever it occurs.

It seems that clowning in primitive societies and elsewhere expresses certain universals of culture and of the psychic life of individuals, that these universals may be expressed in ways that use contents specific to groups or individuals, and that clowning is a convenient, and hence recurring, means of vitalizing awareness of both the universal and the particular by ensuring that they are kept together. One of the universals is the capacity for laughter as part of the mimetic and emotional equipment of every human person. People can laugh at an endless variety of things; most themes of humor are culturally and individually conditioned, but some of them seem to be universal. The anthropologist Julian H. Steward has summed them up under the headings of burlesque of sacred things and persons, humor based on sex and obscenity, humor based on sickness, sorrow, and misfortune, and burlesque of foreigners.[3] Since laughter under the right circumstances is felt to be "good" and is in any case necessary, attempts are made to provoke it in jokes and ridiculous behavior. For the same reason, fools are singled out or single themselves out to provoke it by telling the jokes and engaging in the ridiculous behavior. There is no intrinsic necessity for the fool to become a fixed social role filled by a specific person; nor is there any intrinsic necessity for this role to come to incorporate important social and cultural functions, including ceremonial ones. However, this role does seem to make itself felt in the normal life of a social group and then to get filled by a single person. This may be seen in any school class. And there is usually a tendency, almost equally "natural," for the social authority to try to gain some control over this office of the fool. This may be seen, as isolation and prohibition, in the institution of the stool and dunce's cap in the corner of earlier schoolrooms.[4] The contrary strategy, that of allowing the fool, may be felt as socially and culturally advantageous; this advantage may be seized in one way or another by individuals and groups performing religious functions. When ceremonial clowning emerges in this way, it is the product of a specific invention. But the basic resources utilized by that invention may be found in Steward's universal themes of humor, all of which have a direct bearing on the cultural and religious life of the group. In the rest of this chapter I will discuss the ways in which these themes are taken up in primitive clowning; in subsequent chapters I will consider some of the implications of these themes for cultural life and individual psychology and some of the ways in which they are incorporated in the larger—and less immediately primitive—fool show.

Persons and things regarded as sacred, or in some other way powerful and valuable, are essential to cultural organization; sexual and other materials regarded as obscene represent instinctual energies that must be drawn upon and molded to cultural forms; sickness, sorrow, and misfortune—death should be added to Steward's list—represent destructive realities to be dealt with by culture, warded off, or in some way made acceptable; foreigners are potential enemies and thus constitute a threat to cultural life.

Burlesque of sacred authority was common in Indian America. At a Jemez Pueblo dance a clown is said to have sprinkled his fellows with sand and ashes in imitation of the ceremonial sprinkling with corn meal and pollen. The Zuñi Newekwe clowns speak in Spanish or English before the gods, a thing taboo to ordinary people; once they even rigged up a telephone and pretended to converse with the gods, although the gods are not supposed to speak. Among the Indians of California clowns make fun of the ceremonial leader while he is singing, and Aztec priests are reported to have blown mud balls at the actors in religious ceremonies and to have praised or censured the performance in a jocular manner.[5] All of this behavior suggests that of the fool actor in his semidetachment from the dramatic action of a play, the Aztec priests calling to mind the German stage figure of "English John," who discussed critically with the audience the dramatic action in progress. Burlesque of sacred authority is linked with the other themes listed by Steward and sometimes appears to include them. Thus desecration by clowns may contain obscene elements; it may appear to court misfortune and be performed by figures like the senile Navajo man and his transvestite wife; and it may imitate the behavior of foreigners who should be excluded from the rite with which the clowning is associated.

Insofar as sacred persons and things are important, culture is based upon religious cult; cult, in turn, is partly based on instinct and partly shapes our access to it; thus ceremonial clowning is often sexual. Barbara Swain writes:

> Cult represents vitality making an effort to survive. It is a commonplace that since survival depends in part upon fecundity, one phase of any cult is likely to involve some form of sexual licentiousness. Barenness and the extinction of the race, death and the extinction of the individual, are two fundamental human fears. . . . The outstanding characteristic of the folk fool is his power magically to revive himself and to propagate. He represents the most elementary biological wisdom, shared by men and animals alike.[6]

Thus "calf," "monkey," "ass," and "pig" are used as synonyms for "fool" in the fifteenth-century *Fastnacht* plays, in which the fool is almost always the "servant of Venus," totally preoccupied with the satisfaction of his sexual drives.[7]

Clowning as a form of fertility magic is especially prominent among the Pueblo Indians, owing to specific cultural developments in a hostile terrain and climate. But this aspect of clowning is to be found in a great many times and places. The motley figures still seen in Swiss *Fastnacht* processions, for example, have been thought to be "Leafy Fools," having their prototype in the "wild man" or "green man" who was tried, killed, resurrected, and married to the Spring in a fertility drama once widespread among European peasants. (In Czechoslovakia, where there are also such motley fools, the country women pulled the colored tabs from the fools' costumes and put them under hens to make them lay.[8]) This tradition reaches to Erasmus and, as I have already suggested, to Shakespeare. When Erasmus' Mother Folly says that she is responsible for life itself, she means not only that even "the father of gods and king of men" must disguise himself like an actor "if he wishes to do what he never refrains from doing, that is to say, to beget children."[9] Nor does she mean only that "a Stoic multiplied by six hundred . . . will certainly lay by his gravity . . . and for a few minutes toy and talk nonsense" for the same purpose.[10] She means, as well, that her influence is directly present in the act of procreation, which is performed with "that foolish, even silly, part which cannot be named without laughter. . . . This is at last that sacred spring from which all things derive existence, more truly than from the elemental tetrad of Pythagoras."[11]

The transvestitism so common in ceremonial clowning and in saturnalian festivals has deep roots in fertility magic. In Europe we may think of the Fool and the transvestite Bessy of the Morris Dance. And in East Lancashire in the week before Easter groups of boys dressed as girls and girls dressed as boys went around accompanied by the "fool" or "tosspot" and asked for presents of eggs.[12] The reversal of sex roles activated the demonic, including vegetation spirits, since these roles are fundamental to the cultural life that holds the demonic at a distance.

Fertility is part of the biological answer to sickness, sorrow, misfortune, and death, as is the spirit closely linked with sacred persons and things. This may be seen in the obscenity with which we may greet sudden misfortune. An angry person with a gift for obscenity may pour out a string of epithets naming sexual organs and activities, products and processes of excretion, and names of everything holy. This is an act similar to the licensed fool's desecration, by which conceptions of the holy and of the world as it is organized around them are broken up by the potencies of natural process conceived as magical. The act is an invocation to be understood in the context of the magical attitude toward misfortune, according to which it is always the result of human or spiritual intention rather than chance. Van der Leeuw writes about this attitude, when it is concentrated upon the climax of personal misfortune:

> . . . the death which overtakes a man is no "natural" death; that we die is no natural affair, and for this reason man refuses to permit it. With some difficulty he fastens upon a "cause" . . . ; and when the natives of the Melbourne district lose a member of the tribe by a "natural" death, they . . . set up a sort of ordeal of God in order to discover the "murderer" . . . ; they then resort to the alleged perpetrator's hiding-place and slay him.[13]

The angry man may curse someone or something specific for his misfortune; he may be cursing the world in general; in either case, he is naming an enemy and calling upon a power to attack it and to defend the integrity of his own life. He uses obscene words to express a magical attitude, and the confusion of sacred and profane that he effects with them has an even deeper potency than the words themselves. A similar attitude employing similar means is expressed in a Spanish amulet against the evil eye combining a representation of the holy Virgin and the infant Jesus with the *manus lasciva* or "phallic hand." The hand, making the obscene gesture of "the fig," encloses the crescent moon, suggestive of nature beyond the distinction between the sacred and the profane, yet full of magical influence.[14] The sexual and scatological play of Pueblo clowns —or for that matter, of clowns in the modern circus—would seem to fit under this heading, too, since life not only continues in spite of misfortune and death: it triumphs over them and destroys them. In one sense there seems to be an unbroken connection of attitude between the Melbourne natives and that of people who take as their own St. Paul's affirmation of "death . . . swallowed up in victory" (I Cor. 15:54). Clowns and fools play ambiguously with that connection.

The ambiguity of the fool's relation to the magical force of continuing life consists partly in the fact that he is licensed to invoke it and does so effectively; it also consists in his being himself the victim of misfortune. The Jemez Koshare clowns in the American Southwest, for example, dress in rags; the Jemez Piñon also wear rags and beg for food. And on the last day of the Mountain Chant ceremony of the Navajo there is an impersonation of a dull-witted, decrepit, shortsighted old man who stumbles onto a Yucca plant, howls with pain, and must get his wife, a transvestite made up as a hideous old woman, to pick the Yucca fruit for him.[15] Similarly woebegone figures are to be found in the Heyoka complex of the Plains. The same quality of having been abused by fate may be seen in the tattered dress of many circus clowns and of the early Harlequin; it is also suggested by the tramp costume of Charlie Chaplin. Among Swiss-German *Kraftwörter,* obscene "power words" in the sense that I have been discussing, are *verreckt,* "dead" (used properly of an animal but not of a person) and *siech,* "sick." Such words as "pox" used for abuse and profanity have virtually died from English, but they were very much alive in Shakespeare's time. The horrible indecencies of Thersites in *Troilus and Cressida* have their counterparts in clownish ranting, clowns in various times and places verbally heaping all the imaginable diseases and misfortunes upon each other as though upon scapegoats to be sent out into the wilds or the desert. These two aspects of having magical power and of being a victim may thus be embodied in the knave and butt roles of the knockabout fool pair, the most common and widespread form of the fool actor and his double. This semidramatic form thus seems to have its roots in the magical mentality.

The extreme of misfortune is death, and the fool has an ambiguous relation to it, too. This ambiguity includes that between "funny" in the sense of strange, disturbing, upsetting, and "funny" in the sense of amusing, between similarly divergent senses of the French *drôle* and the German *komisch,* between the German *Grauen,* "dread," and *Lust,* "desire" or "pleasure," between horror and humor. Things that are amusingly "funny" are laughable; horrible things may also be laughable. When we laugh at them, we often do so partly because we do not know what else to do, because we do not find our way to another and more appropriate reaction. Through laughter we achieve a provisional stance, outside belief and disbelief, in the face of the horrible. We also laugh as part of an automatic recoil into life. In *King Lear* Edgar alludes to this reaction when he remarks, "The worst returns to laughter" (IV. i. 6). Iris Murdoch in her novel *The Italian Girl* describes such laughter in a scene that is not at all unique in the history of funerals:

> The coffin-bearers [in a crematorium] stood stiffly in a row at the back. In front of them was the huge figure of my brother, and as I turned I saw him swaying, bending forward and putting his hand to his mouth. I thought for a moment that he was ill or overcome by tears: but then I saw that he was laughing. Monstrous giggles shivered his great figure from head to foot and turned, as he tried to stifle them, into wet spluttering gurgles. "Oh God!" said Otto audibly. He choked. Then abandoning all attempt at concealment he went off into a fit of gargantuan mirth. Tears of laughter wetted his red cheeks. He laughed. He roared. The chapel echoed with it. Our communion with Lydia was at an end.[16]

Similarly, in André Malraux's *La condition humaine* there is a description of a Chinese woman who slaps the face of her dead husband in bed; while it wobbles grotesquely from side to side her children roar with laughter. They are caught in the horror of an unimaginable fact; it is smotheringly close and must be pushed away. In many societies merrymaking after a funeral is sanctioned. The laughter is then mirthful rather than a shocked reaction to horror, and it is institutionalized rather than purely spontaneous; but like the personal outbursts I have mentioned, it probably serves the purpose of putting death at a distance and asserting the continuation of life.

The circus clown is hit over the head with a sledge hammer and rises again in a mock resurrection. (After such a blow Harlequin once picked his brains out and ate them with relish, suffering only an increase of stupidity.) The medieval stage devil emerges from the mouth of death to speak an epilogue. These and countless other instances of the fool's immortality could be considered a form of "comic relief" from the anxiety provoked by a natural fact that is as mysterious as that of birth but that is horrible rather than joyous. But the fool is not only the mock victim of death; he is also the real agent of it. Thus Conrad Pocher, jester to a German Count Palatine, was reportedly given his position on the strength of his jest of hanging a boy on a tree because he was scabrous. Chicot, Mathurine, and Maître Guillaume, eccentric entertainers of Henry III and Henry IV, figured in scenes of intrigue, massacre, and attempted assassination.[17] Nietzsche's tightrope-walking clown in *Thus Spake Zarathustra* bears the threat of death, as do the vengeful jesters of Hugo's *The Man Who Laughs* and one of Poe's tales, "Hop-Frog: or, the Eight Chained Ourang-Outangs." The dwarf jester who narrates Lagerkvist's *The Dwarf* encourages the sordid and idiotic war of his princely master, poisons the prince's enemy at a feast of reconciliation, and incites the prince to the murder of the two young lovers who represent the one point of sympathy and hope in the action. And in *Richard II* the antic jester Death grins at the pomp of the king, whom he will kill (III. ii. 160–70). William Empson and Geoffrey Bush have commented on the similarities between the fool as jester and the figure of the Revenger in many Elizabethan and Jacobean plays, among them *Hamlet;* and W. H. Auden has written an essay about Iago called "The Joker in the Pack."[18] Moreover, imaginative interest in the interrelated powers of the fool to survive death and to kill is still very much alive, as is shown by an impressive work, "The Clowns," in the repertoire of the New York City

Center Joffrey Ballet in 1968. The ballet begins with a cataclysm among clowns, only one of whom appears to survive it. As he tends the bodies of the others, they come to life, and the stage is soon filled with their frolicking. In time they grow hard-hearted and induce a second cataclysm, which is survived only by the same clown who survived the first.

Archaic and magical roots of the deathly aspect of the fool may be seen in the figure of Harlequin, who was once *Herleking* (a form of Wodan), who led a procession of the dead through the night skies.[19] His progress from demon to trickster to clown is paralleled in that of other masked and originally demonic figures who were appropriated to the merrymaking of spring festivals in Europe. Of course, this can be understood as the result of a more or less natural development from dread to joking pleasure. (We can, after all, make jokes about horrible things; in doing so, our provisional stance in the face of them may allow us to disengage ourselves from them and may thus serve to protect the ego from more binding, and often paralyzing, emotional processes.) However, on the archaic level, dread and joking pleasure may coexist. Thus the Zuñi Koyemci clowns are "funny" in the sense that they make people laugh, but they are also the most potent and dangerous of the masked dancers. On the archaic level death and life, too, coexist, in such a way that cults of the terrible spirits of the dead and cults of reborn natural life are seldom clearly distinct from each other. Thus various authorities, among them the ethnologist Richard Weiss, regard the masked figures who perform in dances and processions in the Swiss Alps as derived from cults of the dead and of vegetation and fertility, with the elements from these two sources thoroughly mixed. It is extremely difficult to see a way of answering such questions as the following. Is the loud noise made by such figures intended to awaken fertility, or does it belong to the terror-inspiring of the spirits of the dead? When these figures throw seeds, nuts, and fruit, are these gifts from the spirits of the dead, or do they represent fertility magic based on contact? When they splash people with blood, soot, and dung-water, does this belong originally to the judging function of the spirits of the dead or, again, to fertility magic? And when they beat people with twigs, is this originally a purifying punishment by the spirits of the dead, or is it fertility magic of the kind to be seen when women were beaten in the spring?[20] The same combination of elements is found in early cultic practices in Greece, where the invective that is basic to the dramatic and literary tradition of satire was mixed with, and itself had, fertility-inducing functions. All of these activities have their counterparts throughout the world of the fool show; there are echoes of them in every performance by circus clowns. Again and again fools imply that the mystery of life and that of death are one. The bauble, bat, or slapstick of many fool actors, for example, is used in ways that suggest both of the complexes of meaning described by Weiss.

This duality is still very prominent in the fool in Shakespeare's time, incidentally, as is the magic that we associate with Harlequin. The Duke in *Measure for Measure* uses "fool" metaphorically in a way that draws upon both of these senses. He advises Claudio, "Reason thus with life. / If I do lose thee, I do lose a thing / That none but fools would keep." A moment later he adds, "Merely, thou art Death's fool" (III. i. 6–8 and 11). The fool is presented first as the person in whom the will to live continues longer than in anyone else, then as the helpless victim of death. Here death has the upper hand, but there was also, from before Shakespeare's time and continuing into it, a well-established tradition that combined death and the fool in the same figure. Death's triumph over the fool is generally, as it is for the Duke, a moralistic conceit calling attention to the vanity of wanting to live. The combination of death and the fool in the same figure, on the other hand, results in a darker figure than the fool alone, one that calls to mind the origins of Harlequin. Dürer, Holbein, and other artists employed this conceit in their pictures, and L. G. Salingar sees Death as the "supreme 'antic'" in *Hamlet*. (See Plate 22.)

The *verkehrte Welt,* the topsy-turvy world of saturnalian folly, is usually characterized by a mixture of elements from these two sources of fertility and the world of the dead. Their proximity in the sources of laughter may be seen in the ancient festival of Hilaria, echoed in our words "hilarious" and "hilarity." An effigy of the dead vegetation god Attis was mourned and buried; it was resurrected on the day of the festival, reckoned as the vernal equinox. According to Frazer, "the divine resurrection was celebrated with a wild outburst of glee. At Rome, and probably elsewhere, the celebration took the form of a carnival. . . . A universal license prevailed. Every man might say and do what he pleased.

PLATE 22.  Drawing by Alfred Kubin. According to a late medieval conceit,
Death, himself a fool, makes fools of us all. Here Death has appropriated the fool's
costume, bauble, and cap and drags off the lump that wore them. The old conceit
and this modern picture both imply that the fool survives his own death: abandoning
the *prima materia* of the human image, the fool enters the dimension in which
Harlequin once led a horde of ghosts. A similar form of immortality is implied
when the circus clown jumps to his feet after having been hit over the head with a
sledge hammer.

People went about the streets in disguise. No dignity was too high or too sacred for the humblest citizen to assume with impunity." [21]

It has even been conjectured that the Feast of Fools had its origin in the fact that on Easter morning the story of Christ's resurrection was told from the pulpit in such a way that it included many jokes at the expense of the Apostles, the saints, and the devil. In any case, the *Fabula Paschalis* —Easter drollery, sometimes a tale, sometimes a ridiculous sermon—and the *Risus Paschalis*—"Easter laughter," inspired in the congregation by the drollery of the priest—were part of the Easter church service throughout Christendom for centuries. [22] Easter is the celebration of life in death, in a spiritual as well as a physical sense; though Christ is not primarily a vegetation god, he is partly that, too. Folk traditions connected with Easter contain elements that go back thousands of years; there is a direct link between Easter and such fertility festivals as that of Hilaria.

The burlesque of foreigners is colorfully described by an American Army officer, John G. Bourke, who attended a Newekwe dance in 1881. (His account provides examples of all four of Steward's universal themes of humor.) Bourke writes:

> One [of the clowns] was more grotesquely attired than the rest in a long India-rubber gossamer "overall" and a pair of goggles, painted white, over his eyes. . . . I had taken my station at one side of the room, seated upon the banquette, and having in front of me a rude bench or table, upon which was a small coal-oil lamp. I suppose that in the halo diffused by the feeble light and in my "stained-glass attitude" I must have borne some resemblance to the pictures of saints hanging upon the wall of old Mexican churches. . . . The dancers suddenly wheeled into line, threw themselves upon their knees before my table, and with extravagant beatings of breast began an outlandish but faithful mockery of a Mexican Catholic congregation at vespers. One bawled out a parody upon the Paternoster, another mumbled along in the manner of an old man reciting the rosary, while the fellow with the India-rubber coat jumped up and began a passionate exhortation or sermon, which for mimetic fidelity was incomparable. [23]

This was followed by an orgiastic bout of urine-drinking, an example of antinatural or anticultural behavior not highly regarded by the guest.

One swallowed a fragment of corn-husk, saying he thought it very good and better than bread; his *vis-à-vis* attempted to chew and gulp down a piece of filthy rag. Another expressed regret that the dance had not been held out of doors, in one of the plazas; there they could show what they could do. There they always made it a point of honor to eat the excrement of men and dogs.[24]

The "universals" that I have been discussing are strong human interests that fools in many times and places have demonstratively shared with nonfools. Still, an individual fool actor performs before an audience with values shaped by cultural and historical factors; both the fool and his audience are to a large extent bound by conventions, including those of what is funny. Thus, though ribaldry is a permanent source of humor, countless clowns in the European tradition have reaped harvests from sexual conceits to which we no longer respond. The figure of the woman catching a sixth husband at the funeral of her fifth, for example, is no longer as hilarious as it was in Elizabethan times; nor is the "horn joke." Such materials can be *made* funny, but this requires a reworking of what was once funny in itself. Most jokes, in fact, express the attitudes of a specific group in a specific period and do not survive the death of those attitudes. And though jokes on topics of universal interest tend to keep their vitality, they gradually suffer the fate of those on more ephemeral topics. This consideration raises questions about the abiding elements of folly and their primitive and magical connotations.

Among these questions are the following. If a modern circus clown engages in the same overt behavior as a Pueblo Indian clown, are they really doing the same thing? Do the two similar bits of action have the same meaning? And if the various sticklike appurtenances of earlier fool actors derive from cults of fertility and the dead, is any of this significance still present when clowns knock one another over the head in the modern circus and in slapstick films? Or are we not instead witnessing a continuation of elements that have been emptied of significance, that have become dissociated from the dread that was once close to the pleasure of response to those elements? Are we not looking at survivals that have gained their own charm and appropriateness in the way, for example, that the wedding veil has come to suggest modesty instead of protection from

94

the evil eye or that Hallowe'en has become a celebration of childish
naughtiness rather than an emptying of graves and a deliverance up to the
"destructive element" and to elemental life forces? Such questions require
us to consider some aspects of the relations between universal interests
and the specifics of culture and to consider some characteristics of clown
play with both of them.

We are by now greatly impressed by the variety of human values and by
the complexity and apparent uniqueness of historical and cultural
configurations. But we may also be impressed by the limited number of
really basic problems to be solved by human groups. In these unique
configurations there are focal points of biological and spiritual importance
around which values are organized. With regard to one such point, Yeats
once claimed that "Man has created death"; but before man made it by
making it part of a system of cultural values, and before individuals such
as Yeats devised their own versions of its spiritual meaning, it was a
biological fact. Its meaning may partly be given by culture, but it must
partly be discovered anew by every individual in every period everywhere.
Cultural and personal forms of relation to these points are tenaciously
maintained; yet just at these points, cultural and personal differences
often fade, sometimes very surprisingly. It may, for example, be a slippery
step from taking an enemy seriously to admiring him and accepting him
as a leader, or from decently fearing social authority to hating it enough
to rebel against it. Such shifts of allegiance are subjectively familiar to
everyone from dreams and fantasies. Our relationship to cultural values is,
then, always ambiguous, since conscious commitment and intention have
their limits and since the unconscious speaks in its own voice, which may
be antinatural or anticultural. Though the language spoken by the
unconscious is not single, it makes frequent use of universal motifs. In
any case, the *fact* of these ambiguities is universal. (To deny this would be
to deny the uniqueness and relativity of cultural configurations; it would
be to deny that each is, or will be, laid waste by time.) And when these
ambiguities make themselves felt, they bear some of the primitive and
magical power of the unconscious.

Clowning in the circus is different from that among primitive peoples
in that the former is a show divorced from ceremonial forms invested
with the highest religious and social authority and concerned with basic

facts of life and death. But circus clowns are also concerned with those facts: circus clowns playfully give birth and playfully kill. Both kinds of clowns provoke and play with the ambiguities about which I have been speaking: both act in accordance with specific cultural attitudes and in violation of others and pursue a shifting compromise between allegiance and rebellion. They question the adequacy of cultural attitudes by reminding us of these ambiguities and by adopting other attitudes, thus implying that those of the audience are arbitrary. After all, one *might* talk with the Zuñi gods on the telephone, even if one *cannot;* the culture behind the Paternoster and the U.S. Army coat is powerful and *might* be based on valid premises, even if it *is not*. I have never seen a circus clown appear as a mock Indian, but such a gag is easily conceivable, and in it the clown might triumph over his partners. Both kinds of clowns are semidetached from social authority; what they do is a mixture of the anticultural and of play; they effect in their audiences what could be called a suspension of belief or of value—for example, in the telephone conversation with the gods or in circus-clown skits based on ridiculous premises.

One can even say, with some qualification, that clowns of the circus, like ceremonial clowns, play not only with the ambiguities of the individual and of culture but also with the magical and primitive power alive in those ambiguities; that both kinds of clowns contain, absorb, nullify, redistribute, and redirect this power. With the same qualification one can say that both kinds of fools also effect a suspension of *dis*belief and of *non*value, an opening to a self-authenticating spiritual power that is directly available to clowns and only indirectly, through clowns, to their audience. This is clear in the case of ceremonial clowns who are fun-makers and who are yet awesome spiritual beings of fundamental importance to the culture and surrounded by taboos. In the case of circus clowns that power has become a fiction, but it affects the imagination in ways that grant glimpses of that power, though for us neither the fiction nor the power inspires conscious belief.

At first sight it appears as though the modern circus clown does, in fact, represent a descendant of the cultic clown divested of magical power. After all, the clowns among the Hopi Indians, who are culturally closely akin to the Zuñis, have largely lost their ritual functions and become entertainers. And the same process has occurred elsewhere, often (though not always) as part of a cultural development in which ritual and magical practices lose their importance. This picture is largely true, but it is by no means as simple as it appears at first sight. The complexities that must be taken into account derive, first, from the role of the clown, in many primitive societies as in the modern circus, as a being who makes a funny *show* of extraordinary powers. They also derive from the fact that magical modes of thought are by no means operative only in people who believe in such powers, that such powers may have different meanings in ritual and in the nonritual fool show, and that these different meanings are not always mutually exclusive. And they derive, further, from the possibility that where such different meanings have excluded one another, a collapse or inversion of attitude may occur, whereby what was merely funny suddenly commands awe.

For a carver of masks, a piece of gnarled wood suggestive of a face may invite the carving that will make the face emerge, and the face may invite further elaboration; for someone who has played at clowning, the outline of a gag may invite the careful ingenuity that makes it into art, and the gag may invite elaboration into a skit. The mimetic impulse may become a motive in the development from ritual to drama, as it did in Greece (and in a rudimentary way in Indian America and elsewhere); it may also become a motive in the development from ritual clowning to clowning for fun. In one sense this development means a diminution of the power of the clown. If Lévy-Bruhl's "collective representations," or shared patterns of thought, are taken to represent the "objectivity" of the people who believe in them, this development means a withdrawal from the divinely ordained, collective power of cult to a more subjective, individual, and playful relation to magic, a relation no longer to the reality of spirits but to magical modes of thought. But in another sense this development means an increase of power for the clown, as did the development that led to drama for the actor. This increase of power is most clearly evident in the figure of the court jester, to be discussed in Part III. Whatever the origins and antecedents of the European jester, his role represented a break with ritual clowning. His famous privilege and power of "speaking the truth," even when his master could not do it, was based on the convention that, for the jester, everything, including the most sacred matters, was mere play. This did not mean that his playful utterances could not be taken seriously; in fact, his dispossession and playfulness provided a medium in which "the truth" could be allowed to have its own bite.

When we think of jesters "speaking the truth," we usually have in mind statements addressed to consciousness despite the nonsense in which they might be cloaked. Though this (one-sided) conception of jesters distinguishes them from circus clowns, who pursue nonsense for its own sake, it provides an analogy for the relation of clowns and other fool entertainers to magic. The question of whether such figures have a relation to the demonic and to elemental life forces is partly, but only partly, answered by the fact that what they do is divorced from collective forms of serious relation to such powers. The question then becomes one of whether or not such figures inspire in their audience subjective feelings that would seem to imply a contact with such powers. This question, in turn, is partly, but only partly, answered by the fact that what such figures do is mere play and does not invite feelings appropriate to what is serious, even sacred. However, in this play, as in that of jesters, what were once matters of ritual importance may inspire a momentary thrill. This does not necessarily mean that either the fool actors or the audience have felt that ritual importance, but it may mean that the fool actors have touched the same fundamental human concern that was expressed in ritual. And if the fool even uses some of the devices of ritual in his exploration of that concern, he may be using them for the same reason that they were used ritually: because the mimetic impulse alive in serious ritual and in clowning suggests or even demands them. For example, two musical clowns (Helena Amwrosjewa and Georg Schachnin of the Moscow State Circus) appear as an Amazon woman and tiny absent-minded professor. After she has played a trombone loudly, skillfully, and in horrible taste while he has accompanied her on a piano, they tear off their wigs to reveal the Amazon as the man and the professor as the woman. The effect is stunning; whether or not the purpose of the performance is the same as that of transvestite mummers in earlier fertility rituals, we probably have some of the same feelings toward the clowns as people did toward the mummers then.

In general, fool actors recreate the world—or try to do so and fail—in accordance with the "fundamental apperception" that is alive in everyone. As a result they are infantile; but also as a result they express concerns that were those of myth, legend, and ritual, of the whole enterprise of human culture when it was informed with them. In what fool actors continue to do survivals of the sacred and clownish invention are one in the expression of a magical attitude toward fundamental human concerns. In the life of culture these concerns give rise to certain sets of problems: those of order and disorder or of cosmos and chaos, of "good" and "bad," of the boundary and the center. These continue to be explored by nonritual fool actors. What clowns do may seem mere play, but then the mummers begging for eggs at the beginning of spring may have thought that they were merely playing.

# 6   Order and Chaos and the Fool

Fertility rites of agriculture imply that there is an order in the world (spring comes after winter), that there are forces working against that order (the crops may be poor), and that man can help to assure that the order will prevail (he mimes his involvement in the processes of nature and his commitment to its order). The "contrary behavior" of clowns may also serve that order—a complex matter with which I will continue to be concerned. But if man *can* help to assure this order, is he not *responsible* for it and the forces that work against it? This question is answered by an ancient mythical pattern that has been fundamental to many religions and to the development of drama, especially the genus of tragedy. According to Herbert Weisinger, that pattern is of man,

> projected as god, divine king, or hero . . . struggling desperately and endlessly to carve out of a chaotic and cruel cosmos a world of order and justice. In a sense, man has never succeeded in that effort, nor, in the very nature of the situation, can he possibly succeed. Yet, precisely because he is man, he struggles; he plunges into the terrors of the small moment, he suffers, he dies, but he lives again. For the very struggle to succeed is a success in itself; as long as he struggles against the dark, death, and evil, he holds them off, and for every moment that they are held off, he has succeeded.[1]

Weisinger sees tragedy as based on this struggle as it is explored in the dimension of choice.

> It is not the engagement itself which alone makes man; it is rather the kind of engagement which he chooses to encounter which distinguishes him as man. For he chooses what battle he shall fight and he takes on thereby the responsibility of responsibility; he selects not

any engagement, nor looks forward to any victory, but this one alone, and precisely this: the victory of light, life, and good over dark, death, and evil. He dies that he may live, he falls that he may rise, he suffers that he may learn.[2]

Fools are characteristically unperturbed by the ignominy that comes of being irresponsible. They have a magical affinity with chaos that might allow them to serve as scapegoats on behalf of order; yet they elude the sacrifice or the banishment that would affirm order at their expense. They reduce order to chaos in a way that makes a farce of the mythical pattern. They wrest life from the "destructive element" while ridiculing the ancient dream that victory over it is possible—and while ridiculing even more the idea that victory over it may be achieved through the observance of rules of conduct. Fools induce chaos by violating those rules. They may look on passively, innocently, even benignly, while the sympathetic magic that binds them to it works. Though they may seem innocently detached from it, it may be an active form of their folly. It may be overtly demonic, but it may also take a playful form, and it may emerge as the fool's guiding spirit in a transvaluation of values with him as its center. I have so far mentioned many fools who have attacked rules and by implication the whole principle of order. I wish now to illustrate these other forms of the fool's relation to order and chaos by scenes from modern films and vaudeville. I wish to show the persistence of concerns alive in ritual and of the fool's magic as a reality that again and again requires contemporary expression.

Folly is a disembodied and demonic force in a scene in Chaplin's film *Limelight* (1952), in which he and Buster Keaton are music-hall clowns performing a skit. Chaplin is a concert violinist accompanied at the piano by Keaton. As Keaton is getting ready to play, his sheets of music begin spilling from the piano, the confusion mounting and mounting as though the music were possessed. His piano then starts to disintegrate, slowly and malevolently, and the strings snap and roll up until the guts are an insidious snarl of wire. As the strings break one by one, weird sounds erupt. As soon as Chaplin has begun playing his inanely showy piece, one of his legs shrivels up and disappears into his trousers. He stops, looks down startled, pulls the leg down with his hands till it touches the floor and begins playing again. The leg again shrivels up. The audience howls with laughter.

The laughter is, by implication, at poliomyelitis, at cancer, at automobile accidents, at the ills that ravage mind and body. One could argue that the fools are not quite real for the audience, which knows that they are not really being destroyed. Still, we may laugh at someone who has fallen down before we are certain that he has not broken his leg. In laughing at him, as at the contorted clowns, we are dissociating ourselves from what has unexpectedly happened, and our doing so attests to its frightening character for us. Though we may be laughing at the clowns partly out of the joyful sense of superiority over others, especially in their misfortune, that Thomas Hobbes found essential to laughter, that superiority is made questionable by the fact that we do not understand any more than the clowns do what is happening to them. And we must work to keep ourselves from feeling what it would be like if our legs were to shrivel up like Chaplin's. The clowns become a writhing momument to the limits to the human image, before it yields to monstrosity, a momument to the human will to resist the demons of chaos.

Keaton matter-of-factly fumbles with the sheets, the controlling pattern of the music the clowns intend to perform; he does this as though he hopes that enough fumbling might dispel the mischievous spirit. Once the sheets have been thoroughly scrambled, the possibility that the musical act may be salvaged is lost, but the pianist goes on. When his piano begins to disintegrate, he proceeds to pick at the keys, as though the destructive process might at any moment stop or undo itself. And Chaplin deals with the shriveling leg in a faintly embarrassed way, as though he were committing some lapse of good taste instead of being the victim of something inexplicably terrible. The two fools seem so busy behaving normally that they cannot spare attention for the remarkable nature of these phenomena; they try to push them out of mind so that they can continue performing actions that have lost all point whatsoever. Or have they lost all point? After all, what should two soldiers do if they are ambushed in an isolated outpost?

It is, in fact, probable that we are laughing not only at their inappropriate and pedantic fussing but also at their heroic tenacity, at their dedication to the meaningful continuance of life. There is, as well, something sinister about their heroism. Their participation in the human image, already slight because they are clowns, is violated further and further until we must realize that it is not the human will that is in them enduring and even holding its own against chaos; there seems, rather, to be a secret collaboration between them and whatever is attacking them. They go on being tormented as mice by a cat; if we were the mice, we would have given ourselves up much sooner. The fact that the fools persist, without succumbing to panic and running, makes us begin to suspect that a single intelligence, like that of an unimaginable cat-mouse, is playing with us through them, through their dilemma, and through their attempts to deal with it.

In a sense the two clowns enact the struggle of man against a "chaotic and cruel cosmos," but their enactment of it apparently has little to do with choice, responsibility, victory, or even learning anything. Their ignorance of the moral dimension is not at the moment bliss for them, but it allows them to go on, and it brings to us a sense of expansion, of freedom. The silliness and the sinister overtones do not lessen the heroism of the clowns, and our mockery at them does not lessen our admiration of them. We know that light, life, and good are invaluable, that their victory demands sacrifice and may result in tragedy or, much worse, deliverance up to the demonic or simply to nothingness. The clowns remind us of a truth as ancient and as important: that light, life, and good are not necessarily synonymous and that, in any case, they are not limited to conscious order.

We hope that our means of making and keeping order will be sufficient to fend off chaos. But sometimes the power of those means expresses itself not in accordance with our expectations but rather in queer events that may bear traces of magical intentions, though we are not sure. Almost everyone is superstitious enough sometimes to feel that his purposes are bewitched. Almost everyone who drives an automobile, for example, has had the experience of driving through a city and being stopped by every red light, no matter how often he speeds up and slows down. When this happens, he may make a game of trying to outwit the next traffic light, perhaps by taking a shortcut that the light should not have thought of. When he is stopped by that light, too, he may feel that he has been defeated not by chance but by a conscious intention counter to his own, that the light is not a neutral thing but is playing with him, that someone is grinning at him from the mechanism controlling the traffic lights. A perfectly normal person may have such experiences, but they are also characteristic of ambiguous forms of psychopathology. Someone may, for example, have ideas that strike others as possibly mad, but possibly not; he may have mad ideas but not quite take them seriously; he may have brought them into a kind of order that perhaps is mad, but perhaps is not; he may feel that the world has become uncanny but that there is also something uncanny about the way he looks at it; he may devise a test of himself and it and then wonder how to test the results of his test. The driver may be nearing the labyrinths described by Kafka, in which what should be orderly and just is mindless, though it speaks the language of order and justice; the man having trouble with his ideas may already have entered those labyrinths.

An example of how the world looks when the means of keeping order become possessed in this way is provided by one of the sketches of the comedian Karl Valentin, *Die verhexten Notenständer,* "The Bewitched Music Stands."[3] In this skit Valentin and his partner Liesl Karlstadt are also two clown musicians; they intend to play a trumpet duet. Without sheets of music they both play the same lines of the duet; after they have got the sheets, they do not know how to use them. They hang them on each other's backs and then chase each other in circles trying to read them. The stage manager brings out two music stands, one very large and one very small (to hold their very large and very small books of music). The clowns then seem to inflict their foolishness upon the music stands, which, infected with it, add to their difficulties. Karl Valentin takes the large stand, and his small book of music again and again falls through it; Liesl Karlstadt takes the small stand, but her book is so big that it repeatedly knocks the stand over. As soon as these problems are more or less solved, others arise. The clowns are both ready to play, but Liesl Karlstadt's music stand is so high that when she tries to read the music her hat falls down her back; his stand is so low that his hat falls down over his face. The stage manager takes the two music stands from the stage and comes back with a large, double-backed one. The clowns put their music on the stand and begin to play, but the stand starts to grow taller and taller, so that the two clowns must climb up on their chairs to read the music. But they are still too low, and they resignedly let their instruments sink. Valentin stops the orchestra, asking if the players do not see that the stand is growing. While he is addressing the audience about the problem, the music stand drops to its original height. The clowns remark that they do not need the chairs any longer. As they climb down, the music stand again shoots into the air. They stand under the rack, Valentin touches the stem, and the rack falls on their heads.

The fools try to understand what is happening. Valentin suggests that someone has smeared the bottom of the stand with fertilizer and it has grown. Liesl Karlstadt guesses that there is a string on the floor and that, by pulling it, the stage manager makes the stand go up and down. Valentin proposes that they cut the string. In the meantime, the stage manager takes the music stand away and brings one that does have a string, which runs to the wings. Liesl Karlstadt sees it and pulls it, a shot is fired, the stand collapses, and Valentin, terrified, falls to the floor. The music stand is now too low; Liesl Karlstadt tries to adjust it by pulling the string, and the stand jumps again into the air. The stage manager takes it away reproachfully and brings another. (One wonders by now whether they are his puppets or victims or whether he is a *deus ex machina* fulfilling their wishes in a secret conspiracy.) They put their music on it, and the stand begins lurching in 90-degree turns, spinning more and more quickly as they try to keep up with its movements. The next stand swings back and forth like a metronome. Valentin accuses it of being drunk, and Liesl Karlstadt thinks that it has become foolish and should be put in the icebox.

The stage manager brings a new music stand, the two fools play a short march, and bow three times: at the third bow the music stand collapses. With still another music stand—and after many difficulties—they succeed in playing a duet for the two instruments that are, as Valentin announces, the most different of all instruments in the whole world: an enormous drum and a very tiny harmonica. The music falls from the rack, and the top part of the stand flies into the air and out of sight. They finish playing with still a different stand and begin to leave the stage, but Valentin pauses, whistles to the music stand, and reminds it they are finished; it slides across the stage after them.

105

## The Pattern of Folly

At the beginning of the sketch, Karl Valentin and Liesl Karlstadt display the inability or refusal, characteristic of fools, to master a simple mechanical problem, that of fitting the big book to the big stand and the small to the small. It is a special instance of the general infantile difficulty with measure and proportion. The successive music stands take on an intelligent life, apparently fed by energies belonging to the same problem of size. The fools effect a transformation within the world, and an inversion of the customary relations of mind and matter takes place: the intelligible order of the world is replaced by a kind of foolish intelligence; objects that should be passive become active in the expression of folly. The music stands, that is to say, not only have become human but show the same disrespect for natural laws and normal proportions that the two clowns have already displayed. The clowns broach the question "Why?" but soon drop it as irrelevant. The problem is no longer one of predicting and controlling the behavior of the music stands; it is rather one of taking in *what* the music stands are doing at each moment and of trying to go along with the curious intelligence they display.

Some of the lacking consciousness of these two half-wits has seemingly become active in the world around them. They thus present a foolish picture of certain elemental facts of psychic life. We are continuously deceived about the objectivity of our relations to the world, since they are partly characterized by "fundamental apperception," by "mystical participation" (or subjective identity with the object), and by projection. Thus a good deal of our psychic life takes place outside ourselves, though we do not notice the fact until our relations to the world become noticeably disturbed, and usually we do not even notice it then. Such considerations even led Jung to speculate that the psyche may once have existed completely outside us "in the form of arbitrary powers with intentions of their own" and may then gradually have taken its place within us.[4] Whatever the development has been, we are still acted upon by such powers.

As we look at the consciousness displayed by objects in the world of fools—for example, the music stands of Valentin and Karlstadt—we do not find it to be of an impressively high grade. Of course, the fact that such objects display intelligent will at all may blind us to its quality. (We are less concerned with how well the fools play than we are with the fact that they succeed in playing.) But there is, as we have seen, a practical difficulty about an arrangement whereby the fool has more or less half the consciousness he should have and the world around him the other half. For normal purposes the half-wittedness of the fool is worse than none, because it activates a corresponding half-wittedness in the environment, with the result that the normal means of maintaining order in the face of chaos become means of increasing chaos. The psychic infection coming from the fool tends to invade the parts of the world where problems of order and disorder become crucial, for example, in the forms of social interaction and mechanical implements. Thus it is Keaton's piano and Valentin's and Karlstadt's music stands that become foolish. Chaplin's shriveling leg is an image of what can happen when our means of keeping order fail altogether. The music stand of Valentin and Karlstadt, which follows them off the stage like an obedient dog, shows that the twilight confusion between order and chaos can also, sometimes, resolve itself in the harmless insignificance of a joke.

In neither of these two vaudeville sketches, that of Chaplin and Keaton and that of Valentin and Karlstadt, do the events that befall the fools give the impression of being accidental. In both sketches, objects seem possessed. This fact does not in itself make the queer behavior of the objects meaningful to us, but then meaning is not the immediate issue. What is at stake is life. In the routine of Chaplin and Keaton the fight for continuing life is being carried on as effectively as it could be without the benefit of a new meaning, a new idea of what is wrong or of how to attack or escape it. In the sketch of Valentin and Karlstadt the irrational but intelligent behavior of the music stands is not so threatening that a meaning for it is urgently demanded. It is still possible to interact with that intelligence in a kind of play and wait to see what its final intentions are. Life and the meaning absolutely necessary to it are preserved in the fact that these queer happenings belong in one way or another to fools and not to us. In the words of William Blake, "If others had not been foolish, we should be so." [5] The fool of the fool show is in his self-manifestation sufficient meaning for these events. He will survive and will continue his participation in them, now falling victim to them and again triumphantly getting the upper hand over them. But this mischief-making power can never be really mastered. We cannot master it, because not only does it refuse to accord with our methods of understanding and prediction, but it infects our means of conscious control. The fool cannot master it, because he shares its substance and intelligence. One can come to a relative harmony with this force, as Valentin and Karlstadt have by the end of their sketch (when we see that the music stand was really part of a foolish conspiracy against the audience), but without understanding it fully and without claiming possession of it.

In the act of Chaplin and Keaton, the battle is from the outset one-sided, the fools against a horrible force which would defeat us if we were in their places. In the sketch of Valentin and Karlstadt the battle is much more relative; it is as though a partial incarnation has taken place, the arbitrary and potentially horrible powers of chaos having assumed the playful intelligence of the fool and become undangerously marvelous. This amounts to a humanization of the autonomous power.

Both kinds of experience—that of chaos as an invasion and that of chaos as emanating from the means of keeping order—are partly shaped by subjective interpretation. Both rest on the assumption that the world, here, is basically hospitable to us, even if meaning often eludes us, and that chaos is in its most potent depths extraneous. Chaos should not, we think, break through the wall from the outside; nor should bits of it turn up again and again within our means of keeping order. The fool breaks down the boundary between chaos and order, but he also violates our assumption that that boundary was where we thought it was and that it had the character we thought it had: that of affirming whatever we have taken for granted and in that way protecting us from the dark unknown. In so doing, he allows us to maintain a playful contact with undeveloped possibilities, the "embryon atoms" of Milton's Chaos,[6] despite the chance that they will take the form of queer and hostile objects and events, and despite the foreordained certainty that chaos will break at some point into their development and try to swallow them again, either from the abyss or from some indeterminate point within the ordered world.

When the music stand follows Valentin and Karlstadt offstage, an overt joke is made of the identity between the fools and an object that has in their presence become foolishly alive. More usually, however, the relationship between the fool actor and such a foolishly possessed object remains covert. It is neither a clear relationship of identity nor one of nonidentity; the fool is neither simply the agent nor simply the victim of the freak occurrences, though they seem to take place "because" he is present. Thus in the Chaplin film, *The Pawnshop* (1916), Charlie, working for a pawnbroker, must assess a clock that a customer has brought to be pawned. Elegantly professional, Charlie prods the clock, listens to it with a stethoscope, opens it with a can-opener, and disembowels it. The parts that had till a moment before kept time with mechanical precision become a viscous mass that begins to churn on the tabletop. Charlie pounds it with a hammer; he squirts it with oil, and its illicit life suddenly vanishes. He is neither simply the agent nor simply the victim of these queer events while they are occurring, but in the resolution of the skit there is a crude sorting-out of the two roles. Charlie is in one sense no longer the victim, but he has not really become the victor: he has "broken even" with the folly in which he was implicated, but he has gained nothing from the entire operation and will go on falling into such plights. It is, however, clear—as Charlie sweeps the parts back into the shell of the clock and fastidiously refuses it—that the customer has been made a fool of and is the victim in the sense that he must bear the loss of his clock.

Consciousness proceeds by means of associations among which a selection must be made. The associations that Charlie allows to govern his behavior are in our eyes false, being based on inappropriate analogies. For him the clock is like a patient to a doctor or dentist; it is like a tin of coffee; the mechanical parts are like ribbon to a ribbon salesman; they are like swarming vermin (to be pounded with a hammer); they are like a storm-tossed sea (to be calmed with oil). But no matter what the clock is *like,* it is, in fact, an alarm clock, and Charlie's caricature of the magical attitude results in the destruction of the thing it is for us. And since it is not only the customer's clock but also our notions of what a clock is that is attacked, we, too, are the victims of Charlie's folly.

The ambiguity of the fool's relation to order and to the chaos that erupts from it in his presence is rooted in his lack of self-identity. That is to say, in part, that his defective ego-functioning is of a piece with his

# The Pattern of Folly

deficient ego-identity. Since the fool is "not all there," and since what is there is relatively uncentered, we cannot establish a simple cause-and-effect relationship between him and the queer events that go on around him. He releases a kind of foolish magic and then escapes the consequences of the magic he has released. This may be seen in a circus-clown gag. First Clown (pointing): "Look! Look! Look!" Second Clown: "What? What? What?" First Clown (triumphantly): "A finger!" [7] The collapse that the first clown effects between subject and object takes place at the expense of the normal order of things and is the expression of his own lack of self-identity. The first clown is rewarded by a blow on the head from the second, but the blow is futile since the first clown is "not all there." (The deeper level of his not being "all there" is revealed in the clown gag mentioned earlier: "I wish I were two puppies —so I could play together." The lonely clown is not two, but he also is not one.)

Although the fool as a person (or pseudoperson) escapes, something remains that is also a form of the fool: the mess around him. And in being fooled by it we are drawn into a provisional identity with the fool who has escaped. One element of our reaction to such gags is bafflement; it gives way to the supremacy in disorganization that according to Helmuth Plessner characterizes our subjective experience of laughter.[8] The lumpen or motley, idiotic or mad, fool as clown is the visible form of both that disorganization and that supremacy. We are not drawn into the kind of actual involvement with the fool that Charlie's customer was: the disorganization that the fool effects in us is that of our subjective adaptation to the world.

Another joke, in which there is no overt victim, illustrates this process. Two Englishmen are riding in a train. First Englishman: "I say, is this Wembley?" Second Englishman: "No, Thursday." First Englishman: "I am, too." The Englishmen remain placid in what strikes us as their foolishness; they are no more troubled by their incomprehension of each other than Charlie is by his of the alarm clock. But their behavior inflicts violence upon our assumptions of what people are and of how they ought to behave. In our commitment to those assumptions we are brought to the position of Charlie's customer in the pawnshop. But we also share in the triumph of nonsense over sense. We feel ourselves fooled by the irrational mess that has been made of a conventional conversation; in freeing ourselves from that mess, in which our conscious assumptions about the world have become for a moment stuck, we experience within ourselves the supremacy of the fugitive and irresponsible fool.

The magical force that induces chaos in the presence of the fool often results in a transvaluation of values that could be the beginning of a new order. This process is illustrated by a scene from W. C. Fields's film *The Bank Dick* (1940). Fields drives a car at great speed while a bank robber in the seat behind him points a gun at him; they are chased by policemen on motorcycles. In the course of the pursuit, the controlling mechanisms of the car begin to disintegrate. Unperturbed, Fields throws away the gearshift and the brakes and passes the steering wheel to the robber. The car careens madly but without accident, dodging obstacles, until it finally comes to a halt at the very edge of a cliff. Fields steps out, the criminal having passed out with fright, in time to be greeted as a hero by the arriving police. The magical power that guides the car may be seen as another form of that which horribly afflicted Chaplin and Keaton and which playfully teased Valentin and Liesl Karlstadt. That this power belongs to the fool, or that he belongs to it, is shown by the fact that Fields takes the astonishing course of events completely for granted and that it ends in a triumph for him. In addition, the cliff overlooks water with a sign labeling it "Lake Shosho-Bogomo," a product of the same mind, Fields's, that earlier in the film invented the disease "mogo on the gogogo:" the fool's intelligence has plotted the course that the car takes as though by chance.

The nature of this power as a psychic reality becomes apparent if we regard automobile-driving as an analogy for the functioning of the ego. Driving is not just an act of conscious thought or understanding but a very complicated interaction of conscious and unconscious functions. If a person is to drive well, his car must be in working order, he must know how to drive, he must have a clear idea of where he wants to go and how he wants to get there, and he must have a flexibility of understanding that will allow him to deal with unexpected events along the way. In other words, his driving is not just an act of conscious thought or will but a complicated interaction of conscious and unconscious, of voluntary and habitual functions.

The power of the automobile—the energy used by ego-functioning—may be assumed to derive from deep regions of the unconscious. More specifically, it may be assumed to derive from a constellation of archetypes, of transpersonal, unconscious factors that actively shape our experience. In Jung's view, the archetypes are sources of both instinctual energy and meaning. Unless a person experiences the constellated archetype on the symbolic level (as *Sinnbild* or "image of meaning"), he is immersed in its dynamism. This dynamism may animate states of subjective identity with the world; it may nourish projection, affect, and diffuse and obsessive sexuality; it may make objects unpredictable and adaptation to them extremely difficult; its effects—when meaning is inadequate—are largely destructive. A person's adaptation to the outer world may fail, as when he makes a wrong turn with his car into a one-way street; his adaptation to these inner factors may also fail, with the result that he may fall into magical modes of thought and behavior. The analytical psychologist Edward Whitmont sees magical phenomena as belonging to a field of energy derived from the archetype; he sees this field of energy as constituting a dimension of experience and a characteristic mode of psychic functioning.[9] This view implies a correlation between culture and the individual, between primitive peoples and modern Western individuals in states of regression, that may be too neat (for reasons I touched on in the previous section), but it is nonetheless suggestive when applied to personal psychology.

Fields can be imagined, then, as having fallen into such a magical field, with the dynamism of the archetypal constellation having usurped the controlling functions of ego-consciousness. The automobile is magical in that it continues to run despite its disintegration and finds its way among obstacles (thus implying a breakdown of the distinction between the intelligent subject and lifeless objects); the affect characteristic of strong connection with the archetypes appears in the war between the bank robber and the police. Fields's equanimity in the course of this perilous adventure is appropriate to the foolish characteristic of being only "as though the same as" oneself; what he *really* is—his folly—is at work in the disintegration of the car, in its precarious course despite this disintegration, and in the conflict between the forces of law and lawlessness. His role in the magical field is at first that of victim; then it becomes clear that he is its agent; and finally it allows him to triumph over both the criminal and the police as he—or it—makes fools of both of them.

Both the police and the criminal belong to an order based on certain rules of behavior and certain realities of power. In both culture and individual psychology, patterns of order tend to become rigid and sterile; they repeatedly need renewal. This tendency, too, is partly a matter of our relations to the unconscious. When the symbol or "image of meaning," the manifest content of the archetype, has crossed the threshold into consciousness, it is at first numinous; in time it loses its dynamism, which is also its capacity for provoking emotion. This loss is a natural part of the process by which rational meaning is formed and maintained in consciousness. "It is a fearful thing to fall into the hands of the living God" (Heb. 10:31); but the experience must lose its immediacy if it is translated into the discursive language of theology. However, the process of abstraction is necessary, as it splits the total experience of the archetype into one of a subject confronting an object and thus protects us from the archetypal dynamism.[10] But when the process of abstraction has gone too far, the repressed dynamism asserts itself. Life goes on even when it is meaningless; order must again and again be brought into relation with vital possibilities supplied by the unconscious. These are at first incomprehensible, but they may express what seem to be dispositions in the magical field.

Fields's wild car ride implies such a magical disposition. As we watch him, life revenges itself upon the colorless order that has been made of it, and folly revenges itself upon the nonfoolish values that have temporarily neutralized it. Chaos is spread throughout the normal world until the car halts at the edge of the cliff, as though the magical power that had guided it there were content to disappear again to the "outside," beyond the limits of conscious awareness. The result is a transvaluation of the good and bad figures, the police and the robber, into fools who (as unwitting butts of the folly that has possessed the car) must acknowledge the superior power of the fool (as knave). This reduction of order to chaos in which the magical power of the fool makes itself felt is related to that effected by saturnalian revelers and primitive clowns.

It is striking how strongly inclined people are to believe the rational constructions that, as individuals and groups, they make of the world. Reason is often motivated by unconscious contents, as when scientists explore and systematize owing to their emotional attitudes toward the unknown and toward order; and ideas of what constitutes the proper form of things facilitates action, as when our conception of our territory creates the line at which we will act to defend it. Thus order invites belief, as does that which violates it. However, one can argue skeptically that knowledge of objective order is humanly impossible unless the psyche, including the irrational, is granted the status of objective fact; but this admission opens us to painful ambiguities that we had hoped to avoid through our passion for reason. Thus people are also inclined to trim and connive in their commitment to the order that they believe in. The fool, deficient in normal understanding and in the normal appreciation of order, readmits the magical power of chaos; he makes us surreptitiously feel that a debt of honesty has been paid.

In his clowning the fool plays with some of the irrational hopes that motivate the makers of order and some of the doubts that plague them. If the world were different, we might find certainty in it; the unknown might yield marvels, including a summer of golden plenty or a thought as perfect as a crystal, instead of the threat of death. As things are, we may, like the philosophical Jaques and like Hamlet in the guise of the morose clown, be fool-victims in our inability to understand the world and ourselves and to act nobly. But we may also, like the victorious fool-hero of the chase scene in *The Bank Dick*, commit ourselves to the irrational flow of life. We may feel that queer events (such as those that befall the car) are living traces of a wholeness that is annulling for a purpose our customary distinctions between order and chaos. That purpose transcends the train of the queer events yet seems to inform them and to belong to the deeper nature of things. The fool as magician-actor and "delight-maker" (as one kind of Pueblo Indian clown was called) belongs to it, too.

# 7 The Fool and "Good" and "Bad"

Problems of "good" and "bad" are closely bound up, on the one hand, with those of adult responsibility and infantile irresponsibility and, on the other, with those of order and disorder, of cosmos and chaos. Fools may be "good," either as the saintly and pure in heart or as ironic moralists; they may be "bad," either as victims of the Eighth Deadly Sin that Alexander Barclay took folly to be (in his English translation of the *Narrenschiff*) or as willful agents of evil. More usually, though, the fool as moral agent—as in other respects—is like the child's toy called in German *Stehaufmännchen* or "little get-up man" and in English a tumbler or roly-poly. The toy, often painted to look like a clown, is weighted at the bottom; when it is hit, it rolls and bobs until it stands upright again. Neither in its motionlessness, when it is upright, nor in its flailing to stand upright again is it for us an image of a moral agent acting on behalf of the "good." It is impressive, rather, for its detachment from any moral conflict that we might try to attribute to it with our imagination. The toy is not in conflict with the "bad" person who hits it. It simply reacts with simplicity and economy according to inviolable physical laws and without expending energy of its own. It can take any number of blows; it has endless time to find its upright position under a rain of them, and the "bad" person cannot win against it, so that the conflict between the two is illusory; its winning does not make it "good." Nor can we imagine it as being caught in an inner conflict, since there is nothing in its mechanical construction that hinders it from regaining its balance. Whether anything about it is "good" or "bad" depends entirely on the moral perspective in which it is regarded. Its stability and uprightness may seem admirable if we think of the fools and kings (to be considered later) falling from the wheel of fortune, but its total submission to the determinism of physical laws may seem deplorable if we think of the freedom and surprising wit of many fools and nonfools.

This toy is presumably made in the form of a clown for two reasons. First, it is a model of the fool as butt, as pure victim. (Thus the business of the *stupidus* during the Roman Empire was, according to Enid Welsford, "to repeat the words and make unsuccessful attempts to imitate the actions of others, and to be deceived by everybody. He wore a long-pointed hat, a multi-coloured patchwork dress, and according to St. Chrysostom it was part of his duty to be 'slapped at the public expense.'"[1]) And second, the toy is also a model of something more elusive that we often feel about clowns and fools: their "objectivity," their ability to move with events in ways suggesting that they are somehow following God's or nature's design. (Enid Welsford suggests something like this when she calls Lear's Fool the *punctum indifferens* of the play and attributes roughly the same status to other Shakespearean fools.[2]) The pattern made by the bobbing of the clown toy is also "objective" in that one movement is balanced by a countermovement in a process governed by symmetry in the interests of the "point of indifference" to which the toy should again arrive. This process of balancing also suggests the processes of compensation that, according to Jung, govern psychic life (for example, when the saint has sinful dreams). It suggests, further, certain facts about the nature of the center of the personality that will be considered in the next section. The analogy between the fool and this toy is also borne out by the fact that the seemingly magical outbursts of chaos that occur in his vicinity often seem to reflect this deeper level of objectivity.

In the events of the fool show there is often a kind of logic that is apparently not ours, since it surprises us, and apparently not the fool's, since he is often its victim; it is foolish enough to strike us as a pseudologic, and it is objective in that it breaks order down to create a new balance. The whole process *feels* right to us, though it plays with conventional notions of "good" and "bad." For example, in his film *Cops* (1922), Buster Keaton, driving a horse-cart full of furniture, unwittingly breaks up a parade of policemen filing past a reviewing stand occupied by dignitaries and their wives, *because* (to make a guess at why this feels right to us) these "good" people are so stuffy. An anarchist throws a bomb which lands in Keaton's cart next to him, *because* killing the "good" would be the wrong corrective for their stuffiness. (Instead, they and their parade should be made ridiculous, as they are by Keaton.) He lights a cigarette with the burning fuse of the bomb, *because* it belongs to his character that he live close to danger. He tosses the bomb to one side, where it explodes near the policemen, *because* it belongs to his character that he be dangerous to others, and *because* he must provoke the law if he is to spread chaos through the conventional world. The logic that determines the sequence of events is, then, that of the fool, Keaton as furniture-mover, in a certain situation; "good" and "bad" figures act upon him to supply material for that logic, like blows hitting the clown toy to set it in motion.

This might seem a very special case, since in Keaton's film the categories of "good" and "bad" are so black and white and devoid of important content. I will now take up the fool's relations to these categories when the content *is* important: in the relations between the fool and the Devil in Christian tradition, in the fool's relation to death, and in the fool's relation to sexuality. But first I want to comment on the fool and infantility and the fool and responsibility for social order.

Clowns are thought to provide "wish-fulfillment," to activate infantile patterns of thought and feeling in us and thus to effect a pleasurable release of energy from the work of consciousness. This is the old notion of comic relief restated in accordance with psychoanalytic theory, and it is convincing as far as it goes and when it is not made to go too far. It becomes untenable when it is taken to imply that the infantile patterns were operative before categories of "good" and "bad" were imposed upon the developing personality by adults; and it becomes untenable when it is taken to imply that the relatively amoral magic of the fool show is rooted in instinct alone, rather than in instinct and spirit (the two poles of the archetype).

Several recent psychologists, among them Melanie Klein, have maintained on the basis of strong evidence that no experience, even for the infant, has simply a neutral value.[3] It is true that cultural ideas of "good" and "bad" are instilled (or "introjected") in the course of time, largely at the expense of a more primitive form of judgment based on what Freud called the "pleasure principle," according to which whatever one likes at the moment is "good." But one must distinguish between the cultural *content,* which is acquired, and the *categories* of "good" and "bad," which are inborn. In making this distinction I do not want to imply that the categories of "good" and "bad" are static. From the beginning they call forth certain patterns of behavior and direct energy into them. ("Bad" things make the infant cry.) And as these categories become interwoven with specific content, they gain the character of the person's values as a whole. His judgments of "good" and "bad" may, for example, be rigid, or they may be complex and ambiguous; they may play a role in the making of conflicts of various kinds, or they may protect him from them.

Fools characteristically serve a principle of wholeness that is often difficult to reconcile with categories of "good" and "bad" altogether, since these categories tend to oppose each other, and since either tends to oppose a wholeness that would include them both. In any case, fools serve this principle by violating cultural values; their anticultural behavior may be infantile , or it may be magical, or it may be both at the same time, as it is among the Zuñi clowns. In their infantile behavior fools are not, then, simply reinstating the paradisaic condition of the infant before it had to learn the painful realities of "good" and "bad." Rather, they are acting in accordance with infantile notions of "good" and "bad" *in contrast* to cultural values; the point of the contrast is at least as cultural as it is infantile. Thus urine-drinking and excrement-eating are infantile, but not all infants are as intent on doing these things as Zuñi clowns are; this behavior of the clowns is at least as Zuñi—and based on specific cultural concerns—as it is infantile. However, this leaves an important question: that of the relations of the infantile to the magical with respect to these categories.

In a psychological sense there would seem to be a *continuity* between the infantile judgments of "good" and "bad" and the concept of taboo in primitive thought, these judgments and this concept sharing the qualities of irrationality and absoluteness. The continuity between them is rooted in the "fundamental apperception," the "magical dimension" of the psyche, shared by everyone. But there would also seem to be a *difference* between the "natural" behavior of the infant and behavior based on the primitive institution of taboo; this difference indicates something of the radical change of attitude toward "good" and "bad" that must occur in the course of growing up, even when the cultural forms based on these categories are magical. An infant *must* respond in certain ways to things that it finds "good" and "bad"; a primitive *must* respond in certain ways to a taboo object. Yet the reaction of the primitive contains an element that may be regarded as ethical. Thus van der Leeuw reminds us that taboo has been called the oldest form of the categorical imperative and says about the experience of taboo: " 'Thou shalt'—what one should do is a secondary issue; why one should do it is not a question at all. Confronted with Power, which he experiences as being of completely contrasted nature, man apprehends its absolute demand." [4] In other words, in relation to the taboo object, *I* must do what *it* wants. This presupposes a distinction between "I" and "not-I" or, if we wish to emphasize the element of mystical participation in primitive thought, between "we" and "not-we." In either case, the distinction has not been firmly established in the infant. The anticultural behavior of clowns activates the sense of wholeness that comes from a loss of this distinction. (In sometimes appearing to lack an ego, the fool actors I considered in Part I often have the same effect.) Often such behavior makes us feel the nearness and pervasiveness of magical power; sometimes it makes us feel strongly in touch with the objective order of things.

In being both magical and infantile and in assuming a semidramatic status, the fool becomes a crude equivalent of the *Stehaufmännchen;* he achieves something of its amoral disinterestedness. The fool is often like an infant in that the objects of his desire and aversion do not fit the pattern of values of responsible adults—and sometimes do not seem to fit any pattern at all. The fool is often like a taboo object in that contact with him may result in an outburst of avenging power, as when the dignitaries and the police come near the furniture-moving Keaton. (If the wishes of a Zuñi clown were not granted, the person who failed to grant them could expect his house to burn down; "holy fools" in many places carry an implicit threat of the wrath of God.) But usually when nonfools encounter this power in the fool, it says neither "Thou shalt!" nor "Thou shalt not!" in a way that makes sense to them. It is in the fool the antinatural or anticultural power *of* the infant or child, and it brings us to the ambiguous point at which infantility or childishness ceases to be a condition of domination by instinct and becomes the expression of spirit.

In discussing "imagination," I referred to the conventional idea that children as well as poets, lovers, and madmen have access to a deep truth that is their special province. Christ speaks often of the blessedness of children, an idea that is echoed (often with Platonic and other philosophical overtones) in the work of many poets, such as Traherne, Blake, and Wordsworth. There are, as well, many myths and legends in which the child is not only blessed but is a hero who determines the most important course of events, a motif most familiar to us from the Christmas story. The dramatic events that typically befall the child hero may, as Jung shows, be regarded as illustrating the psychic events that occur in the genesis of the self as an element of consciousness. This archetypal factor is, according to Jung, the totality and the deepest center of the personality, which it transcends. More specifically, it is "the matrix and organizing principle of consciousness," the source of the compensatory movements of the psyche by which a more adequate and "objective" order becomes manifest.[5] In the spatial metaphors that come to mind when we speak of something we believe to be transcendent, the self stands "behind" or lies "beyond" consciousness. Something of the way in which it does so may be sensed in uncanny moments in which I feel that I am gripped by a "not-I" that seems more really "I" than I am. But since the self in Jung's view organizes consciousness, it can and does make itself known as an object of consciousness. The object is a symbol, a mediate form of whatever gives the symbol its power. If one tries to describe what stands "behind" the symbol, one's description is a hypothesis or an article of belief. Jung's hypothesis of the self is partly an attempt to see a pattern in certain symbolic forms and articles of belief. These forms often have the attributes of totality and centrality, divinity is often attributed to them, and they are often felt to provide a basis for the life of a group. The self is, then, the supreme "point of indifference" in psychic life and the power that emanates from that point.

The fool is unlike the divine child in being a magician-actor rather than a mythical figure. Moreover, the divine child has a unitary purpose, whereas the fool's purposes tend to become scattered as though under the influence of infantile drives or of concentrations of power in the magical field. (As Viola observes about the character of the fool, he must, "like the haggard [or untrained hawk], check at every feather / That comes before his eye" [*Twelfth Night,* III. i. 61–62]). The fool does, however, have something of the divine child's transcendence of patterns of cultural value, something of his objectivity; the infantile and magical fool is like a chunk of chaos in which the archetypal divine child is present but unborn, his form and meaning hidden. And the fool, though infantile, is an adult; as an adult-child he is a grotesque who breaks down and fuses order (the human image, that of the responsible adult) and chaos (the infantility thought to be extraneous to adulthood). In the fool show this breakdown and fusion have a more specific content, that of the contrast between young and old, between burgeoning potency and rigid form, between spring and winter, and, most extremely, between life and death; and they have a more specific effect, that of rejuvenation. As we shall see, the hero, too, whether or not he takes the form of the divine child, often brings rejuvenation. But the fool achieves it in ways that bypass the demands of heroic purpose with its implication of cultural value to be consciously created or affirmed. Still, what he does in his infantility has a cultural function. As Jung writes, "If . . . the childhood state of the collective psyche is repressed to the point of total exclusion, the unconscious content overwhelms the conscious aim and inhibits, falsifies, even destroys its realization." [6] And the fool's confusion of levels of "good" and "bad" (for example, when he makes an infantile judgment in a serious adult context) and his obliteration of the distinctions between the categories themselves may have some of the same effects that are achieved when the hero defeats what is bad, affirms what is good, or actively creates a conscious awareness in which these values have new functions.

The divine child may have cosmic functions; there are, as well, other lines of connection between the infantile and the cosmic that have a bearing on the fool show. In certain psychotic states adult people are infantile and experience cosmic delusions; they may smear the walls with excrement and feel at the same time that they are central figures in conflicts very similar to Milton's war of the angels. On the magical level such diverse materials are not at all mutually exclusive, a fact which is important to keep in mind when we consider some forms of clown humor. Clown play with excrement activates personal anxieties in the audience; the violation of inner prohibitions may pleasurably release energies in ways that are described by Freud in his *Jokes and Their Relation to the Unconscious*. But Freud's theory does not, I believe, entirely account for the magical properties of excrement, any more than it accounts for the fact of magical thinking in general. Accidents with excretion are "bad," but they are also more generally a paradigm of our succumbing to chaos; they make us feel infantile, but this infantility is more generally the impotence that we may feel in the face of powers that we cannot control. These powers may be "good" or "bad," as may the act of giving in to them. The clown's difficulties with proportion (for example, those of Valentin and Liesl Karlstadt) express this infantile impotence, but sometimes they also seem to allow glimpses of something transcendent that is expressed in an infantile version of paradox. When Valentin and Liesl Karlstadt perform on the instruments that are, as they explain, of all the instruments in the world most different from each other, a gigantic drum and a miniature harmonica, they are presenting a childish version of a paradox. And one of the most famous tricks of the clown Grock was to open an enormous suitcase and pull a tiny violin out of it. (The recurrent clown skit of the trained fleas, intelligent enough to be talked to by the clown and to balk at his commands but invisible to anyone else, is a variant of this disproportion.[7]) Often the infantile difficulty with size and proportion is unwilled, but sometimes, as in these bits of business by Valentin and Liesl Karlstadt and by Grock, the disproportion is, we feel, willed. Perhaps they will it because they do not know any better; yet the audience is presented with a ludicrous version of the "smaller than small yet bigger than big" that in various traditions serves as a formulation of reality beyond the modes of sense, thought, and judgment.[8] This motif, which may be regarded psychologically as an expression of the self, is dramatized in the child hero. As Jung points out, the impotence of the child has its complement in the child's ability to perform miraculous deeds. The clowns I have been discussing are not heroic, unless there is something heroic about playing a harmonica or a violin that is "smaller than small" or a drum that is "bigger than big," yet they may make us feel that they are not only full of infantile desire but are in touch with a transcendent power that they express in infantile terms. This is not to say that such clowns intend a kind of religious revelation. It is to say, rather, that they activate psychic levels on which such paradoxical expressions are natural. The same levels are expressed in the contrast between the "white clown" and "Chocolate" among the Rastellis. (See Plate 17.) And we sense these levels when the clown Popov gathers up his white cock and puts it back into the suitcase from which it has escaped, only to have the cock, this time black, escape from it again.

By making fun of the idea that the police, for example, as a collective force should and even can enforce the "good" and by undermining the authority of this or that important person, fools break down patterns of cultural and individual values. This foolish play has also been carried on in connection with the Christian Devil, who is one term in a cosmic drama; in which problems of chaos and cosmos become matters of intense individual responsibility, of conscience. Scenes from that drama were translated into a species of human realism, usually with a moralistic intent, on the medieval stage; there the Devil and the fool interacted with each other, and the Devil himself was often clownish, as were Herod, Pilate, and other "bad" characters. In a common form of this interplay the Devil, *not* a comic figure, acted upon the farcical figure of the Vice, the terrible knave and the silly victim developing in the course of time in the direction of the familiar knockabout fool pair. (Late in this process, Feste in *Twelfth Night* compares himself with "the old Vice . . . with dagger of lath," who wrathfully defies the Devil [IV. ii. 132–41].) Some features of these developments are not at all clear; among the questions that have been raised about them are these: What is the origin of the Vice as a fool character in England? Was the Vice always distinct from the Devil? Did the stage fool simply grow out of the Devil or Vice, or was the Devil a fool much earlier? Was the stage fool (in whatever form) a direct continuation of the folk or festival fool? And whatever the developments were in detail, why did they take place? [9]

These questions can be answered only in part, and then uncertainly. The answers that seem to make the most sense imply that the fool activates levels of the psyche on which terms of value that are opposed in consciousness lose their opposition. The fool (as Devil or in other forms) in late medieval drama does not simply represent the admission of the fool of the fool society into the scene of the dramatic action. At least in German drama the Devil was a serious and frightening character before he became a fool. But it does not follow that the theatrical Devil became a fool as a concomitant of diminishing belief in the reality of the Devil off the stage. Nor does it follow that people could laugh at the Devil only because they were protected from him by the sacraments. In fact, people were able to laugh at the Devil, on stage and off, long before he became primarily a farcical stage figure. (The title of Ben Jonson's play *The Devil Is an Ass,* acted in 1616, is a metaphor that preceded the medieval drama by centuries.[10]) After all, the Greeks had laughed at the gods they worshiped, and in late medieval drama august "good" personages of religious importance could be treated farcically. For a long time St. Joseph was both venerated and ridiculed, often by the same individuals. Laughter was then one possible response to the Devil as an object of terror; this response did not preclude others. When the Devil, already laughed at as well as feared, got caught up in clown business on the stage, his connections with the figure of the fool were simply made explicit.

As for the religious background of the theatrical development, there was, as there had always been, resistance to the Christian tendency to divide experience according to metaphysical and ethical categories of "good" and "bad." Thus pagan gods and lesser spirits from both the Mediterranean and the North of Europe tenaciously went on asserting themselves, and some of them reappeared again and again, slightly disguised, from their banishment by the Church. Late medieval rationalism tended to break down that dualism, but the substratum of magic and pagan religion upon which Christianity was imposed resisted that dualism from the first and continued to resist it.[11] The Devil as an imaginative form of one term in that dualism drew upon materials from the non-Christian substratum and allowed them a continuing life; this life could not be *imaginatively* reduced to the judgment that the Devil is categorically "bad." In their continuing life, those materials tended to escape that judgment into the more ambiguous one that we accord the fool. Attributes of the Devil, as a repository of power of spirits and nature demons, converge with those of the fool in the relatively recent yet highly pagan Harlequin. This foolish and diabolical figure represented a complex with very deep roots. Christianity had effected a differentiation between the devilish and foolish components of the complex but had not succeeded in breaking it down to such an extent that the Devil could remain simply nonfoolish. In the larger view, the Devil through his association with the fool again became part of an ambiguous unconscious totality; this included important realities that did not find expression in the cultural world view.

Whether or not evil is made into a cosmic principle, whether it is regarded metaphysically as a *privatio boni,* the absence of good, or as a power in itself, whether or not man is given complete responsibility for it, it has a basis in our natural experience. The relationship between sin and death that is asserted by St. Paul is in one sense a development of the idea that death (at least *my* death or that of someone in my group) is "bad." Death may be necessary to life, but this thought does not make it possible for us to regard it neutrally. Similarly, some of the abundance of natural life that is expressed in saturnalian reveling may be necessary to cultural order, to meaning, but this does not mean that saturnalia can be made into a permanent state. Death and dissolution and an excess of natural energy are attributed to the Christian Devil, who drags souls to Hell, where they burn with his fire. The natural facts reflected in this conception are expressed without Christian moralism by William Blake, who claimed that "one portion of being is the Prolific, the other the Devouring." [12] Neither of these qualities is unambiguously "bad"; in any case, they need to be actively engaged. The fool enacts one typical and recurring form of this engagement.

We have seen something of the fool's way of dealing with "the Devouring" in the mock-heroic resistance of Chaplin and Keaton to the power that attacked them. The medieval stage fool, too, fought mock-heroically against the Devil. But the fool may also deal with this element by attacking our judgment of it as "bad" and by suggesting that folly contains the power to withstand dissolution and death. An example is provided by the proverbial joke about the old Jewish lady who comes home from the doctor and cheerfully reports that she has cancer. She brushes aside the shock that this announcement causes by saying, "Cancer, schmanzer; what's the difference as long as you're healthy?" At the outset of our response to the joke we, too, are shocked at the thought of cancer. The punch line leaves us caught in an ambiguity that might be resolved if some detail at first unnoticed were suddenly to explain her cheerfulness. But there is no such detail; the woman is cheerful in spite of having cancer and knowing that she has it. Our outburst of laughter is partly at her silliness for not grasping the horrible seriousness of her condition; in laughing at her, we partly reassure ourselves of our superior understanding and health. But the joke has another overtone: perhaps she *is* healthy in spite of having cancer or even *by virtue of* having it. Perhaps she has the magical power to withstand the force of dissolution; perhaps she is partly nourished by it, as some diabolical fools are. In any case, "cancer" is for her as nonsensical as "schmanzer"; the horrible element is completely assimilated to the meaningless rhyming and half-rhyming names of fool pairs in the circus and vaudeville. Again, the diabolical and the foolish emerge in her as a single complex. Within that complex, life (or "the Prolific") triumphs over death (or "the Devouring"). The fool's characteristic mediation between the two elements is rooted in a basic—and "natural"—fact of the human condition, a fact summarized in a remark in Vercors's novel *Sylva:* "It is because the human species is the only one which knows that death is our common lot that it is also the only one to know laughter as a saving grace . . . ; during the moment when laughter shakes us we are immortal." [13]

The relation of fools to instinct, to "the Prolific," is at the same time a relation to "good" and "bad"; the value of foolish obscenity is not simple but complex.

Sexuality is often but by no means always a prominent element of what the fool *is;* being his foolish self may mean being overtly sexual, as in various traditions of phallic clowning. Or the fool may imitate the plight of nonfools when they are concerned with sex despite more noble conscious intentions. Thus Groucho Marx as Mr. Hammer in *Cocoanuts* (1929) farcically makes romantic love to the dowager Mrs. Potter (Groucho's long-suffering butt, Margaret Dumont) and paints the vision of "an empty bungalow just for me and you, where we could bill and cow —no, we could bull and cow. . . ." But the fool's relation to sexuality may

126

be one of inhibition and furtherance at the same time. Thus the Koyemci clowns among the Zuñi have cotton cords tied around their penises so that they are incapable of erection; they can be looked at naked "because they are just like children"; it is said of their mythical forebears that "the fruit of sex was not in them"; yet these clowns are in direct contact with the generative powers of nature.[14] Similar motives combine in a different form in sexual jokes about newlyweds who are intruded upon by a stupid hotel clerk who is a Pandarus in reverse but furthers the sexual determination of the couple. Even when the fool is licentious, his licentiousness is not simply a direct expression, despite cultural categories of "good" and "bad," of what is "natural." The fool's relation both to these categories and to nature is compensatory to specific cultural attitudes.

Jokes about excretion and sex usually play upon restrictions, but it is equally possible for such jokes to play upon cultural permissiveness toward these processes. Thus the night-club comedian Lenny Bruce, famous for his "sick" humor, was arrested for violation of a New York State law which forbids any "obscene, indecent, immoral, or impure" public performance. The judges who handed down the decision against Bruce remarked that his language "clearly debased sex and insulted it." This is very far from the view that the explicit dwelling upon sex is itself bad. What was bad to the judges was rather the comedian's attack upon its dignity and nobility by means of gutter words for incest, sodomy, and excrement. The attitudes of the judges and of the comedian are different sides of the same coin, humor such as his finding an audience in the same cultural moment in which the law is interpreted according to a certain permissive attitude toward sex. The New York judges partly represent a variant of the "pastoral" view of nature and sex, which the comedian cynically deflates by treating them in ways that suggest the unpleasant realities of the urban ghetto.

A similar cultural attitude is attacked in *As You Like It* in the dialogue between Touchstone the clown and Corin the shepherd (III. ii). Corin gives an idyllic description of his profession, to which the clown replies:

> That is another simple sin in you: to bring the ewes and the rams together, and to offer to get your living by the copulation of cattle; to

be bawd to a bell-wether, and to betray a she-lamb of a twelvemonth to a crooked-pated, old, cuckoldly ram, out of all reasonable match. If thou beest not damn'd for this, the devil himself will have no shepherds; I cannot see else how thou shouldst scape.

(ll. 69–74)

Touchstone's jest implies that the idyllic innocence of Corin is as foolish and as "bad" as the corrupt values of the court; yet Touchstone abuses the pastoral attitude by means of those values. The court is the god by which Touchstone intends to see Corin damned:

Why, if thou never wast at court thou never saw'st good manners; if thou never saw'st good manners, then thy manners must be wicked; and wickedness is sin, and sin is damnation. Thou art in a parlous state, shepherd.

(ll. 37–40)

Touchstone reduces the whole pattern of "pastoral" values that includes artificial civility and a country-weekend naïveté toward nature. To accomplish this reduction he must be cynical about the sexual processes that fools most often treat as "good."

# 8  The Fool, the Boundary, and the Center

In his fortieth year Erasmus had a personal seal made, a picture of a stone marker with the head of a man; the device was inscribed CONCEDO NULLI, "I yield to none." (See Plate 23.) He believed that the figure he had chosen for his seal was the Roman god Terminus, the genius of boundary stones, which one could not remove without violating the god within them. To him the figure suggested the Platonic remark, "Remove not what thou has not planted," and was a reminder of death (which yields to none). His enemies, however, took it as a sign of his pride (that he, Erasmus, yielded to none).[1] Though the seal expresses a solemn side of Erasmus, it could be taken as an illustration of a remark by Huizinga about the playful *Praise of Folly,* that "Erasmus knows the aloofness of the ground of all things: all consistent thinking out of the dogmas of faith leads to absurdity."[2] Van der Leeuw (following Eduard Spranger) expresses a similar idea even more radically and in a way that also has a bearing on both the seal and the *Praise of Folly:*

> The religious significance of things . . . is that on which no wider or deeper meaning can follow. It is the meaning of the whole: it is the last word. But this meaning is never understood, this last word is never spoken; always they remain superior, the ultimate meaning being a secret which reveals itself repeatedly, only nevertheless to remain eternally concealed. It implies an advance to the farthest boundary, where only one sole fact is understood:—that all comprehension is "beyond."[3]

Erasmus' seal is thus a *memento mori,* and it reminds us how little we understand of final and even of very immediate things. Death and ignorance are boundaries that give rise to religious and philosophical problems, but these boundaries are rooted in natural fact. The cells of our

PLATE 23. Ink drawing by Holbein the Younger of a device designed by Erasmus. The figure is complex and ambiguous in ways that make it an appropriate emblem for the author of the *Praise of Folly*.

bodies are constantly dying and being replaced; we know almost nothing through direct sensation about the universe of bodily processes keeping us alive; in any case, few of them can be controlled by will. The psychic processes on which understanding is based, among them memory, attention, perception, and judgment, also have their specific boundaries. These, too, are relatively unknown in themselves and follow rhythms that also are largely independent of will. Attention, for example, becomes exhausted, and its contents disappear through the boundaries of consciousness. And unconscious contents that we try to hold from attention may break through those boundaries into it, as may vivid impressions of the outer world. In similar ways everything in the world of our experience impinges on the unknown. At every moment the unknown is figuratively and even literally a matter of life and death, and again and again it robs us of whatever justification we might feel for pride. Sometimes we consciously encounter the unknown as a boundary, but whether we do or not, it is there, we are in touch with it, and in our relation to it we are largely fools.

Used in this way the word "fools" has a solemn ring in keeping with the moralist that Erasmus also was but not with the fun of the *Praise of Folly*. In fact, there is a joke that Erasmus missed in his devising of the seal: the figure that he took to be Terminus and a god of death was really Dionysus, a destructive but also highly creative link between man and the sources of natural life.[4] In the seal the phallic element of Dionysus is, as well, assimilated to the phallic character of boundary markers in many times and places.[5] Thus the device also says, in effect, "I, the force of the irrational and of natural fertility, yield to none." We have already seen the same ambiguity between life and death in various fool figures. Erasmus would have laughed at the joke on him, and the special ironic sense that would have made him do so is part of what makes the *Praise of Folly* so rewarding. In the book, in fact, he created his own equivalent of the joke by presenting his moral purpose in a way that makes it finally indistinguishable from the anticultural attitude of those clowns and fools who exploit our relation to the irrational and magical. To do this he broke down boundaries.

Erasmus' seal also implies another ambiguity that is fundamental to the fool show: in making an emblem of the boundary stone, he brought it to the center of attention. As we study the figure, we deprive it of its essential characteristic, that of being on the border, where it is in touch with what is for us the unknown. This ambiguity belongs to the nature of symbolism; owing to this ambiguity, the center of our awareness may divide under the influence of the irrational and the magical. Thus in *A Midsummer Night's Dream,* Hermia, bemused by magic and in the proximity of fools, remarks, "Methinks I see these things with parted eye, / When everything seems double" (IV. i. 186–87). Also owing to this ambiguity and to the autonomy of the unknown, a point at the periphery of our awareness may begin to develop attributes of a center, at first dividing attention but then claiming it completely and for a while keeping its magical character. We have seen that the fool is often double and that he may, as peripheral to the human image, triumph over the "I" that is supposed to accord with it fully. I will now consider some of the ways in which these qualities of the fool are linked with the realities of cultural life and some of the ways in which these in turn are taken up in the fool show.

Culture draws various boundaries between classes (or even castes) of people, for example, those between different kinship, occupational, and ceremonial groups. The cultural whole made by all of these people often (at least when the group lives settled in one place) corresponds to a geographical area with a boundary that demarcates it from a no-man's-land (for example, the sea, the desert, or the uncultivated forest) or from the area of others who do not belong to the group and are hence in one way or another not fully human (for example, enemies and demons). This boundary often corresponds to that between order and chaos.[6] Many fools have strong connections with these cultural and social boundaries, which they are felt to transgress, though the transgression is allowed. Since people have, as well, an intimate relation to boundaries in other senses (including those that I have mentioned in connection with Erasmus), boundaries of class and cultural geography are in the fool show often interwoven with various strands of symbolism.

Karl Kerényi describes the Trickster, a special mythological form of the fool (with attributes of the Promethean culture hero) as *"the spirit of disorder, the enemy of boundaries."* According to Kerényi, the Trickster's

"function in an archaic society, or rather the function of his mythology
. . . is to add disorder to order and so make a whole, to render possible,
within the fixed bounds of what is permitted, an experience of what is not
permitted." [7] If the fool is "the spirit of disorder," he is necessarily "the
enemy of boundaries." But since the disorder of which he is the spirit is
largely contained in his show, he serves the boundary of which he is the
enemy; and in doing this, he sometimes even demonstrates an authority
proper to the central figure of the established order (such as the king, the
president, the chief, the boss). Nonetheless, he is often regarded as a
usurper with no right to be where he is in the ordered world.

Thus according to an English writ, *de idiota inquirendo,* passed in the
reign of Henry VIII and subsequently revised and renewed several times,
the king could grant a subject the profits of the land and the custody of
the person of anyone judged insane. (Court jesters seem occasionally to
have been procured in this way, and it is quite possible that some people
were legally decreed fools under false pretenses.[8]) Of course, some
professional fools have risen to positions of wealth, security, and prestige.
One may think in our time of Grock and Chaplin, though Charlie seems
sometimes to peer out through Chaplin's aristocratic pretensions, not sure
that he has outsmarted the police, and the castle that the successful Grock
built for himself looks like a pompous set for a slapstick movie. Centuries
before, the jester Rahere of Edward I had the wealth and power to found,
after a religious vision, the priory of St. Bartholomew in Smithfield.[9] But
more generally in the history of professional folly fools have either been
their own masters, as in the tradition of wandering minstrels, or have
been pampered or have eked out a precarious livelihood as retainers of a
person of rank, upon whose whims they were dependent. And often the
fool, retained for awhile, chose or was forced to resume his wandering.
Thus the Roman emperor Alexander Severus banished the freaks from
Rome, where they had been pets fawned upon in the aristocratic salons,
and they wandered around the empire, exhibiting themselves for a fee or
for coins tossed to them in the streets. When a fool in the silent films has
an established social position—as a barber, millionaire, or operatic
impresario—we know that his having it is a joking pretense and that his
foolish nature will triumph over that pretense in a way that reveals his
character as an outcast.

133

# The Pattern of Folly

Brilliant explorations of the fool's relation to the social border occur in the opening of one Chaplin film and the close of another.

At the beginning of *A Dog's Life* (1918) the tramp "Charlie" is asleep in a vacant lot next to a fence that runs along the sidewalk. The sun is rising over the city. A draft blows through the knothole onto Charlie's backside; he takes out a handkerchief, stuffs it in the hole, and tries to resume his sleep. A hot-dog vendor sets up his stand on the other side of the fence. The tramp is again awakened, this time by the smell of the hot dogs, reaches through the fence, and steals one. He is just going to begin eating it when he sees a cop's face glaring over the fence. Charlie quickly returns the hot dog, but the cop is not ready to accept this sneaky compromise with justice; he tries to coax the tramp out from the vacant lot and into a confrontation with him. Charlie refuses to be coaxed, and then begins one of the innumerable chase sequences in which Chaplin (like so many silent-film comedians and other fools and clowns in many times and places) tries to escape the powers of the law. The chase first takes the form of the cop's running from the sidewalk around the end of the fence to the vacant lot and back again, with Charlie evading him by rolling back and forth under the fence. At one point, when the cop is standing on the sidewalk with the tramp in the vacant lot, the tramp reaches under the fence and maliciously unties the cop's shoelaces and sticks him with a pin. At last Charlie feels himself safe and triumphant, having exhausted the cop by rolling back and forth under the fence. He stands up, takes a circus bow, only to have his outstretched hand touch the badge of a second cop. He feels it assessingly for a moment before looking around; his self-satisfaction changes into doglike worry, and the chase begins again.

The fence is the border of the social world of the sidewalk and street, in which the cop tries to make his influence felt and the order he represents prevail. The vacant lot is the undifferentiated no-man's-land beyond the border. It corresponds to the wasteland beyond the kingdom or to the heath in which Lear wanders with his jester. The tramp-fool of the film is in a typically lawless and parasitic relationship to the social world; the only way he can (or will) obtain food is to reach through the fence—from chaos into order—and steal it. In doing so, he conjures the cop to the point at which the border has been violated. The cop then tries to extend his authority to the vacant lot, which he now sees to contain dangers enough that it cannot simply be left alone; he must attempt to subjugate them, though they lie beyond his normal jurisdiction. The result of the attempt is that cop and tramp pass with tremendous energy back and forth across the border. The border is thus at the outset apparent as the third term in their restless antagonism, and its violation may be regarded as the precipitating cause, on the magical level, of the struggle that goes on between them.

The border has come alive; when Charlie leaves his refuge in the vacant lot to invade the city, he does so with the ambiguous spirit of the border stirring within him. Under its influence he becomes more and more implicated in the social world; the conflict between him and the cop expands and draws more and more people into it. He is like Dummling carrying the golden goose or like other instances of the "Stickfast" or "tar baby" motif of folklore.[10] For him boundaries are arbitrary in a double sense: though (on the one hand) he *regards* them as arbitrary, he *is* (on the other) an instance of a still deeper boundary, the limit beyond which social rules and rational understanding are no longer effective but the fool's magic is. Although the conflict between Charlie and the cops is irresolvable, he has in a sense never left the border and is detached from the conflict. While *being* an instance of the boundary, he refuses to recognize the rational construction made of it by the cop mentality. He passes through the limits of that construction at will, to the consternation of the agents of the law; yet his triumphs in nonfoolish terms are more often than not snatched out of his hands. This is because the cops are right, in their simple-minded way, in thinking that he belongs to the vacant lot, the outside. But in the more complex view that we have from our seats in the cinema, something of the outside simply *is,* in him, brought to the center of attention, and cop ideas of what should be outside, and what inside, the human world are relative to his self-manifestation. He is impelled by the dynamism of chaos; they are impelled by what they take to be the necessity of reinforcing the wall against the outside and of neutralizing what has broken through it into the world they govern.

Often the only possible resolution of the conflict between fools and nonfoolish authority is either for the fool to disappear from sight into the no-man's-land beyond the border (like a clown disappearing from the stage as pointlessly as he came) or for him to reaffirm his vital connection with the border itself. This second possibility is shown by Charlie at the close of *The Pilgrim* (1922). At the beginning of the action, Chaplin is an escaped convict, disguised as a Protestant clergyman. He flees to a small town, where the congregation of a church is awaiting the arrival of its new pastor, whom they take him to be. The rest of the film is concerned with the misadventure of the preacher-criminal. He is finally caught by the sheriff, who leads him, the sheriff on horseback and he afoot, to the Mexican border and tells him that he can gain his freedom simply by crossing the line into Mexico. Charlie laughs as though at a good-natured joke. The sheriff then orders him to pick some flowers across the border. Charlie, now exaggeratedly naïve, in a way that contrasts with his cunning during much of the action, picks a bouquet and returns with it to the sheriff, as though not comprehending that the sheriff wants to be rid of him. The sheriff dismounts, leads his prisoner to the border, and kicks him into Mexico. At last Chaplin "understands," with a show of grimly farcical idealism, and enters Mexico, joyous at the prospect of a new life; his gestures mime the notion "Freedom!" Suddenly two bandits appear from hiding places on the Mexican side and begin shooting at each other. With the United States to his left and Mexico to his right, Chaplin is caught between law and lawlessness. He begins running down the border line, away from the camera, hopping from one side to the other. Finally, straddling the border, with one foot in each country, he waddles off into the unstructured infinity from which in his early films he often appeared as though by accident and which in the final moment claimed him again.

It is at the border between "the law' and lawlessness that we see the flickering interplay between the fool's unscrupulous cunning and his stupid innocence. The chaotic wasteland of Mexico awakens his childish goodness and his belief in the goodness of the world, after his career as an unscrupulous trickster in lawful America. The fool effects an inversion of our assumed values and shows their arbitrariness. For him they are make-believe; his commitment to them is as provisional as is his assumption of the role of the lawful and "good" or lawless and "bad" nonfool, and in his show those values are completely dissolved in his playful self-manifestation.

## The Fool, the Boundary, and the Center

A succinct instance of this dissolution occurs in a scene in a late short film by one of Chaplin's early fellow comedians, Harry Langdon, who shuffled through his sketches like a bewildered baby. Langdon with a toy pistol in his hand is caught between a jewelry-store robber and a policeman with guns drawn, blazing at each other in dead earnest. With his pistol Langdon pops impotently at one and then the other. Irrelevant as he is to the battle, he is at its center; he does each the inadvertent service of shielding him from the other but also keeps either from doing away with his real enemy, who is hidden behind the fool's soft burlesque of the toughness common to the criminal and the cop. Since they have no special reason to shoot him, and since he anyway bears the fool's immortality, the conflict, which has become one of life and death, is reduced to play and spent in foolish fireworks.

The other side of the threat of the unknown is its promise; the fool as a borderline figure holds the social world open to values that transcend it. However, under the influence of the fool we may be as incapable of grasping these values as we are of annulling that threat. Thus they may continue to elude our normal modes of understanding and remain bound to his show. One of the most impressive examples of the fool as the receptacle and bearer of a transcendent value that, instead of being made accessible to social life, is deranged, distorted, and ostensibly lost in the fool's own being, is Bottom in *A Midsummer Night's Dream*. Bottom is granted a dream by Titania and awakens to report it:

> I have had a most rare vision. I have had a dream, past the wit of man to say what dream it was. Man is but an ass if he go about to expound this dream. Methought I was—there is no man can tell what. Methought I was, and methought I had, but man is but a patch'd fool, if he will offer to say what methought I had. The eye of man hath not heard, the ear of man hath not seen, man's hand is not able to taste, his tongue to conceive, nor his heart to report, what my dream was. I will get Peter Quince to write a ballad of this dream. It shall be call'd 'Bottom's Dream,' because it hath no bottom; and I will sing it in the latter end of a play, before the Duke. Peradventure, to make it the more gracious, I shall sing it at her death.
>
> (IV. i. 202 ff.)

## The Pattern of Folly

In the suggestive but inconclusive words of the critic Harold C. Goddard,

> The moment when Bottom awakens from this dream is the supreme moment of the play. There is nothing more wonderful in the poet's early works and few things more wonderful in any of them. For what Shakespeare has caught here in perfection is the original miracle of the Imagination, the awakening of the spiritual life in the animal man. Bottom is an ass. If Bottom can be redeemed, matter itself and man in all his materiality can be redeemed also.[11]

The scene appears to play upon such a hope; yet that hope founders upon the fool's unintelligibility in our terms, or rather, upon our inability to penetrate and secure with our forms of understanding the element within him that seems to be of value. We would like to know Bottom's dream; we would like to have it for ourselves. The numinosity of the dream effects in him something like the total disorganization of the senses sought by Rimbaud; what lies in it or beyond it he will never be able to tell us. Bottom's dream, too, goes to the bottom along with whatever hope he awakened by telling us that he had it. But perhaps the dream was and is always there, the numinous happening that deranges and deforms him, binding him eternally to the border of the known world; and perhaps that dream is the hidden treasure the fool bears as a social outcast. At the borders of consciousness the fool has seen and heard the transcendent value that, according to St. Paul and Erasmus, is only available to fools. And yet he has not the means to make it intelligible to us. Seeing and hearing and speaking, he is blind and deaf and dumb. From the absolute border of folly, he babbles like the fool he is and was and will be, whether enlightened or not. He bears the value of a transcendent perfection and is the living reminder among us of its inaccessibility. That value remains undecipherable in the chaotic and insubstantial mirror of the fool show.

The content of Bottom's dream is dispersed in folly. This movement is inseparable from that described by the central action as it engages Titania, the Fairy Queen, in whom one of the highest values in the process presented in the play is invested. She has fallen into the folly of being enamored of the ass-headed dreamer. Her awakening from this folly is interrelated with his failure to hold onto the content of his dream and articulate it in nonfoolish terms. Titania and his dream are both sublime; we feel that she must stand in some close relationship (that we cannot define) to the content of that dream. As it slips away from him, she becomes free of the folly of her magically induced infatuation. What we take to be the natural line of division between folly and nonfolly is reasserted.

This entire process of dreaming wise and waking foolish, of being romantically infatuated and then shocked by the absurdity of that infatuation, is a weaving-together of themes that I have explored till now; these may be briefly recapitulated in the light of Bottom's dream. Fundamental to our experience of the world is the distinction between folly and nonfolly, and the border between them may correspond to the other borders that we have considered, those between nature and spirit, "good" and "bad," chaos and cosmos. Every nonfool, partly a fool, takes his nonfolly to be essential to his identity. (His folly is for him the possibility that he may engage in kinds of foolish behavior that he should, with a modicum of luck, be able to write off as accident or as someone else's responsibility, if he has not himself chosen for a moment to play the fool.) He believes in his self-identity and his continuity with himself and believes further that they are not foolish. The fool, on the other hand, is divided in a different way: he is one fool half mirroring another fool half like the doubles within a knockabout-farce pair. He fights for his own identity and continuity, loses them, and finds them again, but he hardly can be said to believe in them: he believes rather in the facts of his own divisibility and of chaos and in a power within chaos that will keep the parts of himself sufficiently in contact with one another that he will be able to go on being a fool. In moments when the nonfool might say with conviction, "I am I," the fool would say in effect—with a nonfool translating for him—"I am *as though the same as* myself." The fool is not so much concerned with meaning, to which some kind of fixed identity is essential, as he is with the continuity of life, of which meaningful life is a part. He will live as long as there is life; and as long as there is, the foolish halves of himself will continue to bob around in some kind of interaction.

Thus in the encounter between the nonfool and the fool—for example, between Jaques and Touchstone and between Titania and Bottom—there is really a meeting of four elements: the nonfolly of the nonfool, the unnoticed shadow of folly specifically related to that nonfolly, and the two separate but interrelated qualities of folly within the fool. In the encounter the nonfoolish identity of the nonfool disintegrates in the way characteristic of the tenuous self-identity of the fool. This nonfoolish identity is then reconstituted in the way characteristic of the fool in his survival of disaster. The process often proves to have been of clear value to the nonfool: he may, for example, re-enter his old situation with a different awareness of its structure or with a different attitude of feeling. It is customary to find the fool responsible for the sequence of events composing the encounter, and it is often possible to trace their dynamism to the self-division within the fool. The film comedians Laurel and Hardy, for example, shift the blame back and forth for the fact that one of them has dropped a banana peel on the sidewalk and caused a nonfool to fall down. The result is not the punishment of the guilty one but a scene, on a scale almost worthy of Cecil B. De Mille, in which swarms of people splash an apparently inexhaustible fund of custard pies into one another's faces. It is clear that they would not have done this except in the presence of the fools; nor would the pies have been thrown in the presence of one of the fools alone. The curiously tentative and fluid self-identity of the fool (like the relationship between two partners in a fool pair) is highly volatile; it is too unstable to contain the energies released by the juxtaposition of irreconcilable qualities within the fool. Those energies spread from him into the nonfoolish world. In this way, as in others, the fool is like the alchemical Mercurius, which was believed to have the power to penetrate all bodies:[12] the fool show spreads from the fool, nonfolly dissolves in it, the tide recedes to the fool, nonfools come to themselves again, and the line between folly and nonfolly is reinstated. Some reasons *why* this encounter takes place may be inferred from what I have said so far, but another reason *why* needs to be considered, as it touches upon one fundamental purpose of the process represented by the encounter.

In an important sense the fool may be said (if we consider the range of his forms and of his doings) to hunger after nonfolly; he often even appears to desire incarnation as a nonfool. Just as silly as the fool's onslaught upon conventions are his attempts to learn what they are and to adapt himself to them. The pathos of many fool presentations lies in the fact that the fool is painfully unable to stop being a fool, though all of his aspirations are for a place on the other side of the border between folly and nonfolly. His attempts to be a nonfool fail because they are disproportionate; they are disproportionate because his participation in the human image is so slight that he cannot adequately imagine being a nonfool (with a bearable and even valuable component of folly) and living a nonfoolish life. His attempts to imagine nonfolly are colored by his sense of what a tremendous leap would be necessary for him to get out of his folly; he makes the leap, it carries him ridiculously wide of the mark, and he lands once again half-outside the human image. Instead of such a leap, he may make many steps, and, as we have seen, they may carry him through the center of the nonfoolish world. The fool may (like Chaplin and Keaton in many of their films) be motivated by the most sentimentally humdrum dream of the "good" *petit bourgeois* life, but that dream is often imbued with a fairy-tale vision of kings and queens, heroes and saints; and it is the tension between this element of supreme accomplishment and value, on the one hand, and his folly, on the other, that finally shatters the realization of hopes that are in a sense pathetically modest. He finds himself within the range of an august potency, but in arriving there he has lost the access to the human image for which he has been searching. Folly and nonfolly are confounded, and so for a moment are the highest values of each. The boundary must be drawn again, and he must be banished.

Titania has no business with an ass-headed lover, and he has none with her. (Ian Kott persuasively emphasizes the obscene, cruel, scatological quality of their meeting, suggestive of "the fearful visions of Bosch." [13]) The fool must be put in his place; but before he can be, the nonfool must escape from his power. In the meantime the world has been made whole in a bliss beyond action and understanding, but from this totality the quest for the human image must begin again, and this entails the affirmation of both human imperfection and a transcendent perfection. It entails action and understanding, and these are realized in the sublime comedy of the marriages at the end of the piece. Foolish and nonfoolish forms of action and of understanding must be separated: Titania must again become Queen of the Night, and Bottom must succumb to the unintelligibility of his dream or to his inability to articulate it. But part of the highest value is at the bottom with him, as is a part of our wholeness, until the fool appears again.

In the moment when we nonfools are overcome by a tremendous joke, it may be that we are close to the impossible marriage of Titania and Bottom; and as we try to recover from our laughter and to find our nonfoolish identities again, it may be that somewhere within ourselves we have touched Bottom, struggling to give expressive form to an ineffable illumination.

As the subject of my conscious experience, "I am I"; what I am has continuity in time and is the center of my world. Yet this identity is in part like the role of an actor, transformed or set aside in dreams (as Bottom learns) and in death. I feel the objects of my experience to be *there* in some of the same ways that I feel myself to be *here*. Yet Erasmus' Mother Folly is certain that "all human affairs, like the Sileni of Alcibiades, have two aspects, each quite different from the other; even to the point that what at first blush (as the phrase goes) seems to be death may prove, if you look further into it, to be life." [14] According to many mythical and religious traditions, the centrality I attribute to myself and the objects of my experience finally belongs to something deeper, to an actor within these shifting shapes of myself and them, to an uncharted firmament. According to these traditions, certain phenomena can and must be attributed to this center; through them it is experienced as a numen with its own powers and purposes. (Jung's descriptions of the central archetype, that of the self, were partly based on materials from these traditions.) On the cultural level, these powers dictate the organization of the space in which their purposes can be enacted.

The site of this microcosmic space and the principles of its organization were often determined by a hierophany. Supernatural signs accompanied or even dictated the founding of many ancient cities. Thus we read in Plutarch's life of Alexander about the emperor's decision to build the city that was to bear his name:

> And when he saw a site of surpassing natural advantages . . . he . . . ordered the plan of the city to be drawn in conformity with this site. There was no chalk at hand, so they took barley-meal and marked out with it on the dark soil a rounded area. . . . The king was delighted

with the design; but suddenly birds from the river and the lagoon, infinite in number and of every sort and size, settled down upon the place like clouds and devoured every particle of the barley-meal, so that even Alexander was greatly disturbed at the omen.

However, the seers exhorted him to be of good cheer, since the city here founded by him would have most abundant and helpful resources and be a nursing mother for men of every nation, and so he ordered those in charge of the work to proceed with it, while he himself set out for the temple of Ammon.[15]

Very often extraordinary events of this kind were not merely signs of supernatural judgment upon an enterprise already undertaken; rather, they supplied both the idea of such an enterprise and its sufficient motive. Rational considerations followed: if the gods decree through signs that a city should be built in thus and such a place, then they must also have taken its mundane geography into account. But the problem posed by such events, whenever they arise, is always fundamentally the same: the exceptional power must either be regarded as demonic—it must be fought or excluded or fled—or else it must be taken as an expression of the center and allowed to dictate the organization of whatever space it requires for its manifestation. If, however, the extraordinary power is regarded as an expression of the center, our access to the center and the nature of its influence upon us are unpredictable. We are at the periphery of the power we would claim for our own. And this is true not only of ordinary people but also of those—for example, priests and kings—who by their office "should" have the greatest possible access to that power. Thus van der Leeuw, writing about primitive kings, remarks that their potency, "whether attached to their clubs or their wisdom, was experienced as a power 'from elsewhere.' "[16]

Mother Folly's remark about the ambiguity of things is true, as well, of the microcosmic center, where the ambiguity "should" be resolved. That center is marked by an object full of mana or by a sign of supernatural disposition. But the center is also in our conception of it the source of established order and uniform power, in contrast with the mana which erupts spontaneously from it and distributes itself in unpredictable waves. These two qualities of the center may be reconciled at least in the sense that both of them are consciously acknowledged, as in the coexistence of the cults of Apollo and Dionysus at Delphi. But the two qualities may also seem to be in foolish contradiction, one the hidden face of the other, and in their illicit interplay they may lead us to suspect that the center is illusory altogether. The access of the social group to the sources of fundamental meaning and power "should" be secure but may not be or may cease to be. Our relationship to those sources may then appear to be a highly charged and unstable system, reflected, despite its grave importance, in that of the fool in his show.

An example of the ambiguity between the numinous point of power, the mana object, and the field of meaning it irradiates—partly *its* meaning and partly the net of assumptions with which we try to secure that power for ourselves—is provided by the Kaaba, the center of the Islamic cult. It is traditionally believed to have been built by Abraham as a replica of God's dwelling in heaven and was erected to house the holy black stone which fell from heaven in the days of Adam. This stone was originally a meteorite that burnt itself out in the sands of the desert of Mecca, and its flaming descent was surely taken as a supernatural sign. The cult of the stone, which preceded the advent of Islam by centuries, has many parallels in the history of religion. The cult object of Diana at Ephesus was also a fallen meteorite; a similar stone was worshiped in addition to Apollo at Delphi; a meteorite, the "iron shield," which fell in Rome under the reign of Numa Pompilius was put in perpetual custody of a college of twelve priests; a meteorite which fell in Alsace was interpreted by Maximilian I as an exhortation to a crusade against the Turks and was hung by him in the village church of Elsisheim, where it can still be seen.[17]

The shrine of the Kaaba thus combines a divinely ordained pattern, in Islamic terms the model of God's house, and a unique object that is on the magical level full of mana. The relation of the stone to the house has, of course, been rationalized: Abraham is said to have embedded the stone in the wall of the building. Yet the stone retains its magical potency, in which the character of its original appearance is dimly present.

When such an object of supernatural or magical power is also construed as the expression of a pattern of meaning, the mutual accommodation between the two elements may in time prove inadequate. The power may fail; in that case, what is judged to be chaos begins to emanate from the means of keeping order. The priests of a moribund religion may, for example, develop dissenting doctrines that threaten the structure of the cult. Or the power may break free of the pattern of meaning and reassert its autonomous life; then chaos invades that pattern in a demonic form. This may happen whenever and for whatever reason the gods or other exceptional powers withdraw their favor from the human microcosm. As a result, a city may, for example, be afflicted with an epidemic disease or conquered by a foreign army.

It is dangerous to forget that extraordinary power is extraordinary; often the bearers of such power have means of reminding us that it is. Thus the high priest, the king, or the military leader may have insignia of might that are reserved for rare occasions. Thus, too, even within a sacred building a part may be closed off as a sanctuary. In some periodic religious festivals images of the gods that are otherwise kept from public view are carried in procession. The rarity of their appearance conveys to the beholder something of the character of their original epiphany. Despite such institutionalized forms for preserving that character within the cult, the sense of the extraordinary may gradually be lost. When this happens, we may complacently assume that the agency of the center is our own and that the nature of the center accords with our reason. This assumption brings us anew into the dilemma of the center and the border.

The fool often plays with this dilemma. Since his grasp of identity, reality, and meaning is uncertain, and since he has a strong connection with borders, it is not surprising that he should. As we shall see, jesters provide examples of this play as they joke about their position at the center of the kingdom. In the broader world of the fool show, such play is more often concerned not with *that* center but with *this,* with the vicissitudes of "I"; yet there are correspondences between the two, so that jokes about "I" are by implication jokes about that deeper center. Here I wish to consider a circus-clown skit that could be about the workings of the ego but could also be a prosaic burlesque of the relations of a person or a group to a content of great importance. I choose it because in jokes of jesters about kingship and in the traditions of holy clowning there is simply a stressing of implications that are already present in more mundane forms of foolery.

In this circus-clown skit the "straight man," playing a role similar to that of the stage manager in the piece by Valentin and Karlstadt, offers a clown 500 francs to play a trumpet solo. The clown readily accepts, though he cannot play a trumpet, and engages a second, trumpet-playing clown, whom he hides in a box. The second clown should play while the first pretends to do so. This trick on the "straight man" depends upon a system of communication between the other two. The clown pretending to play should stamp his foot once for the music to begin and twice for it to stop. Of course, the system breaks down: the clown in the box plays when he should not and does not when he should.[18]

The trumpet-playing clown is the bearer of exceptional power in relation to the other two, who cannot provide their own music. Yet access to that power must in one way or another be rationalized so that it seems to belong to the second; he is in the position of the priest or king dependent upon mana "from elsewhere." The "straight man" is in the position of the ordinary person in relation to that power; he wants meaningful access to it, an access that accords with his understanding of how things "should" be. As the audience knows, the clowns—one bearing the exceptional power, the other trickily assuring the "straight man" of access to it—will fall into the trap they have constructed with such rational ingenuity; the suspense lies in the question of when and how the structure will revert to folly, like a house falling around their ears.

The fool is not content, merely because he refuses or is unable to grasp the distinction between chaos and cosmos, to remain excluded from the social world from which he is an outcast. He demands incarnation within a space and time that is also ours and in which he is "allowed" to live his foolish life. And there is an authority behind this demand: it is that of the center in its ambiguity. In his immediate relation to the center and to the authority he derives from it, he has similarities with a symbolic figure of fundamental importance, that of the king. There is, moreover, a deep and long-standing connection between the two. That connection, which has been amply borne out in the interplay between countless actual kings and their jesters, is a fundamental imaginative form. The form is that of a fool-king, divided within himself for the purposes of his self-manifestation as the fool is into knave and butt. The king has his kingdom, based on an eternal order; the space and time of the fool are based on a queer relationship between, on the one hand, a different eternity, that of the

146

accidental and fortuitous, and, on the other, whatever conventional space and time he can wheedle from the hands of those who wield social power. The fool begins, socially, as the outcast, the parasite, the tramp, though he may in the course of his show prove himself more powerful than the king and in a fuller relation than the king is to the intelligence and vitality of the world that embraces the microcosmic kingdom in a larger whole.

# Part Three    The Fool and the Kingdom

There's nothing in a play to a clown, if he
Have but the grace to hit on't; that's the thing indeed:
The king shows well, but he sets off the king.
        (Thomas Middleton and William Rowley, *The Changeling*)

If every fool wore a crown, we should all be kings.
                                        (A proverb)

# 9   The King, the Hero, and the Fool

The title "king" may call to our minds Alexander the Great, Louis XIV at Versailles, a fat African chief mounted on the back of a slave on hands and knees, a mild man in a business suit dedicating a power station, a chess piece, a playing card, or a doddering ogre in a fairy tale. We are content to give the same title to these various figures, because in important ways they are alike, and our imagination easily grasps this likeness. It is true that the institution of kingship is thousands of years old, that the world has changed greatly in the course of this time, that the major flowerings of the institution are long past, and that kingship is always, practically, a matter of *this* people in *this* time and place. Still, there is a great uniformity among the diverse forms of kingship; in an important sense it is a single cultural complex. (Such writers as Frazer and A. M. Hocart were right in seeing this, even if they misinterpreted or gave the wrong emphasis to certain phenomena.) The title "king" draws its resonance from an archaic pattern of belief, according to which the kingship is only secondarily a political office and is primarily magical and religious. The man in the business suit is "allowed" to go on being king, somewhat in the way that fools were once "allowed" to serve as jesters, only because that pattern still appeals to the imagination even though it no longer inspires conscious belief. I am concerned with it here because it is the context from which the fool draws his highest symbolic value.

Hocart oversimplifies matters when he conjectures that the "earliest known religion is the divinity of kings"; [1] nonetheless, the institution was of great religious importance, since it shaped conceptions of the supernatural and of human relations to it. And much more concretely, it determined human relations to the natural. Thus in the ancient Middle East and elsewhere the divine or semidivine king was thought to generate the fertility of crops and cattle. That fertility was so important, and despite the king's superhuman status so precarious, that in some societies he may have been put to death in order to ward off the dangers that would accrue if his strength and potency were to diminish.[2]

In this chapter and those following I will discuss the fool's relations to the king and the hero regarded as typical figures who, like the fool, have had important roles in the institution of kingship. It is clear that there are heroes where there are no kings. It is also clear that such broad types cannot be precisely defined and that not all instances will fit whatever definitions we do adopt. We might, of course, ask, If a mythical culture-bringer is heroic, is a wit in an eighteenth-century comedy or an anti- or nonhero in a nineteenth- or twentieth-century piece of fiction heroic in the same way? The question would be fruitless, because it disregards the purposes and limits proper to a discussion of such typical figures. In them one sees traits that are recurrent because they are culturally and psychologically important. I will stress that importance by calling attention to some of the functions of these figures in archaic kingship. With that importance in mind, one may profitably note variations in the recurring traits and in the contexts in which they occur, but that is not my main purpose here.

Cornford, accepting Frazer's designation of the king in this early period as the archmagician, describes the forms of social organization and thought consistent with the operations of the royal magic:

> Because at one time human society and nature formed one solid system, the head of society is *ipso facto* the head of nature also; he is the source of law, which governs the elements no less than mankind. In this sense, he is pre-eminently "divine." His judgments or *"dooms"* . . . are, as Hesiod tells us, inspired. The word *Themis,* like its cognate, the English "doom," means both "judgment," "decree of right," and also the oracular utterance of Fate; once more we find what *ought* to be undistinguished from what *must* and *will* be. The king is the spokesman of the world-order, of destiny and law; for he is the seer, and moves in the world of supersensible, sacred things, in immediate and perpetual contact with that power in nature which is the magnified reflex of his own august potency.[3]

The kingship is thus from the outset the means by which the forces of nature are made to conform to a pattern of ordered fertility. That pattern is in the archaic view eternally present as a model; yet it must be discovered in the realm of the sacred and then established and maintained in the human world, "carve[d] out of a chaotic and cruel cosmos," in Weisinger's words.[4] Thus the king is not only the magician, the prophet, and the lawgiver; he is also the hero, sometimes meeting with a tragic fate. He is the center of magical operations that have the effect of maintaining the vital power of the kingdom, but at the same time those operations, with the king participating in them, are a drama with a metaphysical and moral content. In the person of the royal actor, man is, according to Weisinger, "engaged in a cosmic struggle in which he is made to face up to his opponents, that is to say, chaos and evil, without equivocation or the minimizing of their reality and effect; he forces himself to meet, to be temporarily conquered by, and then to vanquish his antagonists, and in the process he wins through to the greatest victory of all: he changes himself." [5]

The divine and human king is, then, the central actor in a process by which the cosmos is established and maintained. That process is twofold: it is the furtherance of an elemental dynamism that expresses itself in natural fertility, and it is the delineation of the meaning pre-existent within the world. In the symbolism of kingship the potency of the king, whether it derives from his divine right or his individual actions as the head of state, actively maintains the order of his realm against the chaos from which it is divided in the magical field.

For a reader of anthropological studies of kingship the sacred signs which led to the foundation of a particular kingdom are only a few of many which have led to the foundation of many kingdoms. However, the founders of any one of these kingdoms accepted the signs upon which it was based as absolute, and the kingly office has an absolute claim on the members of the group. The burden placed upon the king in this conception is tremendous; although the power of the center is granted to him, his access to it must be fought for, sometimes tragically, sometimes even desperately and ignominiously. Thus van der Leeuw writes, "In relation to men . . . the king was the power bearer, while in relation to power itself he stood in need of it; and in occupying this dual position he became the original type of all the mediators between God and man." [6] Although the king is the bearer of salvation, he may become engaged in a struggle to save himself from the ambiguities between his person and his office and within the office itself. He is subject to personal failings and senescence; he can also become the victim of shifting dispositions within the magical field, whereby a point other than that which he occupied shows signs of being an even stronger center—for example, when his army is defeated in battle or his kingdom is incorporated into another. He may sustain himself in office by the pretense of a power no longer proved in its effects. This pretense may lead to such tragic absurdity as that of Lear, who, having resigned his office and divided his kingdom, calls himself "king" and is addressed by the title, as he rants on the heath. When any king fails his office, he becomes, at least for the moments of that failure, one of the "counterfeit kings" who recur in Shakespeare; [7] like an unconvincing actor he may fall to the mercy of the clown, who, having no fixed place in the action, is free to occupy the center intended for the king but abandoned by him.

When Lear is stripped of everything but his fool, he is in one sense left with a silly plaything, a sign of his impotence and of the futility of his fate. But in another sense his fool belongs not only to the essence of what the king is and has been as a man but also to the ambiguities of his office: when the Fool insinuates that Lear is a fool and says, "All thy other titles thou hast given away; that thou wast born with" (I. iv. 148–49), he is, of course, alluding to Lear's personal folly in giving away his kingdom, but he could also be naming (from the fool's point of view) the essential identity of any king beneath the insignia of his office.

The origins of the royal jester are, like those of the king, lost in antiquity. The earliest known to us is the Negro dwarf jester in the court of Pharaoh Pepi I. This jester could "dance the God," and in an appeal to the pilot who should bring the boat with the soul of the king to the islands of Osiris the Pharaoh claims identity with his jester and hopes that it will ensure his soul a fair voyage and a welcome reception in the other world.[8] The custom of keeping a jester was widespread outside Europe; in fact, the court of Charlemagne, which abounded in entertainers, was in contact with that of Harun al-Rashid, who kept the well-known fool Buhlul al-Madjnun, "Buhlul the Madman." But when we think of the king and his jester, we are calling to mind a picture which began to take substantial form in the European Middle Ages. (William the Conqueror had jesters, but the custom of keeping them had been established in England by the brief reign of Edmund Ironside in 1016.) An attempt to trace that picture to its sources is made impossible by the fact that there are fool entertainers in virtually every society and that the highest classes are usually in one way or another patrons of these entertainers.

We find the picture of the jester beside the king natural and fitting. We expect the two to play together (after all, the jester is a plaything) and are not even shocked when the play goes so far that the king becomes the knave or butt of the farcical fool pair. There are many anecdotes and stories in which the king adopts such a role. The show that the two perform together has been allowed by the king and is thus an expression of his will; in relation to that will, which can also decree that the jester be dragged from the royal presence, whipped, and sent without supper to sleep with the spaniels, the fool is apparently of no importance. Thus the interaction between them is the shifting of planes that only touch in the no-man's-land of jokes (which has something of the spacelessness and timelessness of other forms of the fool show).

However, this picture may also assume a dark form. If we are not caught up in laughter at them, and if we are not convinced of the power behind the king's will, the pair may suggest to us a weary conqueror and a rebel prince with whom he has had to come to an uneasy settlement, the king clinging to his throne, the prince biding his time. This character of the bond between the king and his jester may, in fact, be one of the topics of their jokes. (In Michel de Ghelderode's play, *Escurial,* a king and his jester exchange roles in a grim game in which their mutual hatred and rivalry are openly expressed. Finally, both shout, "My crown! I am the king!", and the king puts an end to the game by having the jester strangled.[9]) In tolerating such jokes the king partly affirms the royal power that the fool pretends to deny. Thus the office of the jester fulfills some of the same functions as the ritualized rebellion in which political subjects express actual and possible resentments against authority. The fact that the rebellion is allowed and even encouraged implies that the social institutions and the persons in power are strong enough to tolerate it; thus it serves the interests of authority and of social cohesion.[10]

And yet, having imagined the king and the fool as liege lord and ambitious prince, or as two comedians squabbling sullenly in the wings of a stage, we may feel that these jokes express not only the power of the king but also that of the fool. We may wonder whether the king has really, in an act of free choice that he can afford, admitted the fool into his presence or whether the two are not carrying on a sacrilegious clown routine to which the king is an only half-willing partner. We may, in short, entertain the possibility that the fool's bravado does not just mime infantile delusions of omnipotence but has serious implications for the office of the king. We may even imagine the *king* as the agent of make-believe, saying, "Look at my jester; look at me! Though the jester imitates my bearing, my tone of voice and even my movements in the most solemn rites, I defy you to see any similarity between us! Though I am duped by his tricks, I defy you to think that my being outwitted is anything other than an expression of my will! And though I sometimes flail out at him, I defy you to see in my rage a loss of dignity!" Of course, even if such assertions of authority rely on make-believe, they may still accord with the purposes of the ritualized rebellion I have mentioned. (When the king was a syphilitic semi-imbecile, a jester even more grotesque may have served as a useful stage prop, disarming criticism by making the king look more nearly normal by comparison and thus making the make-believe of kingship possible.) But in another sense the reflection of the king in the fool may be felt to deny the royal claim that there is one center and that it belongs to the king and to him alone.

In the kingship the exceptional power which is the basis of the royal claim should in a sense be domesticated. The kinds of forces which might, for example, be put to the use of sorcery should be transformed to the well-being of the kingdom. In modern terms the difference is something like that between lightning and the electricity that lights a lamp. The babbling fool is one prototype of our relationship to numinous powers. The king, too, must remain in touch with them; he must draw upon them when they promise to be useful and counteract them when they threaten to be destructive to the kingdom. The fool stands beside the king, in a sense reflecting him but also suggesting a long-lost element of the king that, we may imagine, had to be sacrificed at the founding of the kingdom, an element without which neither the king nor the kingdom is complete.

156

## The King, the Hero, and the Fool

At the foundation of the kingdom much had to be excluded, not all of it because it was necessarily "bad" but because boundaries had to be drawn at the limits of the effective power of the center. For example, to make an ordered life within the kingdom possible, laws must be proclaimed that exclude many kinds of human behavior. These limits are also obvious in the military sense that the kingdom can include only those territories that can be subjugated and defended against attack. Nonetheless, the kingdom is not self-sufficient, those boundaries may have to be defended, and the kingdom may profit by commerce and other forms of friendly relations with the lands that have been excluded. But in the archaic view, those lands are to a lesser or greater extent inhabited by demonic powers; beyond the boundaries of the kingdom the magical field is still alive.

The king's task of assuring his people that the sources of their power are secure and that the operations of those powers are uniform is ambiguous. Things do in fact happen that do not conform with the world as it should be. Therefore the king must have contact not only with the central power but also with the randomly scattered sources of unusual events in the magical field beyond his boundaries. If those sources cannot be vanquished and assimilated, at least some measured contact with them must be kept. Thus, for example, the king or his ministers may seek information from ambassadors, spies and travelers, prophets and soothsayers.

The kingdom must deal with specific magical influences, but it must also deal with the *generic fact* of such influences—with the possibility that they may appear, with the necessity of constantly making allowances for them in thought and imagination. The fool as jester provides an institutionalized link with them. As mascot, decoy, and scapegoat he symbolically and in a general way embodies all of the processes by which vitality and meaning are dissolved and holds them relatively centered within his person. He represents the *possibility* that such processes may become effective within the kingdom. This is simply another way of expressing the possibility that the kingly office and other institutions may lose their power and meaning and that the realm beyond the borders of the kingdom may again become threatening. The jester diminishes the threat playfully by holding the possibility of the threat up to the

157

imagination. He also counteracts the threat by embodying the principle of wholeness, by reinstating in measured form the primeval condition before the separation of the kingdom from that which it excludes.

Just as many fertility gods (and goddesses) die and are resurrected in a way paralleling the course of nature through the barrenness of winter to the renewal of spring, so the king as the representative of the central power has enacted the same process. And since barrenness is a mockery of the king's power, the king came very early to have a double, who embodied the threat of natural catastrophe and was deliberately mocked by the people. The institution of the mock king, a lowly person who was given for a short time some of the king's authority and was then abused or even killed as a scapegoat, is a differentiation of roles within the more archaic complex of the single king, crushed beneath his burden and then supernaturally revived. Christopher Sly, robed as a lord, is a late but distinct recollection of the ritual mock king. He is dragged drunk to the part assigned to him after he has reminded the Lord of death—death being both the threat from which the archaic king and mock king were, together, to protect the people and the threat from which the mock king was to protect the king.

The mock king was not always a fool, but by the nature of his office the fool as court jester became a kind of mock king. Moreover, the fool of fertility festivals not overtly and officially connected with the kingship shared the mock king's character as scapegoat and was often explicitly made into a mock king, though one who remained (for instance, in local harvest festivals) positionless with respect to the distant king and was full of his own life-bringing magic.

Enid Welsford conjectures that the European festival fool, who enacts the role of the scapegoat, has a different provenance from the court jester, who was originally a kind of mascot with powers of protection from the evil eye. Nonetheless, both figures, in her opinion, "originate in the notion that a grotesque fool can be used as an abusive scapegoat, a kind of living mascot." [11] Scapegoat and mascot are, in fact, complementary functions; moreover, the role of the scapegoat is clearly relevant to the fact that the king is destined to die, and the role of mascot is clearly relevant to the fact that the king is the repository of powers to be guarded. The fool and the mock king are thus sometimes separate, sometimes interrelated forms in which a fundamental fact about the kingship is imaginatively expressed: the king has a kind of double—either an adversary, such as death or winter, or the protective genius of his person or his office. The court jester, unlike the fool or mock king of the festival, is a permanent embodiment of this double. Since the court jester is in many ways whole and complete within himself, though he is peripheral to the human image, he brings the king into active relationship with a level of wholeness beyond the king's personal claim to power and beyond the separation of the kingdom from what it excludes. Thus it is not surprising that in the differentiated form of the jester familiar to us from the European late Middle Ages the mascot has reassimilated many elements of the scapegoat: we feel them when Lear threatens his Fool with the whip.

However, when the fool has the upper hand, he and the king assume complementary fool roles. The formal parity between them is the basis of a burlesque of the kingship that may proceed in various ways using various materials to accord with various foolish intentions. Yet the burlesque begins and ends with that parity and with the joke, "The fool is a king; the king is a fool"—with the ordained king brought into conjunction with the fool, who is as irreducible and as absolute as the king.

The parity between the fool and the king seems sometimes a commonplace yet sometimes a potent joke that must be spelled out as though to define and so contain it. Thus kingly titles and dominions were often bestowed on court jesters by their masters. Those dominions were assumed to be of inferior worth to those of the kingdom; but any unassimilated realm is a potential threat to the kingdom, especially if that realm lies relatively near at hand. And just as the fool bases his jokes on incongruous elements within his master's domain, so he may also reveal unexpected powers within the inferior realm assigned to him. The conceit of the coexistent but unequal kingdoms may flare up at the real king, if only in a joke. The custom of royal titles for fools was highly developed in Russia under the czars, and often the fool was made the center of mock solemnities in which the kingdom was shown to be composed of the fool's motley. Thus in 1739 the Empress Anna is reported to have celebrated a feast on the occasion of the marriage of her court fool—in fact, her own son, dispossessed because he had become a Roman Catholic—to a disreputable woman. The guests represented all the races in the Russian Empire and were placed in sledges drawn by every kind of animal, including camels, while the bride was the fool's wife and at the same time that of any man who wanted her. This disruptive, chaos-inducing element of the fool show was allowed to emerge fully only upon such occasions. But the potentialities of such disruption were implied in the titles of one permanent jester of the czar: the fool was called variously the Patriarch of Russia, the King of Siberia, or the King of the Samoyeds; he was either a counterpart of the central king or a king in his own right over realms nominally part of the kingdom but distant from the center.[12]

The Russian jester's titles can be seen as a concession to the truth of Rabelais's remark that those who bear the crown and scepter are born under the same constellation as those who wear the cap and bells.[13] Insofar as Rabelais is right, the fool cannot simply be banished, as both king and fool have conjoint roles in the larger workings of the planetary system: although the king is often symbolically associated with the sun, the sun will set, the kingdom will have to endure the timelessness between its setting and its rising, and the king will have to submit himself to death and renewal. Thus it is an ancient custom for time to be reckoned from the accession of the reigning king; the practice survives in English official documents.[14]

Despite the royal claim, the kingdom is, then, delivered over to a realm, with its own intelligence, that exceeds it. The king must not only accept but enact a conjunction between the two realms; yet he must do so in such a way that he dictates terms that leave him relatively in control. If the king does not succeed in dictating them, the fool may, by means of his magic, effect a merger that amounts to a dissolution of the kingdom in the chaos of the fool show. The grotesque fool pageants in imperial Russia are a dramatization of that conjunction; the energies that erupted in the Russian saturnalia are nascent in the titles of the jester who was "Patriarch of Russia," "King of Siberia," and "King of the Samoyeds." The saturnalian mock solemnities that were often performed under the czars were signs of the royal power. And yet these proofs that the central power can withstand impulses threatening to it are at the same time proofs of how strong those impulses are.

## The King, the Hero, and the Fool

It is finally not the king as sun that is supreme but the planetary system that governs the rising and setting of the sun, its disappearance in clouds and night, and its eclipses as well as the waxing and waning of the moon and all the figurations of the stars. This is implied not only in the fact that the Russian jester was king over realms within the boundaries of the kingdom but more or less beyond the king's actual control; it is also implied in the fact that the persons chosen for the jester's office in Russia were often foreigners. At one time he was a Pole, at another a Portuguese —as though the czar sought the power of people coming from beyond the boundaries of the kingdom so that he could subdue elements within the kingdom that were not really responsive to his own power.

There is thus a sense in which the joke of the jester as mock king *always* finally turns against the king and reveals the deficiency of his power to substantiate his regal claim. This reversal of the joke may be seen in a story about the Caliph Harun al-Rashid. He once gave his buffoon Buhlul a document by which Buhlul was made governor of all the bears, wolves, foxes, apes, and asses in the caliphate. "It is too much for me," Buhlul answered, "I am not ambitious enough to desire to rule all your holiness's subjects." [15] The Caliph had offered him a position that comically and on a ridiculously inferior level paralleled his own; at the same time, the subjects to be governed by the fool were representative of forces that could in any case not be fully brought under the control of the caliph. In his rebuttal the fool not only reduced the entire human population of the caliphate to the level of animals; he also implied that the caliphate consisted only of forces that the caliph could not really control. By playing upon the inadequacy of the king's power, the fool made a mockery of the kingdom: a kingdom composed only of bears, wolves, foxes, apes, and asses would be like one in which all the fools wear crowns. It would be no kingdom.

The king's power is deficient because he is mortal in relation to the eternal model that he embodies. Thus the jester may joke about the fact that the king must die. As the butt of these jokes, the king must submit to a momentary transposition of his tragic role into the realm of farce. According to common metaphor, desperately important to clowns and comedians, good jokes are "killing." Obversely, the acosmic forces of contingency, natural sterility, and death are counteracted by the joke against him. That such jokes can have a magical character is borne out by the procession in which the Roman conqueror habitually returned to Rome to receive a triumph. He rode in a chariot at the close of the procession, surrounded by dancing gold-crowned clowns and satyrs, who made obscene gestures and coarse jokes, many of their taunts being directed at him. One satyr in female clothes screamed in his face, cursed him to the last generation of his sons, and invented a rude genealogy for him. While the conqueror held a rat's foot or a dried cockerel's comb as an amulet against the evil eye, a gold-crowned slave holding the crown of Jupiter Capitolinus above the victor's head whispered again and again, "O Conqueror, look behind you, and remember you are mortal." [16] This slave had attributes of the fool-jester, and in the *quattrocento* he was painted in the familiar trappings of one (though the older texts do not explicitly identify him as one of the clowns). Moreover, according to Suetonius, the dead Roman Emperor Vespasian was followed in the funeral procession by his jester or *mimus,* Faco, who "even mimicked the dead man's meanness by asking how much the funeral arrangements cost. When he was told that it would amount to 100 sesterces, he said he would rather be thrown into the Tiber." [17] Thus the mockery of the king is partly a reminder that insofar as the king is lacking in modesty, compassion, and generosity of spirit, his individuality is a joke. But as is clear from the insults poured upon the emperor already dead, the abuse goes deeper than satire merely to exhort a ruler to be aware of his duties. It is magical in the same sense as the rat's foot or dried cockerel's comb of the emperor was: it is the invocation of a germinal wholeness independent of the structure of the kingdom and the misfortunes that could befall it. The role of the royal jester, later, could accommodate elements that are dispersed in these Roman triumphal and funeral processions: the medieval jester combines functions of mockery—as mock king he is mocked and mocks the king in turn—and of the magical amulets that complement the official insignia of the collective order. In his immediate access to hidden powers the jester survives the death of the king.

The fool helps to maintain a relativity between the king and his office and between that office and the facts of life and death. But this function of the fool may entail a danger both to the fool and to the king. The folly of the jester may go too far or in the wrong direction or appear in the wrong time and place and prove as unwelcome as any other incursion of chaos upon the established order; then the fool may have to suffer the king's revenge. A Kaffir chief, for example, had a jester who made a funny remark when the king was assembled with his counselors; the chief ordered the jester killed, because he had made him laugh.[18]

This danger to the fool, one of his occupational hazards, is merely a reflection of his danger to the king. This mutual threat is keenly visualized by Robert Payne, who writes:

> The Roman Emperors took care that the great mimes should be close to the throne. . . . They had the power to turn people against the Emperor, and they were known to be afraid of nothing. . . . The court jesters of the middle ages were sometimes roped to the throne by little golden chains, perhaps for fear they might escape and jest before the people. Dimly, it was recognised that they possessed powers denied to the Emperor. They were closer to the sources of life. They spoke when they spoke at all—for mostly they claimed a prodigious indifference, and were silent for long periods—only at moments of illumination, and so they were cousins to the [sibyls] who lived mysteriously in caves and uttered prophecies over braziers. The Emperor was thought to have absolute power over the empire, but he knew [that] with one word, with one laugh pitched to the exact pitch, the clown could destroy the kingdom, as a singer will destroy a wineglass.[19]

Earlier Alexander the Great had seen his end presaged in an apparition of a mad fool on his throne. Alexander had been playing ball and having himself anointed; just as he was going to begin dressing again, the young men with him saw a man in the king's robes with a diadem on his head sitting silently upon the king's throne. For a time he did not answer their questions; then, coming to his senses, he explained that he had been in prison for a long time, that there the god Serapis had appeared to him, freed him from his chains, and commanded him to assume the king's throne, as he had done. Alexander had the man killed, but, as Plutarch observes, the king "began to be low-spirited, and was distrustful now of the favour of Heaven and suspicious of his friends," and he died soon after.[20]

However, the fool also embodies the possibility that someone or something will survive the failure of the king's power and help others to survive. With respect to the "normal" life of the kingdom, the interchangeability of the fool and the king is a joke. But with respect to the king's mortality, to the half-lie implicit in the assumption that he is strong and wise, and to the subjection of all creatures within the kingdom to chaos, accident, illness, and death, that interchangeability is both an admission of danger and an expression of hope in the face of it. The fool may be a harbinger of death, as the madman was for Alexander, but the fool may also allay the fear of death by an immediate representation of life.

From the moment of his coronation the king begins to lose his heroic power: supposedly contained, it leaks, and it does this whether the leakage is apparent now or whether it will suddenly be discerned much later in a dramatic failure of the king. Once crowned, the hero comes more and more to fulfill the pattern of the "old king," destined to be superseded by the "new king"—a process enacted in ritual festivals of the seasons.[21] This shifting of roles within the drama of the kingship is only partly an expression of the fact that the king, full of power at his accession, must try to maintain that power while death draws nearer. It is also an expression of the fact that it is hard for the king to be the stationary embodiment of the center and at the same time to pursue conquests in regions remote from it. Still, in a ritual and magical sense, the king *is* the bearer of heroic power even while he remains stationary at the center. (In the same way, the court jester *is* the stream of saturnalian folly from which he has been singled out.) But power concentrates in points other than the official center, and these are the province of the hero, whether he is a loyal subject or an enemy of the reigning king, whether he is the young king blessed by the old or an adversary moving toward the king with violent intent upon his life. In his book about kingship,[22] Philipp Wolff-Windegg describes the old and young kings as complementary types. He characterizes the old king as striving toward law and priestcraft, the young king toward conquest and military leadership, the old king as having a relationship to rules, the young to the extraordinary.

Like the title "king," that of "hero" calls many figures and even kinds of figures to mind; and like the king, the hero is on the most primitive

level a semidivine being. The actual kingdom needs heroes, as it needs
kings; as with dramatic types sharing the same stage, various patterns of
relationship between them are possible. Of these, the accommodation of
the hero to the kingship in the form of the "young king" is fundamental:
it is the simplest expression of the fact that the power of the hero, too,
must ultimately be bound to the center. Moreover, the king and the hero
as representatives of the center must act, and their actions have a
significance that goes beyond their importance in the maintenance of the
kingdom. The significance of the two figures is different but interrelated;
this is implied in Cornford's remark that "in the king and the hero we
have found transitional forms, which make, as it were, a bridge from the
daemon of the group to the individual soul." [23] Whether or not the hero is
a "personality" in the modern sense, he is individual in having exceptional
strength, intelligence, and will. But how can this power be made to
preserve the center rather than run rampant in its destruction? Some
Greek and American Indian heroes had powers that did not further the
life of their peoples. These heroes used their powers, rather, in wanton
displays of self-will, opposed to the demands of the center; they provoked
the wrath of the gods and were stricken down. Such stories touch upon
the problem of allegiance to the center and of finding the measure of will
proper to that allegiance. This problem assumes certain forms in the play
between the fool and the king; for the hero the problem becomes one of
meaningful individual action when the demands for action are not clearly
circumscribed by the forms of the kingly office.

   To be a hero is to be committed to a heroic purpose and to try to realize
that commitment in action. The fundamental task of the hero in the
maintenance of the kingdom is that of active engagement with chaos and
the demonic. The hero must validate his power in real effects that reveal
or affirm some undiscovered or forgotten facet of the general structure of
the world. He must be successful, although his success need not be of a
kind that was expected or even wanted. He may, for example, try to win a
battle but be defeated; yet in dying nobly he may reveal to others a kind
of commitment without which the human cosmos is doomed.

   Heroic actions contrast with both the tricks and jokes of the fool show
and the rituals of the king. Thus when Aristotle speaks of "the imitation
of an action," he means the forms, universal in their significance, assumed

in the lives of people who are heroic—if not in the sense of being literally semidivine by descent, then heroic in being exceptional in their attempts to find and live out their fates. Fool and king are bound to the ritual forms of their office, but the hero must become an individual; he must encounter the unknown and wrest from it the line of his destiny. When the larger form of his action emerges to view, it is often clear that he has redeemed some part of chaos and some part of his own folly. That folly is negatively the possibility that he will foolishly fail in his role as hero. But positively it consists of qualities essential to his heroic purpose, such as his openness to the queer and unforeseen and his mockery of conventional opinions when they are shortsighted. He redeems his folly by finding the right relationship to it, by allowing it expression without letting it possess him completely.

The folly of the hero is evident in fairy tales and other stories about the exploits of a fool-hero who remains a fool but succeeds in a heroic purpose. This is the motif of the Grimm story, "The Golden Bird," in which the two older of three brothers undertake a quest, fail, and are followed by the youngest, a fool, who succeeds in winning the princess. Even when the hero is not a fool, he may have virtues that are at first undistinguishable from folly. The border line between courage and foolhardiness, for example, is sometimes very thin, and purity of heart may entail blindness to personal advantage even when that advantage is a matter of success or failure in the heroic purpose or even of life and death. Like the fool, the hero may have queer ideas (many heroes were once considered fools); but the queer ideas of the hero turn out to be generally valid. In the course of a quest the hero demonstrates strength and resilience in the face of folly (thus manifesting qualities necessary, in another context, to the ego in its relations to the unconscious). This demonstration is part of what proves the hero's claim to the throne.

Thus the hero's demonstration of kingly qualities is part of a gradual differentiation that also causes his folly to gain a voice separate from his own, to consolidate, to become a human partner with whom one can have a dialogue. The king at the center and the court jester beside him are a picture of the result of this process, the king being free to allow the jester because the king is (symbolically) detached from his own folly and that of the world. This detachment is important, because folly needs to be included among the things the king sees clearly. In his need to "See better" (I. i. 157), Lear, for example, had to allow his Fool to be his spiritual guide. Such blindness as Lear's represents the decay of an adequate vision, but in the pattern of the young and old kings such vision grows out of what could be called the creative and purposive semiblindness of the hero. The hero is often partly blind in that his single-mindedness is a kind of one-sidedness and in that he closes his eyes to some of what are supposed to be "facts." However, his blindness goes even deeper: although his actions express the demands of the center, he shares our ignorance of its essential nature. If, for example, the kingdom is invaded, heroic ways must be found of reaffirming its structure; in attempting to find them, the hero may at first thrash in the dark, as ignorant as everyone else as to what should be done. But once he has found these ways and acted upon them, he may in retrospect seem to have fulfilled the will of the center. Such ignorance is in a sense absolute: the solution to the problem is either found or it is not found—the will of the center is either known or it is not known. Yet practically, there are distinctions of kind. The ignorance that is formalized in the "normal" view of things is essentially different from the ignorance of the fool who violates it. In breaking out of the conventional view of what purposes are worthwhile and what means are appropriate, the hero immerses himself in the materials of the fool show. His passion and purification of purpose earn him an identity separate from that of the fool; yet the fool show may still erupt in his path, since the nature of the center remains unknown.

Action is the material of drama. Heroes move upon the stage, but, as they do so, the fool, we may imagine, watches. Sometimes the hero fails tragically in his purpose, and when he provokes our pity and terror, the fool may laugh. The fool may even appropriate the trappings, gestures, and purposes of the hero. As a burlesque mock hero he may touch us in a way that is not tragic but is poignant and even sublime.

The scepter of the king and the sword and spear of the hero are signs of authority held in the hand as extensions of the hand's capacity for grasping and forming. In the archaic kingship the royal hand is one of the conventional signs of the king's authority; it appears as such in many graphic representations.[24] Swords and spears are pointed and have cutting edges; they belong to the hero and may be taken with him, wherever he goes, to be used according to his purpose and the needs of the moment. The scepter of the king, on the other hand, is capped with a sign of his authority, usually an equivalent of his crown; the whole is invested with the symbolism of the world axis or world tree.[25] The scepter is thus like a sword or spear that has been crowned and sheathed and fixed at the center, as the hero-king has in a sense come to rest in becoming king. With his weapon the hero serves the purposes of the center but does so at a distance from it, as when he fights dragons or human enemies. But the task of the hero is not only to defeat chaos and reaffirm the order that radiates from the center; it is also to take whatever boons are to be won from chaos. There are countless representations of this process: the hero may, for example, win a distant treasure to be given to his king, or he may conquer a monster that is destroying crops or food animals or poisoning a well. The deeds of the hero with his weapon often result in fructification or spiritual renewal of the kingdom; those deeds connect the center with the periphery in ways that are essential to the kingdom as a whole.

Finally, then, the life of the kingdom both streams from the center and pulses from heroic acts of engagement with the chaos that surrounds the kingdom. And an awareness of this duality, and of the king's dependence upon the hero, may lead to an ironic and even mocking view of the king's authority; it may also direct attention to the duality within the office of the kingship. No matter what the king pretends, he is passive as well as active, feminine as well as masculine, victim as well as ruler; though he should be destined to triumph against chaos, the contest is in a real sense precarious. This duality of the king as both active and passive is clearly shown in a picture of a European king from the twelfth century. (See Plate 24.) In his right hand the king holds a spear-pointed lance that is at the same time the tree of life or world axis. The paradox upon which the kingship as a symbolic form rests is apparent in this emblem. The functions of penetrating, discriminating, and killing and those of nurturing the life of nature to fruition are complementary; if they are brought together in such an emblem as this, the union of these functions makes action in a nonsymbolic sense impossible. A spear may be a magically potent emblem of power at the same time that it is a weapon of

PLATE 24. King with sprouting lance, illustration to a twelfth-century manuscript. The instrument of active conquest is here emblematically combined with the world tree, symbolic of the fixed center and of natural fertility.

the hero, but the sprouting lance is no longer a weapon. The forms of the scepter familiar to us suggest a similar union of functions, the rod (of phallus and spear) being capped with the ring or round (of the feminine vessel).

The fool's bauble is, like the king's scepter, phallic. (In John Cleland's *Memoirs of a Woman of Pleasure* the "fool's bauble," the phallus of an idiot, is "the prerogative of majesty which distinguishes that otherwise most unfortunate condition" of mental deficiency.[26]) The fool's bauble is also like the king's scepter, and unlike the hero's sword and spear, in having hermaphroditic overtones, since the bauble often combines a rod and a lump of a kind that is traditionally regarded as feminine and maternal. But the combination of male and female in the office of the kingship expresses the fact that the dynamic polarities within the kingdom belong finally to the center and accord with its meaning, even if part of its life and meaning are wrested from the chaos outside the kingdom. The fool's bauble, on the other hand, is hermaphroditic in the sense that polarities have not yet been differentiated within it, and its meaning is both that of the center of the ordered world and that of the chaos that surrounds it. The head of the phallic lump of the bauble contain materials that could, we may imagine, develop into the crowned rod of the royal scepter. However, just as the fool almost attains the human image but does not quite, so the lump of his bauble swallows again the capacities of activity and authority that could develop out of it.

In the archaic kingship the king is a center in that he is divine or semidivine, in that each subject invests part of his person in him, and in that he links the kingdom to the ground of things. In a symbolic sense the king is often the focus of a religious, political, or philosophical system built upon an experience of the archetype of the self. Such a system is the result of abstraction, which leads to the senescence of the king, from whom the numinosity of the archetypal experience gradually fades. The outcome is described by Jolande Jacobi:

> When the content of a symbol is exhausted, when the secret contained in it is either made entirely accessible to consciousness and rationalized; or when it has vanished from consciousness—i.e., has succumbed wholly to the unconscious, and the symbol has accordingly lost its

archetypal opacity and numinosity—all that remains behind is the husk of the symbol, which then forms part of the collective consciousness. The contents of the collective consciousness are, one could say, empty shells of archetypes, simulacra of those of the collective unconscious, their *formal reflection*. Although they lack the numinosity of the archetypes, their action is *quasi-archetypal*, for their "ideals" are at first numinous—like the archetypes—but in time they are replaced by propaganda and pressure of opinion. . . .[27]

The symbolic king may even degenerate into something like an obstructive and ill-adapted instance of the "superego" formulated by Freud. This degeneration may be seen in fairy tales in which the king appears as a stiffly self-righteous tyrant, his presence strangling and suffocating everyone around him. If this degeneration takes place, the instinctual potency so carefully guarded in the primitive institution of the divine king may fail, or the kingdom may become defenseless against the dangers embodied in demonic or human enemies. The dynamism to replace that which has become exhausted at the center of the kingdom invades the kingdom from without. The new dynamism must manifest itself through what the king judges to be the forces of chaos, because the potency at the center that held chaos out is the force by which meaning is established and maintained, and this meaning is the basis of his judgment of what is chaotic and what is not. And, since the self is in one way or another continuous with the ego, when the symbol of the self becomes drained of content, the ego may suffer inanition or be overwhelmed by unconscious impulses of various kinds. Thus in a fairy tale in which the king is an old tyrant, his subjects may be swallowed up in lethargy or attacked from without. And if a person is living according to a set of sterile opinions unrelated to the realities of himself and the world, he may dream that he is in such a kingdom (or an equivalent of it).

The hero, in contrast with the reigning king, often represents the ego-forming tendencies that are part of the life of the self. Despite everything that is given, we must in suffering try to find our way in the world: this is so because the search is part of what human life *is* and because what we are is not only what we are given but what we make of it. With singleness of purpose the hero shows the dedication required in some measure of us, too. In the process he discovers new or forgotten sources of life and meaning and helps them to be assimilated to the common weal. Thus it is clear that the fool must often stand in a relation of burlesque counterpoint to the hero: the ego-functioning of the fool is defective, and he enacts the dilemmas that arise when the demands of the ego are ignored. But these may also be the demands of the self for the establishment, maintenance, or renewal of individual consciousness.

The self and the ego compose a system by which consciousness is brought to birth and organized within the larger field of the psyche (which is unconscious as well as conscious), and within and without this system the fool has a life-furthering role. Ego and self are, seen in one way, related as part to whole; the part is necessary to the whole—and is necessary precisely in its difference from that whole. This may be seen in the analogy of the hero who owes allegiance to the king but must draw on his own individuality in the royal service. The symbolic fool is in one sense peripheral to this system and in another essential to it. If the hero represents symbolically the ego-forming tendency of the self, the fool partly counteracts that tendency. But in doing so, he draws the developing ego, sometimes beneficially, back to its sources. The role of the fool in the formation or deformation of consciousness may be understood by means of a concept presented by the analytical psychologist Alfred Plaut, that of the "archaic ego component." The concept is part of an attempt to answer some of the questions that arise about the relations between the ego and the self. According to Plaut, this archaic ego component is effective in undifferentiated states "in which neither ego nor self are clearly discernible." He postulates that other component parts, including the nucleus of what we customarily think of as the ego, are somehow added to or split from this archaic element. Under favorable circumstances, "the components are integrated into a unified if unstable system: the ego to which we commonly refer." This archaic ego component is both the same as the ego and different from it; it "registers on behalf of the individual what is happening and reacts to events without being able to focus sharply enough to make one feel the space-time continuity expressed in 'this is happening to me now.' "[28] This blurred focus of consciousness may come into play in times of stress, exhaustion, sleep, illness, and (Plaut conjectures) at the very beginning and ending of life. This idea owes something to similar thoughts by Michael Fordham and to Erich

Neumann's concept of the "ego-self" axis, by which Neumann means the capacity of the self to function *for* the ego when the ego is temporarily out of action or has not yet come into action.[29]

Plaut's concept is intended as a working hypothesis in the exploration of certain psychopathological states that are characterized by loss or diminution of the powers of the ego and by the emergence of kinds of psychic functioning that we can crudely describe as magical. The fool is to a large extent governed by magical modes of apprehension and action and has a position at the boundaries of life and death resembling that attributed to this archaic ego. If the king may be said to symbolize a collective-conscious world view based upon an experience of the self, and the hero the ego-forming tendency within the frame of collective consciousness, the fool mimes and induces the undifferentiated psychic states out of which both collective and personal consciousness emerge into relatively centered forms. Those stages, too, belong to the total life of the self in something of the way that the seemingly nonsensical play of the jester belongs to the meaningful activity of the king. Although the immediate effects of the fool suggest the workings of the archaic ego component, the fool is finally as much a symbol of the self as the king is, the fool presenting us with the dynamism and meaning that exceed our grasp of the totality and centrality of the self but that belong to the self nonetheless. The fool enriches the king as a symbol of the self by making a constant game of our tendency to take the symbol for granted. And when the king loses his power to symbolize an experience of the self, that experience is available by way of compensation through the fool and the dissolution of consciousness that he effects. Moreover, the fool contains the seeds of a personal identity that may develop so that it is not simply defined by collective consciousness and identical with it.

# 10    The Fool and the Woman

A crude but useful distinction between comedy and tragedy can be drawn
with respect to its outcome: tragedy ends with the death of the hero,
comedy with his marriage. Although this distinction does not accord with
everything we customarily assign to the genus comedy, it is true, as
Cornford has pointed out, of virtually all the comedies of Aristophanes,[1] it
is true of all the comedies of Shakespeare, and it expresses one of the
dominant concerns of comedy of most kinds in most times and places: the
concern that the world and society continue. Geoffrey Bush writes of
Shakespeare that "the end of every comedy is marriage, in which the
dream of order is triumphantly attained. . . . The plot of comedy is
matrimony, which carries all in its path; and in the formality and
ceremony of a wedding the order of society is made perfect."[2] Although
Touchstone marries in his fashion, Shakespeare's fools (such as Bottom,
Dogberry, Jaques, and Sir Andrew Aguecheek) generally remain
unmoved by the train of marriages in the comic denouement. As Bush
interprets this fact, "The fool is not in progress towards himself, the fool
is always himself, and he preserves what he is by ignoring a world
rushing headlong toward weddings. The fool is a fact, and he is the only
fact that cannot be governed by the comic dream . . . ; he is the reminder
that the moment of perfection realized by the comic dream is only
pretending."[3]

   The fool sees through this pretense or is unable to comprehend the
form of perfection that lives by means of it. He is outside the rush of
weddings, outside the personal encounter between man and woman. His
sexuality, like everything else about him, assumes forms expressive of his
indeterminate status on the border between cosmos and chaos. He is full
of self-furthering life; the seeds of that life have assumed neither definite
shapes nor clear connections to one another or to the structure of the

174

world. He is neither simply male nor simply female; and when he is
ostensibly male, he is so without being able to establish an intimate and
enduring connection with a woman. Like the phallic herm of Erasmus'
boundary stone if it were to be torn from the earth, he is too whole, yet
too fragmentary, too positionless, yet too much like a lodestone drawing
everything to itself, too exaggeratedly yet too scarcely human to come to
whatever rest and completion is to be found in marriage. In general, the
fool's sexuality finds only those forms of expression that are tangential to
the hero's course of wooing and winning the maiden. From his position
on the fringes of the social world and of the human image, the fool mocks
the conventional relations of man to woman and keeps visibly alive the
sexual morass from which the form of marriage emerges or upon which it
is imposed. Being on the periphery of the encounter of man and woman
that leads to marriage, he most frequently assumes the roles of the
mother-bound son, the hermaphrodite, the bawd and lecher, the partner
of a fool double almost identical with him, and the yearning lover of the
angelically pure woman.

The mother-boundness of the fool is the most abiding form of his
relationship to the feminine. Just as the fool who has acquired clear and
complex lineaments tends with the passage of time to die and revert to the
primal lump, so the fool who intrudes into the fateful encounter between
man and woman tends to escape to his mother again. In the late Middle
Ages and early Renaissance the fool festivals of the Church and,
somewhat later, the secular fool societies were dominated, most notably in
Dijon, by the figure of Mother Folly, who lived on in the pages of
Erasmus. The fool societies were governed by fool figures who played the
priests and nobles of the normal world, but behind these burlesque figures
of conventional—and masculine—authority Mother Folly reigned
supreme. (See Plate 25.) During the fool festivals special fool coins were
frequently issued by the "Pope of Fools" and used as currency. One of the
coins suggests the abiding double relationship between the fool and the
mother to whom he still belongs and between the fool and the powers
that govern the social world. The coin is stamped with images of the fool
pope with double cross and tiara and of a fool in fool dress reaching with
his bauble to touch the pontifical cross; on the reverse appears the
Mother of Fools attended by a grotesque person wearing the hat of a

PLATE 25.  An insignia carried in the
fool festival at Dijon. Mother Folly
tends her nestful of fool babies by
giving them wine to drink.

cardinal. This reverse side is inscribed with the stereotyped legend, "The number of fools is infinite." [4] If the authority of the Pope is shared with the fool, as the king's is with his jester, then the Church as the Bride of Christ becomes the Church as the Mother of Fools. The momentary abrogation of the Pope's authority in the joke of the fool festival allows the representation of the feminine within the cult, the Virgin and the Bride of Christ, to be opened to kinds of femininity that are excluded from that representation. Within the cult, selfless maternal compassion is represented, but jealous rage is not; chastity is represented, but whorishness is not; silently contained inner knowledge is represented (as in the story of the Annunciation), but mindless chattering (for example, that of Joyce's washerwomen) is not. During the fool festival the walls of the pure feminine vessel admit for a moment the coarse and seemingly chaotic vitality of the Mother Nature to whom the fool belongs. Through the consecrated walls of the Church the fool before the altar affirms his connection with the live earth.

The Mother of Fools is officially represented in the late medieval traditions of folly; more generally in the larger world of the fool show the fool's relation to his foolish mother is only hinted at. And if it is enacted or narrated, it is so only for moments and not in a sustained and consequential manner. After all, the fool's self-sufficiency and solitariness are among the qualities that set him most apart from us, implicated as we are in networks of mutual dependency, including those of families. Yet the fool's relation to his mother, though she is invisible, is fundamental to his show. This is so despite the fact that clowns and fools are at least as much grotesques as they are children. Among the clowns we have seen in the circus we may recall one or another who struck us as, simultaneously, a toothless infant and a wizened lecher full of ancient malice. If we speak of his mother, even as a figure of speech, we must mean a mother who is as anomalous as he is and quite possibly as grotesque. The fool's self-revelation is at the same time a revelation of her. He is still tied to her, and we sense her behind and around the fool we meet; or he is somehow even still within her.

A vestige of the ancient Mother of Fools survives in the modern circus as a clown mother, usually a transvestite man, with babies in a buggy, often twins or triplets, identical with one another and (despite their difference in size) with her. But even when Mother Folly is not visible, we feel her presence in the fool show. We do so, to begin with, because we imaginatively put ourselves, or simply *are,* in the shoes of the fool, and we feel that that is partly the place of the child or even infant. The world surrounding the fool, like that surrounding the infant, is ruled by magic; events seem to the fool, and to us as we watch him, to be happening for the purpose of thwarting or fulfilling his immediate wishes and to be doing so in ways that do not accord with our rational understanding of causality. For the infant the blurred focus of those events is its mother; insofar as the fool is an infant, the magic of his world is that of "the mother"—the fool's, the infant's, and ours.

The figure of the mother is a present fact of the psychic field that constitutes our experience. Our image of the mother has been formed to a large extent by our earlier experience as infants, but that image is alive in us now. Since Freud's explorations at the beginning of the century much psychological attention has been paid to the dynamic effects of the mother image in adult modes of dealing with reality. Those effects are present in all of us, but their source remains hidden. In a normal person both the operation of the mother image as part of his present experience and the infantility of his relationship to it are secrets kept as well as he can keep them, usually even from himself. In the clown that relationship is lived out in what would attest in a nonclown to a pathological lack of inhibition. What he uninhibitedly enacts is intimately familiar to us, but his show is more immediate and full of life than our conscious memories of our infantile pasts.

Some psychoanalytic writers, among them Michael Balint, have traced the influence of the mother image throughout our adult experience of objects in general. Balint describes "ocnophilic" tendencies to cling to them and "philobatic" tendencies to flee from them and seek refuge in the "friendly spaces" between them. Since people are also objects, these tendencies define forms of personal relationship. He finds these tendencies grounded in a person's connection with the "good" and "bad" mother of his unconscious experience. His description especially fits the circus clown's successes and disasters with physical objects and other people, as the clown tries to find them and flee from them, as he seeks cosiness, food, and simply fun, in the process having to deal with the unpredictable nature of the world, including that of his own body (and often especially its excretory functions). Thus we have the impression that the whole world is for him "mother," but, insofar as the mother is "good," he unexpectedly finds "bad" things in her, and, insofar as she is "bad," he finds "good" things in her. In doing so he reveals a clownish version of a fact that the infant must slowly and painfully learn, that the "good" mother (who gives it warmth and nourishment) and the "bad" mother (who scolds or abandons it) are one and the same person. The child must come to understand that he has a relationship to a person whose "good" and "bad" actions make a pattern and who is "good" despite her "badness." The clown reveals something that is both the same and different: the relatively amorphous "good-bad" of Mother Folly.

Though the fool tries to pick pieces of goodness out of the world that is for him the "mother," he is usually unable to bring his experience into any kind of focus. Thus his (and our) sense that the world is for him permeated or even identical with "the mother" does not issue into a clear and persistent image of that mother, whether she is simply "good" or simply "bad" or relatively "good" or relatively "bad." This sense of a personal presence that cannot be brought into focus is familiar to us without the fool. It is an attribute of the unconscious, a dimension of things that has some of the characteristics of the mother in the infant's or small child's experience of her. Jung agreed with Freud that the mother-child relationship is highly important in the genesis of psychopathological states; yet Jung early came to feel that in dreams, myths, legends, fairy tales, and works of art the figure of the mother often has a significance that cannot be reduced to the personal mother of our own experience. The mother often seemed to him, rather, to symbolize the unconscious as the larger background of consciousness. Thus the fool of the fool show not only reminds us of the children we have been but also seems to represent a part of ourselves that has never really belonged to our personal identities. He poses problems not only of the genesis of those identities but also of their vicissitudes at every moment in relation to the unknown. We are all children in the face of the unknown, and this fact, too, is part of the content of the fool's role as a child.

Another recurrent and important representation of the fool's continuity with the feminine of nature and the unconscious is that of himself as a hermaphrodite, his hermaphroditism amounting to a symmetrical stylization of that continuity. (See Plates 26–28.) In the history of folly the hermaphroditism of the fool has been chiefly expressed in two forms: the reversal of sexes (as when the male clown wears a female costume) and the division of the clown into himself and a female alter ego. The reversal of sex characteristic of saturnalian festivals, including the medieval Feast of Fools, provides the basic notion of a Harlequin play by Italian comedians, first performed in 1682. In it Harlequin is the proprietor of two adjoining shops, a draper's and a lemonade shop. In the draper's shop he appears as a woman, in the lemonade shop as a man; he flits back and forth between shops and between male and female disguises. (It is the moment of his reversal of sex in this play that is illustrated in Plate 26.) A customer, Pasquariello, becomes enamored of Harlequin-as-woman, with the result that Harlequin-as-woman and Harlequin-as-man get into a fight, with Pasquariello taking a drubbing between them.[5] A similar ambiguity of sex is displayed in an *entrée* by the English clown Billy Hayden, who chattered, from the back of a donkey, "I, too, was once a pretty young lady. A witch came by with an ugly little boy. She took me, the pretty little girl, out of the perambulator, and she put in my place the ugly little boy. And ever since then I've been an ugly little boy."[6] The hermaphroditic-fool theme recurs in a moment near the beginning of the Marx Brothers film *A Night at the Opera* (1935). The blond mute Harpo is in the dressing room of a pompous opera singer and has been trying on some of his costumes. The singer bursts in and orders Harpo to take off the clown costume he has put on. From beneath the clown costume emerges the uniform of a naval officer, and from beneath that a woman's dress. His transformation into a woman is perfectly in character. Though Harpo is forever chasing girls and at times even suggests a maniacal rapist, his sex remains indeterminate: that of a virile and lewd Shirley Temple. Though Charlie Chaplin is much less a sexual pseudomorph than Harpo Marx is, there have been moments in which Charlie's gender has seemed dubious. In *City Lights* (1930) Charlie, undressing in a locker room, becomes kittenish and bats his eyes girlishly at the tough boxer he is supposed to fight, making the boxer ashamed of his own seminakedness. In *A Woman* (1915) Charlie puts off his characteristic clothes and mustache to become a transvestite and for a while convinces

PLATES 26 and 27. The first plate shows Harlequin as half-man, half-woman;
the second shows the Alchemical Mercurius standing on the winged globe of
chaos. The hermaphroditism of the fool, like that of Mercurius, is an expression
of the fact that complementary and opposing qualities of many kinds coexist
in him. This hermaphroditism implies a very rudimentary stage of formal
differentiation. At the same time, the hermaphrodite is a uniting symbol, with
the power to reconcile the contradictions inherent in the human condition. This
convergence of man and woman in the hermaphroditic Harlequin may be
contrasted with the courtship and marriage of nonfoolish dramatic couples.

PLATE 28. A contemporary version of the age-old motley for fools being taken off by the Swiss clown Jörg Schneider in a strip tease suggesting the hermaphroditism often apparent in fools. The contrast between crude materials in the body of the garment and a finely worked border was common in costumes of jesters: the contrast in this clown's dress is in keeping with the confusion of his sexual identity. At the end of the strip tease, incidentally, he is wearing imitation leopard-skin shorts, echoing the animal elements to be seen in several of the other illustrations.

others in the film that he is a woman. And W. C. Fields in *You Can't Cheat an Honest Man* (1939) disguises himself as a bearded lady. There are traces of this hermaphroditic quality of the fool, as well, in the often repeated clown gag in which a clown dances with a large rag-doll dummy of a woman whose feet are attached to his, so that the only life in her is what ripples through her from his movements.

When the fool's hermaphroditism recedes from view, he often stands forth as the bawd and lecher. King Lear's jester, who has done some thinking about the snares of folly, sermonizes against sexual imprudence; the fool as clown, however, often revels in it and gets away with the grossest indecencies. Our permissiveness toward them derives, on the one hand, from the impersonality and generosity of his sexual interest—it is not so much that he wants this or that woman for himself as that he wants sexuality to flourish in everyone—and, on the other, from the attribute of fertility magic in that interest—he wants natural life to continue and magically furthers it, in himself, in us, and in the world. (See Plates 29–31.)

Just as the fool's ambiguous relationship to the feminine is formally stylized in his own hermaphroditism, so that hermaphroditism is in turn stylized in his interaction with a female double of himself. (See Plate 32.) Thus Harlequin, or Arlecchino, often appeared with a double, with whom he sometimes found amorous consolation for his failure to attain women above his reach; she was called Harlequina, or Arlecchina, and was a form of Columbine. The hermaphroditic substratum of this pair is shown in the fact that one of her principal pieces of business was to disguise herself as various male figures to hide the fact that she was a woman. (In the English pantomime, in which this pairing of Harlequin and Harlequina continued, Harlequin was sometimes played by a woman.[7]) A similar doubling of the fool figure occurs in Papageno and Papagena in *The Magic Flute*. Papageno and Papagena present a neat solution—yet one that touches many complexities—of the important formal problem of how the fool can succeed in reproducing himself outside the encounter of man and woman that leads to marriage and the establishment of a family. The hero, Tamino, must undertake a heroic quest, which is at the same time an initiation, to win the heroine, Pamina, to wife. Papageno, the clown, is ordered to stand aside from this process. He, too, finds and wins a girl, Papagena, but she is a double of himself; thus he enters the encounter between man and woman but at the same time circumvents it, Papagena having (aside from her difference of sex) no identity other than his. At the close of the opera there is a comic

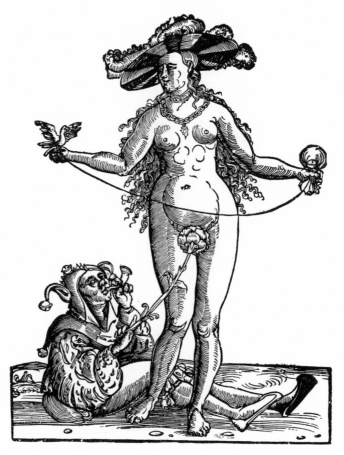

PLATE 29. Woodcut by an unknown German master, based on
a poem by Hans Sachs. The fool and sexual desire. The fool,
tickling the woman with a flower (symbolic of fertility), is
provoking desire in her and in all those who hear his horn and
turn to see her. Her attention is not upon him but upon herself
as desiring and desirable; passively half-lying behind her, he
shows no signs of intending to satisfy the desire he has
awakened. Though there are representations of satyr-like fools,
seizing this or that woman as willing partner or victim, the role
of the *Kuppler* (bawd or matchmaker) is a more essential
expression of the fool's relationship to sexuality. He magically
furthers the procreative urge through a mimic spectacle in which
he may or may not play the role of the man seeking sexual
union with a woman. (In the commedia dell'arte Harlequin
intrigues not only on behalf of his own lechery but also on behalf
of everyone else's: he is the universal pander.)

# The Fool and the Woman

PLATE 30. Drawing by Urs Graf. The fool and fertility. This picture echoes the conventional notion that women make fools of men: every lover of a woman and every man who believes himself to be the father of his own child should be crowned with ass-eared cap and bells—if he has not been already. More immediately, however, the picture calls to mind the transformation of this conceit by Erasmus, who contended that folly is the motive force behind all procreation. The exhibitionism of this fool (carried over in the young mother's displaying of her leg) violates the conventions of the family portrait and effects a reversion to the level on which societies of phallephoric fools magically and impersonally induced fertility. Mother, baby, crow (on the fool's right shoulder), and fool make a hermaphroditic *lumpen* whole. Here that lump is giving birth; in the same moment the sexual elements (dominated by the fool) that have led to this birth are reasserting themselves, perhaps to engender more fools.

PLATE 31. Jacob Jordaens, "The Consequences of Wine" (engraved by Paulus Pontius). The ass-eared fool to the right squeezes the breast of the matron seated before him, while she wipes the backside of her baby.

counterpoint between the marriage of Tamino and Pamina and that of Papageno and Papagena. As the fool pair contemplate their future, it consists of flooding the world with little doubles of themselves (Papagena being already a double of Papageno), the children to be named Papageno, Papagena, Papageno, Papagena, in apparently endless succession. The hero and heroine enter into a royal marriage; if they have children, we can only imagine that each child will have its individual destiny in relation to the pattern of the kingship and the kingly drama. Papageno-Papagena, on the other hand, will reproduce itself (or himself or themselves) in spawnings in the sea of Mother Folly's womb, and each new fool will be a replica of the hermaphroditic clown that Papageno and Papagena together are.

# The Fool and the Woman

PLATE 32. The Swiss cabaret comedians Walter Morath and Voli Geiler in the costumes of Pierrot and Columbine. The geometric pattern of his costume is repeated in hers in the bodice and in the border of the skirt. Their costumes thus suggest the consubstantiality frequently characteristic of the fool and his female counterpart. Often the fool cannot "get the girl" because he is partly identical with her.

# The Fool and the Kingdom

The yearning of the fool for a woman is often ill-defined: he blindly gropes after an inchoate something, often hoping that it will serve as an object of his random and diffuse sexuality. Yet the fool often suffers painfully acute yearnings for a woman who would be, like the morning star, above the urgent mess of his inarticulate will. In the tradition of kingship she is sometimes the queen, but more often she is the king's daughter, destined for the hero. In the broader fool show she is, whatever her social position, angelically sublime. Of course, he cannot win her for himself.[8] With or without a rival for her hand, he fails to win the pure woman simply because he is beneath her. The fool's thwarted love is a theme that recurs throughout films of Chaplin, especially those that have a seriocomic element in addition to the farce that characterizes his earliest films. In *City Lights* (1930), for example, Charlie undertakes a silly yet touching variation of the heroic quest; he does so out of selfless love for a blind girl, for whom he must raise money so that she can have an operation that will allow her to see. The final frames of the film consist of an encounter between them after she has had the operation. There is mockery, disbelief, and wonder in her eyes, as she suspects, cannot believe, and is forced toward belief that it is the baggy-trousered tramp who has helped her. The close of the film is Charlie's face blown up to the size of the screen, looking at her in hopeful fear and pained and selfless love. This ambiguous resolution is as close as we can imagine them coming to a full, mutual, and sustained encounter.[9]

The meeting between the fool and the pure woman he loves is abortive because the fool is a fool. Stumbling into a situation in which he does not belong, he has crossed purposes with the hero; he has got caught up in a line of dramatic action that goes counter to his role as performer of the discrete events of the fool show. But the entanglements and thwarted meetings of the fool and the pure woman also express something deeper. Although the fool seems to be, and is, beneath the woman he yearns for, she often enigmatically seems to belong to him. Both the form and meaning of their affinity, a secret bond that is at the same time a wall of taboo, is suggested by a remark made by Nietzsche's Zarathustra. Speaking of "the most contemptible of all things . . . the *Last Man*," Zarathustra comments that "a man must have chaos within him to be able to give birth to a dancing star." The pure woman, often full of redeeming grace, is such a dancing star far above the chaotic fool (the child who is also the Last Man); she is the form of the freedom that he mindlessly enacts, the spiritual counterpart of his baseness. Something of this bond we have already seen in the relationship between Titania and Bottom.

It is readily understandable that the pure woman whom the fool loves in vain should appear in the form of the daughter of the king: the king's daughter is for both the fool and the audience the paragon of the woman who is for him and for us unattainable, since she belongs to the heroic and royal drama. Her relationship to the fool must be seen against the background of this drama, in which the cosmos is at stake.

Quite as archaic, so far as we know, as the figure of the heroic king is the rite of the royal marriage, the microcosmic re-enactment of the union between a god and a goddess, between a god or goddess and a mortal, or between forces of nature. The form of the royal marriage most familiar to us, from fairy tales and several plays of Shakespeare, is that between the hero and the daughter of the old king. The royal marriage is on the archaic level an act furthering the fertility of the entire kingdom, the royal couple fecundating it through a kind of magical mimesis. Their marriage is, as well, the reconciliation of divergent and potentially antagonistic forces that in their interplay could reduce the kingdom to chaos. This is evident when, for example, the royal marriage assures peace between kingdoms that otherwise would be at war. Their marriage is the ritual investment of life with order and order with life: for the moment of the wedding, things are in their proper places and the world is whole.

The position of the king's daughter at the center destines her for a royal marriage, either with the king of another realm or with the hero who will replace the old king, her father. Thus she often symbolizes both the vessel of natural fertility and the soul at the center. Both are essential attributes of the life of the kingdom, attributes that cannot be governed by the lie of will to which the king is subject. If in a fairy tale the old king is holding his daughter in thrall, there are invariably indications that the kingdom is not strong and whole; it is, for example, beset by famine, a dragon, or human enemies. Thus the nubile daughter of the king, to be guarded yet given away at the right time to the right man, poses a dilemma for the kingdom as a whole, and that dilemma is rooted in something relatively autonomous with respect to the institutional structure of the kingdom: the dilemma expresses both a fact of nature—the moment of ripeness being as ineluctable and even as absolute as birth and death—and a fact of the spirit that "bloweth where it listeth." In the marriageability of the king's daughter the autonomy of the spirit for a moment combines with that of nature; spirit and nature demand the same fulfilling act. What happens in this moment—whether the old king holds onto her, whether she is given to the wrong man, or whether the hero can find his way to her—indicates the state of the kingdom and determines its future. Both the king and the hero may fail to meet the demands upon them; the cause and result of their failure may be folly of one kind or another. This elusive moment is one of the times when the entire enterprise of the kingdom as the living embodiment of the cosmos may revert to the chaos and finally the insubstantiality of the fool show. The danger is posed by the fact that all three figures—the old king, the hero, and the king's daughter—are in different ways consubstantial with the fool.

The consubstantiality between the fool and the king's daughter (as one form of the redeeming woman) is not obvious, owing to the gulf that we sense between them. That gulf is real enough, rooted as it is in the fact that she belongs to the center in a different way than he does. She belongs there by established right (at least until she is given away in marriage), whereas he is only allowed there and belongs to the outside as much as he does to the center. Yet despite this difference between them, both figures are for all practical purposes at a remove from the active life of the center, each of them being a bearer of forces apparently, though not really, autonomous with respect to that life. Moreover, the fate of each of them is ostensibly in the hands of the king, who can have the fool whipped and his daughter locked in her tower. But each of them poses a problem for him and for the kingdom. The problem is one of the king's balance, and that of the whole kingdom, in relation to the larger life of nature and the spirit that the kingship as a process should adequately dramatize. The king's relations to both his fool and his daughter must be based upon the living order of the kingdom and upon an awareness that they belong to it and not to him. If the king loses this awareness, his reign is doomed. He may (as in many fairy tales) be forced to yield not only his daughter but his throne to a heroic suitor whom he regards as an enemy. Or worse (for

190

the enterprise of the kingship that he was to further), the entire structure
of the kingdom may (as in *King Lear*) revert to the chaos of disordered
nature and the fool show.

In *King Lear*, in fact, there are suggestions of a deep and mysterious
relationship between the Fool and the redeeming daughter of the
King, Cordelia. Our first introduction to the Fool is by way of the
information that Cordelia has departed for France; she has opposed the
King, and the Fool will also oppose him, in a different way but partly for
the same reason she did: that his folly has broken down the basic forms
(not only those of the kingly office but also those of simple decency and
common sense) that make the continuing life of the kingdom possible.
And in the final moments of Lear's madness—and of his life—the Fool
and Cordelia seem to combine in his imagination, as though he has
become aware, at least unconsciously, that together they are the one thing
that has mattered (or should have mattered) to him. The relationship
between Cordelia and the Fool is covert in that they never appear on stage
at the same time. This fact is part of what has led some critics to contend
that the two roles were played by the same actor.[10] Even if this hypothesis
cannot be proved, the fact that it has arisen attests to the vividness of the
connection that we, too, may feel between Cordelia and the Fool.

## 11 The Tragic Dimension of Folly: *Hamlet*

According to an anecdote, the cross-eyed Ben Turpin fell into his métier as a slapstick comedian in the silent films from the tragic heights of Hamlet, as he tried on the stage to play the role straight. Whether or not the story is true, the image of Turpin as Hamlet is horrible, funny, and somehow legitimate. Hamlet's "To be or not to be" soliloquy has been burlesqued by many comedians; if Turpin were to have done it as a gag, we might have seen Hamlet's consciousness, which Henry James called the widest in all of literature, reduced to the mindlessness of a frightened chicken and his traipsing about the stage sped up to become part of a frenzied chase.

The pathetic sublimity of Hamlet, like that of Romeo, invites the clown, the noble words and gestures that he apes suddenly seeming themselves clownish pretense. In openly or surreptitiously establishing his parity with the hero, the clown presents a vision of the clod that will survive all winters as the heroic consciousness rooted in the same soil will not. The clown assumes the heroic role in the service of folly; the parity between the clown and the hero is also a contrast that supplies the fool show with materials and energies.

The clown's attraction to the heroic role is partly based on the quality of greatness that the hero shares with the king; but in addition, the hero, freer to act than is the king, stationary at the center, provides a suitable alter ego for the clown in his mobility and his urge actively and concretely to explore the unknown. The image of Ben Turpin as Hamlet accommodates the clown to the role of the hero in an even more specific sense: the presence of the clown within the character of Hamlet is not only a general fact about the heroic nature but belongs to the uniqueness of his character and to the deepest truth of the over-all action of the piece.

Since the time of Dr. Johnson several writers have seen similarities of

192

one kind or another between Hamlet and the fool. Coleridge remarked that in *Hamlet* the character of the fool is divided and dispersed throughout the play, an idea that has also been developed, among others, by Francis Fergusson, Geoffrey Bush, L. G. Salingar and Harry Levin, who have described the ways in which Hamlet for moments becomes a part-incarnation of the foolish presence that can be felt in the background of the action.[1] Bush writes: "There is no fool in *Hamlet;* Yorick [the jester of the late king, Hamlet's father] is dead; and it is Hamlet himself who . . . puts on an antic disposition. . . . With a 'crafty madness,' Hamlet 'keeps aloof.' Like the fool, he is both within and without his situation; it is not only his misfortune, but his tragic privilege, to stand at one remove from the world."[2] This description would fit Lear's Fool, the *punctum indifferens,* as Enid Welsford describes him, of the Lear story. But the difference between Hamlet-as-jester and Lear's Fool parallels that between Hamlet the dispossessed young king (or king-to-be) and Lear the dispossessed old king. Hamlet is called upon to act, though he cannot find a metaphysical and moral basis for the action demanded of him; Lear (after his initial folly) is deprived of the basis he had for action. Thus, although Hamlet and Lear superficially share the fate of the dispossessed, there is an essential difference in the demands placed upon them by their dispossession.

Hamlet's dispossession has come through no fault of his own, but he is left with the imperative of an action that will affect the whole body politic. Lear is dispossessed partly through his own folly, though behind his treatment of his daughters and his division of the kingdom stands his senility as a natural fact; and the range of action that is left him is primarily personal, with little direct consequence in the affairs of state. Hamlet must search for a metaphysical and moral basis for his action, because that basis, as it is provided naturally in the primitive kingship, has failed and become the lie of the person of the king, Claudius, against his office. Hamlet must find his way from his own position, with its personal motivations, to one from which he can act for the general weal. Thus the purification of purpose he must undergo in a sense leads in an opposite direction from that of Lear—from the personal to the collective, rather than the reverse; and it is in this necessity that he adopts the ambiguous, helpful, and disruptive role of the fool.

193

## The Fool and the Kingdom

The background against which Hamlet acts and clowns is the
rottenness in the state of Denmark; more specifically, it is the corruption
of the center, which is expressed (whether as cause or effect or both) in
Claudius' killing of the rightful king and the "unseemly haste" with
which Hamlet's mother entered into her union, in any case incestuous,
with the usurper. What is at stake in the action is the kingdom itself; the
concept of kingship that informs the play is alive with the mythical
significance of the center with its ritual and magical overtones.
Rosenkrantz' speech about "the cease of Majesty," for example, draws for
its effect upon the primitive sense of the king as the embodiment of the
cosmic center:

> It is a massy wheel,
> Fix'd on the summit of the highest mount,
> To whose huge spokes ten thousand lesser things
> Are mortis'd and adjoin'd; which when it falls,
> Each small annexment, petty consequence,
> Attends the boist'rous ruin. Never alone
> Did the king sigh, but with a general groan.

(III. iii. 17–23)

As Fergusson writes (following Dover Wilson): "Hamlet has lost a
throne, and he has lost thereby a social, publicly acceptable *persona,* a local
habitation and a name. It is for this reason that he haunts the stage like
the dispossessed of classical drama." [3] And this dispossession—quite apart
from his melancholy and the other flaws critics have found in his
character—maims his capacity for action, since in the archaic conception it
is precisely the hero's relation to the throne that not only defines his
actions but ultimately makes them possible. And the problem of the
center upon which the movement of the play is based may be seen in part
in the absence of the fool. Just as the kingdom lacks an adequate king, so
it lacks anyone in whom folly assumes a redeeming form: the hero is not
really abetted by his folly, and there is no helpful jester. The ambiguity in
the person of the king is reflected in Hamlet's fluctuation between the
possibilities of heroism and those of folly.

The action of the play, the killing of the false king, requires a hero; but
the problem on which the action is based, the hidden malady of the state,

194

is one with which the hero alone, without the blessing of his folly, cannot deal; a vicious circle ensues that draws Hamlet again and again into the "imposthume" that he should stand outside and lance as though it were a monster or human enemy outside the kingdom. The vicious circle comes from the fact that the integrity of the center needs to be restored, but the abscess at the center destroys the basis for the action needed. It is, of course, possible for a hero to set himself against a corrupt or failing monarch and to assume the throne himself: even the crime of regicide may be regarded as justifiable under certain circumstances, especially when there is confusion as to who is the rightful king. But for a hero legitimately to oppose the reigning king, he must have a clear and undivided allegiance to the ground of the kingdom, to the center prior to its embodiment in that king. Hamlet is caught in the uncertainties which permeate the whole kingdom, in which none of the main characters is sure of his relation to anyone else, as may be seen in the elaborate spying on one another that engages them. Moreover, Hamlet's allegiance is divided between his dead father and his living mother, who, he feels, might not be spared if he were to give his capacities for action free play. He must admonish himself:

> Let me be cruel, not unnatural:
> I will speak daggers to her, but use none;
> My tongue and soul in this be hypocrites.

> (III. ii. 413–15)

in the same moment in which he is fighting to overcome what he feels to be hypocrisy. And insofar as the Oedipus complex, following Ernest Jones's interpretation, is central to Hamlet's dilemma, he is in his personal feelings toward his mother caught in a variant of Claudius' incestuous relationship to her.

The whole kingdom needs to free itself of the murk and disease that envelops and covers the center and obscures the working of the cosmic principle; thus Hamlet must purify his motives in an affirmation of allegiance to the ground of the kingdom, the archaic level of the kingship that overrides considerations of personality, including that of the reigning king. The purgation of the kingdom is, as Fergusson demonstrates, to be achieved through what he calls the ritual and improvisational elements of the play. The ritual elements are in part formal actions, magical in intent, arising from the primitive basis of the kingship and affecting it in turn; they are like attempts at self-healing by a physical organism. He writes: "If one thinks over the succession of ritual scenes as they appear in the play, it is clear that they serve to focus attention on the Danish body politic and its hidden malady: they are ceremonious invocations of the well-being of society, and secular or religious devices for securing it." [4] The improvisational elements of the play consist most importantly of Hamlet's clowning and playing of the madman. By stepping outside the main course of the action, Hamlet taps the fool's ability to suspend and even dissolve personal feelings when they become too sticky: he gropes for the freedom found by the mourner who laughs at a funeral. The ritual and improvisational strands would ideally be united in the figure of the court jester; but the position of Yorick stands empty, except insofar as it is illegitimately filled by Hamlet—as does that of Yorick's royal master, except insofar as it is illegitimately filled by Claudius.

The role of the clown seems to Hamlet to provide him with the sought-for position of a *punctum indifferens* in the midst of the action, but the role is a trap from which he must fight to get out, though he fights in vain. The fool becomes the *punctum indifferens* through the renunciation of action; and to renounce action in face of the threat of raging chaos is to become a fool either in the sense of the failed hero or in that of Lear's jester. Lear can become interchangeable with his fool, because the fool in his incapacity for action and his humble and shrewd acceptance of that incapacity leads Lear toward the moral condition in which he may find whatever salvation is open to him, a state in which he must leave off posturing as the personal agent of a might he does not have. But for Hamlet the necessity is to become the personal agent of a power that he does not have but should have. It is the power of the hero only partly differentiated from the fool, a state in which the hero is open to the dispositions of unseen powers and to the unexpected possibilities in the present moment for action, in which he is free from the inertia of his personal feelings and deaf to the play of reason when it is not immediately relevant to the task at hand. As Hamlet assumes the role of the fool actor, he becomes dissociated from the kind of folly that would have furthered heroism. It is appropriate to the nature of Hamlet's dilemma that at the peripeteia of the action, the play within the play, he should retire to a position between the Danish audience and the players. It is appropriate because the crucial members of the audience are infected with the disease of the state and because the enacted killing of the king points both to the source of that disease in the past and to the task demanded of the hero in the future. If (from Hamlet's viewpoint) the essentials of the action can be reduced to drama, there is a chance that the real world, momentarily focused in the spectacle, will become irradiated with the relative clarity and consciseness of the playlet and that Hamlet will be jarred from his own dramatic role-playing to become an actor in the world.

Fergusson writes about the play within the play that it is

> a "ritual" in that it assembles the whole tribe for an act symbolic of their deepest welfare; it is false and ineffective, like the other public occasions, in that the Danes do not really understand or intend the enactment which they witness. It is, on the other hand, not a true ritual, but an improvisation—for here the role of Hamlet, as showman, as master of ceremonies, as clown, as night-club entertainer who lewdly jokes with the embarrassed patrons—Hamlet the ironist, in sharpest contact with the audience on-stage and audience off-stage, yet a bit outside the literal belief in the story: it is here that this aspect of Hamlet's role is clearest.[5]

Moreover, when the mousetrap springs, Hamlet, who has been the failed hero, emerges not as a hero but as a failed fool. And even if he is, as a result, moved to action, part of his energies must continue to leak into the role of the unsuccessful fool-as-mock-hero, to which he has unwittingly committed himself.

The play within the play is superficially like jokes that jesters have made about the weaknesses, vices, and even villainies of their masters, but those jokes could be permitted and laughed at because the king and the jester were each in his place according to a convention that supported, even while mocking, the king's pretense of power. That Hamlet in his complex reaction to the playlet is on the verge of laughter is in keeping with Freud's idea that a joke often contains some kind of illicit material (of a sexual or aggressive nature) and that the person telling the joke uses the reaction of the hearer as a justification for his reveling in that

material.[6] But a good joke does provoke laughter. According to the
plausible notion of Helmuth Plessner, laughter is an autonomous reaction
to a situation to which there is no answer according to one's habitual ways
of thought and feeling and which is at the same time unthreatening;
Hamlet's play is threatening in the extreme. It is like a joke in which the
malice of the teller toward the listener is splashed like acid, the grimacing
teller caught without the jester's mask of innocence, inconsequence, and
unrelatedness. It is also like a joke with an even more specifically sinister
purpose, which the teller gratuitously and pointlessly reveals—as when
one politician or businessman intends to cheat another, makes a joke
about cheating him, and, instead of luring him into the belief that the
possibility of his being cheated is only a joke, puts him into a panic. Like
the joke in Freud's description of it, the play within the play can be seen
as an attempt to objectify Hamlet's anxieties, to justify them, and at the
same time to relieve them in a wish-fulfilling fantasy. If the point of such
a loaded joke does not open into the impersonal freedom of folly and thus
meet Plessner's criteria for what is laughable, the joke is no longer a joke
but an act of aggression or of self-immolation or of both. Hamlet's
entertainment is both; it goads the king, and its point spreads like poison,
working from him to Gertrude to Polonius to Laertes to Ophelia.
Hamlet's position at the edge of the stage is that of both the clown and
the stage manager and master of dramatic illusion. Dramatic illusion, the
clown's presence, and heroic purpose cancel one another out in the offense
of a bad joke that makes the teller a marked man.

In Fergusson's summary, "The performance of Hamlet's play is both
rite and entertainment, and shows the Prince as at once clown and ritual
head of state."[7] But the reunion of the two separate figures of clown and
ritual head of state in the larger pattern of the kingship is the culmination
of a long process. In becoming the hero in a public sense, the hero divests
himself of that folly until the moment of his full power, when at his
accession that power is bound. Then his folly re-emerges embodied in the
fool actor as jester, who will re-establish his connection to the foolish
ground from which he has separated himself. Hamlet, wise much before
his time in the way the old king should be and lacking both the king's
position and a jester of his own, must stumble in and out of the folly
which he tries simultaneously to divest himself of and to enact. His course

198

from this moment leads as though inevitably to the scene in which, in Fergusson's words, "Hamlet jokes and moralizes with the Gravedigger and Horatio. He feels like the gag-man and royal victim in one." [8] The skull of Yorick, the late and rightful king's jester, is like a lodestone to which he is drawn throughout the action, while intending instead to earn his right to his father's throne. The death's-head and skeleton are traditional emblems of the fool in the sense that death makes a fool of life's joys and purposes, as may be seen in graphic representations by Dürer, Holbein, and others.[9] And even more in keeping with the fundamental action of the play, the hero-prince's familiarity with the cynical Gravedigger as they contemplate the skull of the jester is a final epiphany, outside the course of consequential events, of the disintegration of the social structure, the death of the body politic that now can only await renewal from without.

However, Yorick's skull is an emblem of Hamlet's folly in a more personal sense as well. James Kirsch is convincing in his suggestion that the death of Ophelia means symbolically the death of Hamlet's soul; [10] by the time Hamlet encounters the grave-digging clowns he is himself one of the living dead. Moreover, the fact that the skull is unearthed in the grave intended for her implies a relation between the jester and the girl as factors in Hamlet's fate. In this light the skull may be taken to represent a single ambiguous psychic content that has expressed itself in both Hamlet's clowning and Ophelia's madness. Through his clowning he has sought, as Yorick surely had before him, to sustain the value of his father's kingship and to accommodate it to the circumstances of the kingdom. But even if Hamlet could somehow have managed the illegitimate amalgamation of princely and foolish roles in which he was caught, his clowning would still have remained contaminated by the self-destructive actual madness of Ophelia, since he was bound to her by affective ties, and these, in turn, entailed projections of psychic determinants within himself.

The character of this amalgamation of roles, and its self-destructive motivation, may be seen in Hamlet's famous question, "To be, or not to be . . . ?" (III. i. 56). The ego has no right to ask such a question; asking it is a form of psychic self-mutilation—in psychoanalytic terms, of self-castration—the deliberate abandonment of any possible basis for action. If we draw ourselves up enough to reject Hamlet's pathos, we may see this question as an intellectual equivalent of a clown's attempt to take a step with one foot while standing on it with the other. Or we may treat Hamlet's pathos more respectfully by regarding the question as an intellectual equivalent of Ophelia's suicide. This crucial question of the dispossessed royal person will give way in *King Lear* to another: "Who is it that can tell me who I am?" (I. iv. 50). The Fool's answer there—"Lear's shadow" (l. 251)—means in part that *the jester,* facing death *with* his royal master, serving as *Psychopompos* or *Seelenführer,* as guide to the living soul, can tell him who he is. But here, in *Hamlet,* the dead jester seals the Prince's doom. Just as Hamlet has been unable to find his way through his personal entanglements to a living connection with the center, so he has failed to achieve a connection with folly as the play of life furthering heroic purpose. In Yorick's skull, joy is dead and laughter silenced. In Yorick's skull, too, the force is at last objectified that has blocked Hamlet from assuming his father's throne and marrying his destined bride. (This objectification takes place somewhat in the way that a feeling-toned unconscious complex of archetypal character is sometimes revealed in the course of psychotherapy.) Hamlet's encounter with the skull might thus have signaled a new and more adequate differentiation of his motives and purposes, if it were not too late. But death has already won—and death's accomplices and foes, the grave-digging clowns.

# 12 The Comic Dimension of Folly: Buster Keaton's *The General*

In the character of Hamlet the ambiguity between heroism and folly is tragic; in other dramatic and fictional characters (for example, Don Quixote) it is comic. In the more farcical forms of comedy the ambiguity tends to disappear altogether, the heroic being reduced to burlesque. And when the ambiguity is present in them, it is embodied less often in one character than in two or more (for example, in servant and master). Occasionally, however, the ambiguity is embodied in a single comic character who in part behaves farcically. Such characters have been more common and more successfully realized in the cinema than on the stage, perhaps because the cinema can create a fluid setting that is a serviceable compromise between the abstract space of the fool show and the more particular space of drama. (A clown may perform against almost any background, his tricks and jokes rarely representing actions in a definite time and place. In drama, on the other hand, some definition of time and space is usually required, even when the piece is highly formalized and nonrealistic.) In the cinema no one has explored this ambiguity, allowing it to yield to farce, more masterfully than Buster Keaton. I want briefly to compare *Hamlet* with Keaton's poignant, beautiful, and very funny film *The General* (1926), though this means shifting from one period to another and one set of conventions to another and pausing in our concern with kingship and the king. There is a basis for the comparison: the film is concerned, as *Hamlet* is, with the division of the realm, and the main figure of the film, like that of the play, is a fool-hero. Moreover, though there is no king in the film, at moments Keaton fulfills some of the functions of the jester to authority. The comparison must result in what Kenneth Burke has called "perspective by incongruity"; in it we may focus attention upon Hamlet as well as upon Keaton.

In *The General* Keaton is Johnny Gray, a locomotive driver somewhere in the American South just before the outbreak of the Civil War. At different moments we see him with two photographs which express his

201

loves and aspirations. One photograph, of his vapidly sweet girl friend, hangs in the cab of his locomotive (named "The General"); the other, of himself in front of the locomotive, is a present from him to her. In the first minutes of the film we see him being adored (in his capacity as locomotive driver) by little boys, who follow him into the house of the girl. He tries shyly and stiffly to court her in their presence; embarrassed by them, he tricks them into leaving and resumes his courting, just as shyly and stiffly. The film is occupied with the realization in action of his love and his commitment, on the one hand, to the boyish ideal of himself as a hero and, on the other, to the girl whom he hopes to win with that heroism. What the audience senses as foolish from the outset is the contrast between his and her stereotyped, conventional opinions of what the world is and what people are and should be and the freakishness of the events that must, simply by virtue of the presence he emanates, befall them.

War is declared; Johnny Gray tries to enlist in the army but is refused (because he has the essential job of locomotive driver, though neither he nor she understands the reason for his rejection); and she turns him down in favor of another man, who succeeds in enlisting and later even in being wounded. Through many queer turns of events, Johnny Gray, alone in his locomotive, unwittingly penetrates the enemy lines and rescues the girl, who has been captured in the meantime by the Union troops. He becomes the hero of various fantastic and successful military operations and even manages singlehandedly to capture the enemy general and deliver him up. Through his burlesque heroism the fool wins the girl.

In keeping with the borderline position of the fool, Johnny Gray is, through much of the action, behind enemy lines, disguised as one of the enemy; this leads to situations in which the Confederate troops take him to be on the Union side. Moreover, all of his military exploits are illegitimate in the sense that he does not really belong to the Confederate Army, even though at one point he is wearing the uniform of a Confederate officer. It is as though the urgent and expansive boyish dream that had been compressed into the role of the locomotive driver has now broken loose and dictates not only a course of heroic action but the outcome of the war. And that fantasy of action comes to an appropriate culmination in the final scene. In it Johnny Gray, having won a uniform and a rank by his exploits, is reunited with his locomotive and the girl. He sits with her on the side of the locomotive; while he kisses her, he salutes the passing soldiers in gestures as mechanical as the movements of his locomotive, which begins of itself to move into a tunnel.

Johnny Gray's folly by no means simply negates heroic action. Indeed, he does succeed in winning the girl; moreover, at the close of the film the war seems well on the way to being won (in foolish violation of historical fact) by the South, and he is acclaimed a hero by others for his part in this turn of events. This does not mean that the fool is a hero in fact. His resourcefulness, daring, stubborn will, and purity of purpose issue not into actions but into mock-heroic events of the fool show. His folly leads him into foolish dilemmas, but it also gets him out of them again; it is in the long run, and measured by the standards of practical success, as effective as real heroism would be.

In a crucial scene this ambiguous folly assumes a form strongly suggestive of both the fool as mock hero and the court jester in his relations to the king. The Confederate troops are trying to hold a position against the Union Army, which intends to cross a river. The Confederate general on a horse is directing the action with his sword. Beneath him, Johnny Gray, having completely lost his identity in the excitement of the battle, is imitating the gestures of command in the momentary delusion that he is himself the general. Keaton gives orders for a cannon to be fired. In that instant a Union sniper kills the cannoneer. This mishap repeats itself with a new cannoneer. The third time that Johnny Gray gives the order, he whips his sword out of its scabbard, the blade breaks off, flies through the air, and plunges into the sniper's back. The cannon is at last fired, but by this time it is pointing almost vertically into the air. Johnny Gray dances back and forth, expecting the ball to fly straight up and down and trying to choose for himself a position in which it will miss him. Instead, the ball hits a dam and releases torrents that force the Union soldiers to retreat.

In this scene (as in others in the film) folly has accorded with what would have been a heroic purpose if the fool-hero had been a hero instead of a fool. Since he is a fool, the possibility of heroism becomes material of the fool show. Thus, after the victory at the river, the Confederate soldiers parade in triumph back to the town with Johnny Gray at their head, appearing a hero and presumably imagining himself as one. But as they arrive at their headquarters, he peels off, the moment of apparent glory having burst like a bubble, and returns to his locomotive. So, too, at the close of the film Johnny Gray (by then really a soldier and recognized as a hero) has ended up with the girl, but it is only in a very special sense that he can be said to have won her. Part of what has brought them into each other's arms by the close of the film is his foolish heroism. But just as importantly, they are brought together by her demonstration that she, too, is a fool: at the beginning of the film she was prissily and nonfoolishly conventional, but in the developing action she proves herself to be at least as foolish as he is and hence the right mate for him. Thus, just as the fool may assume the borrowed guise of the hero, so folly, as events in an energetic field surrounding the fool, may further heroic purpose; it may do so in a way that circumvents the agency of a hero. Johnny Gray remains curiously insubstantial; what he does never becomes the expression of a human will that must undergo passion and purification of purpose. Thus the end of the action is like the beginning, and what has been achieved is something that the audience instinctively recognizes as the reality of a fool's wish fulfilled in fantasy.

At the close of *Hamlet* Fortinbras orders the body of the fallen prince to be borne like that of a soldier to the stage, "For he was likely, had he been put on, / To have prov'd most royal . . ." (V. ii. 389–90). Fortinbras commands that the body be taken up and given military burial, since "Such a sight as this / Becomes the field, but here shows much amiss" (V. ii. 393–94). But in fact, Hamlet was not "put on"; he died before he reached the throne, and the carnage of the final scene is not upon a battlefield but within the royal court. Both Fortinbras' orders and the reasons he gives for them signal the return of conventional order, but Hamlet did not belong to it, and his life and death can be fitted to the career of a soldier only by treating the action as closed and by ignoring the complexities of his role within it. He "should" both have assumed the throne and proved himself in battle; in fact he was forced by circumstances and his personal nature to a position at the edge of events, where folly and heroism are a play of energies that have yet to find their foolish or heroic form. Johnny Gray occupies a similar position but in a very different way.

The action of *Hamlet* and that of *The General* proceed on vastly different planes and call forth different kinds of engagement on the part of the audience. The character of Hamlet is humanly real in a way that makes us suffer a recognition of ourselves in him; insofar as he is a fool, his folly is part of a complexity that has a core in which real suffering, moral as well as physical, is possible, and the action touches such a core in us. His clowning is partly an expression of his nature and partly an answer to the dilemma in which he finds himself, but he assumes his clownish stance at the point at which he as an agent is caught in the world. And insofar as his clowning is a desperate evasion of his dilemma, the evasion, too, belongs to the fact of his being caught and returns to it again, and we return to it with him. With the kingdom at stake, Hamlet needs to act heroically but can find neither within nor without himself the line and form of the action demanded of him. In him, action is replaced by suffering; but in that suffering the kingdom remains at stake, because he is the one singled out to act—and, failing to act, to suffer—for the whole. In *The General,* on the other hand, the action is an articulated revelation of the fool we know Johnny Gray to be from our first glimpse of him, and no more seems to be at stake for him or for us than is in a harmless joke. (The fireworks of the action reduce the other characters to scattered part-embodiments of the foolish butt.)

Yet on the level of the action divorced from the emotional attitude it awakens in us, what is at stake for both Hamlet and Johnny Gray is the integrity of the realms they are called upon to defend. The realm of each is threatened with division: like Hamlet, Johnny Gray must try to counteract that division, but in *The General* it is present and actual, not a murky threat, and Johnny Gray's allegiance is simple-mindedly clear. The division of the realm draws each of them to the point in himself at which he is a fool-hero confronted with the necessity of action for the common good. Both remain, each in a different way, fool-heroes instead of becoming heroes in the primitive sense; and their different ways of responding to the necessity for action are based upon their different relations to the center. In *Hamlet* the hero's relation to the center is established in a way that Johnny Gray's is not: Hamlet is a prince, the rightful successor to the throne (the succession having been, moreover, promised to him by Claudius, the usurper), and the burden placed upon him by the malady at the center is his by his rightful, publicly sanctioned position. He is called to action by these facts of his position and by the ghost of his father. Johnny Gray is not called to action in the same way. Of course, when the sequence of foolish events in which he is caught up hurls him behind enemy lines and puts him in possession of the enemy's plans, he must make what he can out of his unique opportunity for heroism. And in the eyes of the little boys who admire him at the beginning of the film he is already a hero. But according to the conventions of the adult society pictured in the film he is far from being in the position of a military general in whom hopes for the success of the entire campaign are focused. And though any man might enlist, in the secret wish of becoming a hero, Johnny Gray is not even a soldier. In the excitement, he and the other characters lose sight of this fact; yet the irony of it adds to the impression of foolishness that his exploits convey to us. For all practical purposes he is *as though the same as* a soldier, although his circumvention of official forms of allegiance puts him in something of the position of the jester who both has and does not have full human status in his dealings with the king. And apart from his role of being *as though the same as* a soldier and from the glory reflected upon him from his locomotive, he is neutral—gray, like his name—a social cipher individually alive only as a fool. This initial position contrasts with that of Hamlet and leaves Johnny Gray free to act as a fool or a hero or both, whereas Hamlet's very real position as a prince binds him to the problem constituted by his divided loyalties and his unclear relationship to the embodiment, itself unclear, of the center in Claudius. Hamlet's position inhibits his action.

Johnny Gray is mercurial and active enough to create a line out of the welter of freak events that befall him. But he lacks a nonfoolish identity, and without it the position of hero that he has won by the close of the action is no more his than are the uniforms of both armies that he has worn at different stages in becoming that hero. Hamlet, on the other hand, is mercurial only in spirit. When he cries that his too solid flesh should melt, he is railing at what keeps him from following his spirit out of his dilemma, which is as real as his body. He is caught in that dilemma

partly by being the person he is and partly by being a person at all, bound
to the reality of being a complex character in an ambiguous situation, as
Johnny Gray is not and could not be without ceasing to be a fool.
Hamlet's fooling is partly a mask of his suffering and an attempt to break
out of it and find a basis for action. Johnny Gray's foolishness belongs to a
fool who despite his heroism cannot win for himself a suffering identity.

Johnny Gray is a simpleton; that Hamlet is not, even if he is partly a
fool. But unlike Hamlet, Johnny Gray reveals extraordinary capacities for
quick and complex action; he is more decisive, even more intelligent,
than we, or Hamlet, would be in the situations into which he falls. But
there is for us an absurd disproportion between his violent expenditure of
ingenuity and what in our judgment it finally adds up to, between the
enormity of his exertions to "break even" with the perilous condition of
being a fool and our pejorative judgment of that condition. His labors at
nonfoolishness are more or less, but not quite, canceled out by the foolish
events in which he is caught, and our feelings about him and what
happens to him are more or less, but not quite, canceled out by our
judgment that he is "only a fool." Thus Johnny Gray suffers in the
ancient tradition of the sad clown, and, although he suffers, we laugh at
him.

Hamlet touches and convinces us as a dramatic character. Johnny Gray
remains semidramatic; and even though his actions conform to a plot,
they belong even more to the dimension of the fool show unbounded by
the stage.

# 13 The Sovereign Fool: *The Tragedy of King Lear*

As the butt of his jester's jokes, the king is a fool; when the play with his jester is past, the king is a king again. But the king may be a fool in other ways as well. Far from being mere play, his folly may induce the anarchy that results when, in Yeats's words (in "The Second Coming"), "the centre cannot hold." The flood of chaos may contain a pattern, but it is one to which the king is not central. His folly may express the turning of Fortune's wheel, with everyone and everything turning, too, and with each coming, like him, to a new position. In the meantime he shares the disorientation and even the dispossession of the fool, and he and the fool may even end by trading places. (See Plates 33–35.) This development is explored in *The Tragedy of King Lear*.

Lear's Fool has been regarded in many ways: as a clown, an idiot, a madman, an oracle, an ironical philosopher who tells the bitter truth, a proponent of learned ignorance, a whipping boy, and a good-natured saint who owes his being to the ideas of Erasmus. Each of these viewpoints has been intelligently argued; each of them is relative to one particular interpretation of Lear and of what happens to him. The crux of the play is the question of whether or not Lear achieves enlightenment and, if so, what kind of enlightenment it is. I will here consider the ways in which the form of the kingship is dissolved in the fool show. In this connection I will comment on the Fool's relation to Cordelia and to the theme of "nothing" and on the King's relation to the disintegration within the kingdom. I will examine in the light of various kinds of clowning four important moments in the play: Lear's mock trial of his daughters, his reported appearance in weeds, Gloucester's imaginary leap from the cliff, and Lear's belief that the dead Cordelia lives. My purpose will be to present the role of the fool actor as an intermediate term between Lear's silliness and madness and whatever enlightenment he achieves—that is to say, as a provisional form of a new and more adequate identity.

We are introduced to the Fool through the information that he has

PLATE 33.  Illustration to the *Carmina Burana*. Wheel of Fortune with rising and falling kings. Though the king is at the center of the kingdom, his reign is in part a process with another center not subject to his power. This deeper center is here occupied by the crowned Goddess of Fortune. She alone remains stable as the wheel turns; the supremacy of the top king, crowned and on the throne, is a momentary illusion that she will shatter.

Wer sitzet vff des gstückes rad
Der ist ouch warten fall /mit schad
Vnd das er ettwann nåm eyn bad

Won gluckes fall
Der ist eyn narr der stiget hoch
So mitt man såch syn schand vnd schmoch
Vnd sůchet ståts eyn hōßern grad
Vnd gdencket nit an gstückes rad

PLATE 34. One of the illustrations to the original edition of the *Narrenschiff*. Wheel of Fortune with rising and falling asses. The figure to the left has the fool's-capped head of a man and the legs and tail of an ass; the figure to the right has the legs of a man and the foreparts and head of an ass. In the figure at the top asininity has completely triumphed over the normal human image; the figure is clumsily trying to seize the ball of fortune. The entire picture represents the incarnation of man in folly. The supreme and blissful moment of being a complete ass—before falling again into the inferior realm of man— is as unstable as the moment of the king's ascendancy in Plate 33. (In the interests of symmetry one would expect a purely human figure at the bottom of the wheel; the figure is missing, because there is no one who is not at least half an ass.) The wheel with the three asses is moving counterclockwise, symbolically in the direction of unconsciousness, in contrast to the clockwise movement usual in pictures of the wheel with four kings. The two wheels represent different aspects of the same process; the tension between them is one source of the life-energy of the kingdom.

been pining since Cordelia's banishment and thus that he loves her, as Lear no longer does. In banishing her, Lear intended to reduce her to "nothing," this being the recompense that she had earned by answering "Nothing" to his demand that she demonstrate her love for him. In his jokes the Fool superimposes upon the King the "nothing" that came between the King and Cordelia: ". . . now thou art an O without a

Ich bitt üch herren groß/vnd kleyn
Bedencken den nutz der gemeyn
Lont mír myn narrenkapp alleyn

vō abgang des gloubē.
Wann ich gedenck sümniß/vnd schand
So man yetz spürt/jn allem land
Von fürsten/herren/landen/stett
Wer wunder nít/oß ich schon hett
r .iij.

PLATE 35. Also from the *Narrenschiff,* an illustration to the lines: "I beg you lords, great and small, / Think only of the common weal, / And leave my fool's cap to me alone."

figure. I am better than thou art now: I am a fool, thou art nothing" (I. iv. 192–94). The Fool now becomes everything to the King, but he retains complex relations to the "nothing" on which the action rests: not merely the "nothing" of Cordelia's answer but "nothing" as a fact of the mind or of the world. In a sense the kingdom, too, rests on "nothing," and this is what allows it to be dissolved in the fool show.

One important overtone of the "nothing" in the play is suggested by the maxim, *ex nihilo nihil fit,* "Out of nothing comes nothing." [1] This can be understood in several ways; it can be taken, for example, as denying the paradoxical Judeo-Christian doctrine that the world was created out of nothing. This doctrine (which is relatively uncommon in creation myths [2]) is used theologically to emphasize the otherness and power of the Creator and the futility of attempts to know ultimate things. But transposed to the level of kingship, as it is in *King Lear,* the idea may be used to emphasize the lie of the royal will. Though the king may have magical and even divine power, he has it in the face of crude matter, chaos, and evil—of whatever opposes that power. Another king than Lear might say, "Nothing comes of nothing," and mean that the king must act and that his actions are real and have real consequences because they meet with real resistance. But when Lear says this to Cordelia, he means, in effect, that there *is* nothing but what he allows to exist. This abandonment to magical thought also leads him, throughout the early part of the play, to deny the evil of his older daughters. He treats the real world as though it were nothing, and it begins to *become* nothing, since despite his infantility he has maintained the archaic power of the kingship. In the fool that the king has become we again see something like a burlesque of the mythical figure of the divine child, though here that burlesque is grotesque and tragic. Cosmos dissolves in chaos, reality dissolves in illusion, and heroic action dissolves in the queer events of the fool show.

When the Fool protests that he is a fool and hence something, he is disguising for a moment a deep relation between folly and "nothing." This relation is another important overtone of the "nothing" that rings throughout the play. Fools are often "nothing" in that they are not fully human and even not real in the way that nonfools are. We have seen this quality in fool actors; it is also present in card games (there are many of them) in which the fool or joker has the value of zero and is removed from the pack. But the zero represented by the fool card is often not simply nothing, but nothing plus an undetermined number. Sometimes the card may be brought into the game and even have the highest value ascribed to it. (The insistence of Lear's Fool that he is not "nothing" but *something* may be understood in this way.) The same ambiguity characterizes the fool in the Tarot pack. In the lore about the Tarot cards the fool is sometimes regarded as the last card, sometimes as the first, and sometimes as being outside the sequence of the cards and forming a link between the last and the first, making the linear arrangement of the cards into a wheel.[3] The complexity, elusiveness, and importance of the fool in the Tarot symbolism is well expressed by Charles Williams in his novel,

## The Sovereign Fool

*The Greater Trumps,* in which the Tarot cards come to life. Among them is "that which has no number and is called the Fool, because mankind finds it folly till it is known. It is sovereign or it is nothing, and if it is nothing then man was born dead." [4] The fool is thus a form of the religious and metaphysical "nothing that is everything"; we are again at the paradox that we have felt in clown skits based on the convergence of opposites and the theme of "smaller than small, bigger than big." [5]

In *King Lear* the "nothing" out of which "nothing will come" and which yet is something, even everything, could be called the *Sovereign Fool.* I mean by this a state of mind and soul and body that is dramatized by the King and the Fool together. "The fool" is sovereign or it is "nothing" in that it is ultimately paradoxical and in that it may assume any value; this means that the fool may enter into many different kinds of relationship with the king. In the traditional forms of the kingship the king and his jester are a *coincidentia oppositorum* combining contradictory and even opposed meanings; whatever form their relationship takes, it has a high symbolic value. We may think of the play between the king and his jester as symbolizing (in part) consciousness and unconsciousness in an interaction that accords with the complex structure of the psyche. (Plaut's notion of the archaic ego component and Neumann's of the ego-self axis are sometimes helpful to an understanding of that interaction.) But all of this implies that the king is a king and can carry out a king's basic functions. If he does so badly, he may be compensated by the fool. But if the king completely abdicates in favor of folly, the psychic system of which he is symbolically the center breaks down; there is a dangerous mutual contamination of consciousness and the unconscious. The resulting state means renewed contact with sources of life and meaning; but it also means dispossession and ruin, since the life from these sources is, to consciousness, partly destructive, and meaning from them is partly deranged. The dangers of this state can be allayed only when the king and fool regain their separateness from each other, when the king ceases to be "nothing" to the fool's everything. By the *Sovereign Fool* I mean, then, the total assimilation of kingship by folly. Lear's kingdom is in this state from the beginning of the play—or at least from his banishment of Cordelia—but the state is at first largely potential.

213

## The Fool and the Kingdom

Finally Lear must become again a "figure," and the "nothing" of the Fool must be allowed to break down their separateness only for moments at a time. The first great step in Lear's return to being a "figure" is the actualization of the state of the *Sovereign Fool*, though this means the disintegration of what he has been. On one level of his character he is at the outset threatened by an eruption of material governed by psychotic processes. The eruption may have the positive result of providing images of his real situation in the world, and some of these images may prove essential to a more adequate adaptation. The storm may break up the identity of subject and object, the object now being a powerful unconscious content; this breakup is a precondition of further consciousness. In any case, the calm before the storm seems closer to death than the storm does. And when the outbreak has come close enough, when the processes leading to it have gained the ascendancy, there is no turning away from it.

By the time the storm breaks on the heath, the *Sovereign Fool* rules the kingdom. The storm is Lear's madness; it is also the dissolution of cosmos in chaos and of reality in illusion. Whether Lear wants to be or not, he *is* still King (as well as a "player king"). But in the absence of a living order (based on justice and mercy) within the kingdom the power of his kingship can take only chaotic forms. He can no longer *act* in a kingly or a heroic way; he can only try to realize that "when we are born, we cry that we are come / To this great stage of fools" (IV. vi. 183–84). And on that stage he can openly assume his foolish identity, no longer the silly butt, duped by himself, by his Fool, by his evil daughters, and by the gods and forces of nature, but now an agent of folly in a fuller and deeper sense, of a wholeness that the kingdom has lost. As he moves toward that identity, the kingdom is sustained by the fool show. If no other redemption proves possible, there is always this, that "The worst returns to laughter" (IV. i. 6). And laughter is seldom so stiff or so maniacal that it does not express a kind of foolish sanity.

The King's movement toward his role as a fool is also a gradual discrimination from it; in accepting that he is a fool, he learns what a fool is. Thus the state of the *Sovereign Fool* is also a state to be achieved—as it is achieved on the heath. But this discrimination must begin with Lear's autism as precondition and as material. Before he can again become a king interacting with his jester, he must learn to accept the reality of people and things in their otherness. This otherness is first translated into the minimal terms of fool revelers or of a clown troupe, the members of which may act out of a mystical participation with one another rather than out of a consciousness of one another as persons. Among this group—of Lear, the Fool, and Edgar—the *Sovereign Fool* is divided; distinctions between subject and object, reality and illusion, love and hate, justice and mercy, can be explored in tentative, playful, and irrational ways.

As a member of this group, the Fool has a fool identity that is relatively simple. (So far as we know, he has no other name than "Fool.") The fool identities of Lear and Edgar are more complicated, Edgar's by the fact that he is a sane nonfool, Lear's by the fact that he is a mad king. It is for this reason that the impetus toward the discrimination between the king and jester within the *Sovereign Fool* comes first from Lear's Fool. And for this reason, too, the Fool's view of the royal office is of interest to us. The tenor of his view becomes apparent if we compare Rosencrantz' speech about kingship with one by Lear's Fool. Rosencrantz calls majesty

> a massy wheel,
> Fix'd on the summit of the highest mount,
> To whose huge spokes ten thousand lesser things
> Are mortis'd and adjoin'd. . . .

> (*Hamlet,* III. iii. 17–20)

The image suggests (and contrasts with) the Fool's counsel:

> . . . Let go thy hold when a great wheel runs down a hill, lest it break thy neck with following; but the great one that goes upward, let him draw thee after. When a wise man gives thee better counsel, give me mine again. I would have none but knaves follow it, since a fool gives it.

> (*King Lear,* II. iv. 71–75)

The Fool would not believe the claim that the wheel of majesty is fixed, and not on a mere hill but on "the summit of the highest mount," since the claim denies what he knows to be the relativity of all degree, whether social or metaphysical, and since he has the already dispossessed Lear beside him. The Fool knows that the wheel will roll down to a plain on which all men share the equality of homeless idiots, madmen, and jesters. He admits that his advice is superfluous to a "wise" view of politics and that he is knave as well as fool and thus has the self-sufficiency and natural cunning to survive where conscious values have been broken down or have not been organized into a structure. For nonfools, to reach this level is to renounce the world or to be debased; for the Fool, it is to affirm both the "nothing" of the "destructive element," linked with winter, disease, death, and nonbeing, and his capacity for making a bridge between this "nothing" and the fullness of natural life.

The Fool's occasional lewdness establishes an irreverent tone that adds to the mockery of social degree, but it also points to a highly important element of the reality the King must face, and it has a bearing on the Fool's view of the royal office. These meanings are focused in the Fool's jokes about the codpiece, the often ostentatious covering of the male genitals in Renaissance garments. His doggerel beginning "The cod-piece that will house / Before the head has any . . ." (III. ii. 27–28) recurs to the problems raised by Gloucester in connection with his bastard son in the first scene of the play. Now that problem is elaborated in more general terms: sexuality makes people foolish, the Fool seems to say, and this foolishness may have dire consequences. In his preoccupation with sexual imprudence the Fool calls attention to sexuality as a dissociable force; he asserts that he embodies it and that his embodiment of it is balanced by the King's embodiment of other forces: "Marry, here's grace and a cod-piece; that's a wise man and a fool" (III. ii. 40–41). The autonomous force of sex, which pursues its life evilly in Edmund's relations to Goneril and Regan, is here presented as contained in an emblematic image suggesting the parallelism between the king's scepter, with its implications of divine power and order, and the fool's bauble. But the symmetry between the two components of the Fool's image depends upon the king's having grace and wisdom. These Lear does not have, at least not simply and directly. The image of sexuality as contained in the interplay of fool and king is a description of how things are ideally, not of how they are now. And things being as they are, Lear still has convulsions of horror at sex ahead of him:

216

## The Sovereign Fool

Down from the waist they are centaurs,
Though women all above;
But to the girdle do the gods inherit,
Beneath is all the fiends';
There's hell, there's darkness, there is the
     sulphurous pit. . . .

                                        (IV. vi. 124–28)

Thus the relativizing function of the Fool, his "objectivity," is
exhausted *neither* in his pointing out to the King that the King is more
foolish and the world more real than he is aware *nor* in the Fool's gnomic
and sometimes apocalyptic counsels of how the world is and how one
should behave in it: the Fool also presents a vision of fool and king as an
irreducible system with its own form and dynamism to which events in
the world are relative. The Fool must balance the King in a kind of
"handy-dandy"; [6] thus he is the spokesman not of reason as an organic
structure but of that structure in its fragmentation and of the fragments
in their relation to the irrational center that keeps them from being
simply "nothing." At the same time, the official representative of the
center, the King, is brought to the state of the fool card in the Tarot pack,
positionless, hovering between an ending and a beginning. The only
action that is still possible is that which serves the discrimination of the
roles of king and jester within the *Sovereign Fool*. Otherwise, there can
be only passion and incoherence.

The turning point of the action is the climax of the storm and Lear's
immersion in as much madness as he can stand before he falls exhausted
into sleep. This is the first moment I want to speak about in which the
role of the fool actor has an important bearing on the action.

The whole scene is, as Enid Welsford observes,[7] a variant of the
traditional *sottie,* in which those of high social station are debased to the
level of fools or in which fools even take the places the great ones have
vacated. In the course of this *sottie* Lear becomes a magnificent figure.
But this is not to say that he arrives at a purification of purpose, at an
insight that makes the audience feel that the mind of the hero has cleared,
that he has knowingly paid the price he had to pay, and that the moment
has now come for the forces of renewal to begin building amid the

wreckage. He goes on ranting about his daughters, giving vent to his injured vanity, enjoying his madness. His pleasure is justified in that the storm of his mind must run its course before there can be any clarity again. But his enjoyment of his madness is also self-indulgent. He has discovered a demonic equivalent of the majestic glory he has lost; he wants to blaze and be extinguished with the flames.

Since the storm is Lear's madness, everything that happens to Lear on the heath happens within him. The two points of connection between Lear and a reality that is not purely private are provided by the Fool and Edgar: it is the reality of the fool show. The height of the *sottie* is Lear's mock trial of his daughters. As he arraigns the absent Regan, the Fool throws off a brilliant line: "Cry you mercy, I took you for a joint-stool" (III. vi. 51). In the Fool's gag we can see something of the way in which the fool show functions to sustain Lear and to help him draw anew the boundaries of himself. The gag is, on the one hand, a piece of the deflating common sense characteristic of the Fool; it is, on the other, a further step into folly—a clown equivalent and transposition of the further step that Lear would like to take into his madness. Through the gag, Lear's imaginings, now part of the fool show, are made to incorporate a bit of the real world extraneous to his wish and will. The joint stool violates the space of those imaginings, that of delusion and hallucination, in the same way that the stage fool does that of a dramatic scene in which he intrudes. The real joint stool is a negation of Lear's purely private world, an intrusion of the Fool's "nothing" into it. At the same time, the joint stool draws the audience even further into *die verkehrte Welt,* the topsy-turvy world of the fool show.

The world in the play is topsy-turvy, not only in that the King has been openly debased to the level of the Fool and enacts his folly with a fool's abandon, but also in that reality has been broken down and reconstituted in the semi-illusion of clown tricks and jokes. It is less important for the further development of the action that Lear does not consciously realize this than that the Fool, Edgar, and the audience do. It is as though the actors of the mock trial draw closer to the audience, to the position of the clown who, at the front of the stage, jokes with the spectators, at the same time that the action opens to depths of horror.

218

## The Sovereign Fool

At the close of the mock trial, with Edgar assuming the role of Lear's jester, the Fool disappears from the play, giving no reason for his departure and no hint of what is to become of him. His parting remark is, "And I'll go to bed at noon" (III. vi. 85)—which is a way of announcing that the world will soon be completely turned upside down and inside out. It may be that the tempest has, as the Fool had predicted, turned everyone into fools and madmen. If this is so, the Fool must leave if he is to preserve his essential freedom, which depends upon his being partly outside, a link between the action and the folly beyond it—or between folly and an action yet unborn. Even if the King may be restored to some slight measure of sanity in the world, he can only become whole, and be again the reigning king, in some transcendental sense, outside the action of the play. We have become fools, too, to the extent of believing that he will endure; and we may imagine that the Fool has departed to be united once again with his master (and fool double), not on the heath and not at the throne of Lear's ruined kingdom, but elsewhere.

Of the three characters who have enacted the *sottie* on the heath, one, Edgar, already had a secret bond with the audience, and that bond is essential to the resolution toward which the tragedy moves. To the demented Lear, Edgar was "the thing itself" (III. iv. 105); to the Fool, he was at first a demon and then another fool; to the audience, he was a sane man pretending to be mad. The possibility of being mad and not mad at the same time is shown. But it is not shown to Lear, who never penetrated the deception; it is shown to us. What will be restored is a way of seeing. It will not, finally, be Lear's way of seeing; it will be that of the audience. The audience will be left, like Edgar, to make what it can both out of what Lear has seen and out of what Edgar and the audience have seen that Lear has not. Edgar is a nonfool who has entered and explored the role of the fool actor against a background of madness. Lear is a fool who should be a nonfool and a reigning king; he has entered and explored the role of the fool as madman against a background of cosmic disintegration. From Edgar's viewpoint the audience will have glimpses of the transcendental sense in which the King is still a king.

The second of the scenes I want to connect with clowning is that in which Cordelia reappears and the King is described as he now is:

## The Fool and the Kingdom

As mad as the vex'd sea, singing aloud,
Crown'd with rank fumiter and furrow weeds,
With hardocks, hemlock, nettles, cuckoo-flow'rs,
Darnel, and all the idle weeds that grow
In our sustaining corn.

(IV. iv. 2–6)

He has become, that is to say, the mock king of the Whitsun mummers.
As we have seen, one of the fundamental things at stake in the primitive
drama of kingship is the "sustaining corn," nature as ordered generation.
Many kinds of counterpole to this principle of ordered generation have
been imagined, and various kinds of relations to this counterpole have
been explored. It has, for example, been placated and attacked; it has been
allowed to possess the king (in an African first-fruit ceremony), and it
has been embodied in a variety of mock kings, some of whom are fools.
Weeds are to the "sustaining corn" as the fool is to the king; on "this
great stage of fools" Lear has become immersed in the autonomous life of
nature; he has become an offering to it; he is a king in the sense that he
draws it to some kind of center in himself. Earlier he had insisted upon
his *rights,* which were (he thought) his by virtue of the kingship he had
renounced; now he assumes again one of the *duties* of the king in the
primitive sense, that of dealing in one way or another, in person or by
proxy, with the forces of chaos that have eluded him or that he has
released. In his dealing with them he is not only a scapegoat: the "idle
weeds" that threaten the "sustaining corn" are full of magical potency,
which he brings into conjunction with the human image—or at least with
that remnant of it that he embodies. He becomes full of the power of the
grotesque mascot. If such a mock king is to serve the human image and
the "sustaining corn," he must have or find clear lines of connection with
the reigning king; the king must stand behind the drama. This Lear no
longer does: he is at the center of it. And there he remains, a focus of
whatever meanings may emerge before the final disintegration.

There is also an element of clowning in the queer resolution of the
Gloucester story, in which Edgar convinces his blind father that he has
jumped over a cliff and been saved by a miracle. This scene has
embarrassed many critics. Among those who have defended it is Ian Kott,

who treats it as similar to a clown trick or to a moment in the so-called theater of the absurd of Beckett and Ionesco.[8] Kott's view is in keeping both with the fact that other important moments in the play have clownish implications and with the strong presence of folly, in various senses, in the ending of the play. Folly is not redeemed in that ending; rather, folly itself is a redemptive force, which begins to reach its culmination by redeeming Gloucester. About this redemption it must be insisted that clown miracles are miracles: they are miracles to clowns, and they are miracles to an audience that has entered the fool show and brings to bear upon it the attitude it demands. The form of Edgar's trick on Gloucester is "absurd" and clownish, and its content is fundamental to the fool show: it is the fact that life goes on and that its doing so, even in the moments leading to death, is a miracle. That miracle is "seeming," but it is also grace. This grace in "seeming" also characterizes the final moments of Lear's life, in which he believes that Cordelia is alive, then seems to become aware that she is dead and, in the last words he speaks, to question the fact of her death.

Immediately before Lear's death we are again reminded of the Fool, who has long ago departed from the action, as Lear remarks enigmatically, "And my poor fool is hang'd!" (V. iii. 305). Critics have argued that Lear is referring to Cordelia, that he is referring to the Fool, and that in his madness he can no longer distinguish between the two. But this confabulation points to something deeper still. Harold C. Goddard[9] has called attention to this deeper element:

> Surely the whole point of the phrase ["And my poor fool is hang'd"] is that Lear is referring to both Cordelia and the Fool. . . . He has *wedded* them would be the better word. . . . Surely this is the main reason for Shakespeare's banishing the Fool from his play—that he might reappear united to Cordelia on his dear master's lips:
>
> Where dead men meet, on lips of living men.

Goddard poses this wedding of Lear, Cordelia, and the Fool as parallel to the wedding of Goneril, Regan, and Edmund (who has had adulterous sexual relations with both) in death. Edmund has summed up this convergence in the phrase, uttered as he is dying, "I was contracted to them both. All three / Now marry in an instant" (V. iii. 228–29). And

221

# The Fool and the Kingdom

Goddard's suggestion of this parallelism is reinforced by the fact that the sinister marriage described by Edmund is also a kind of folly, though in that marriage the element of folly as lewdness is paramount, as is implied by an earlier interchange between Edmund and Goneril. Edmund has pledged his love, or lust, in the oath, "Yours in the ranks of death" (IV. ii. 25), with the connotation then current (and fashionable in literature) of the "little death" of sexual climax. To this pledge Goneril has answered, "My fool usurps my body" (IV. ii. 28). There is reason to speak of these parallel convergences (of Edmund, Goneril, and Regan and of Cordelia, Lear, and the Fool) as marriages, despite the facts that the characters come together in groups of three rather than in couples, that the groupings are adulterous and incestuous, and that they mark the departure of the characters from social life (as the basis of meaningful natural continuity) rather than their entry into it. They are marriages in the sense that the characters within each group have chosen one another and are, to use Edmund's word, "contracted" to one another for better or for worse.

Goddard's view may be taken to imply that at the close of the play there is a reconstitution of the typical pattern in which the old king, his daughter, and the fool make something like a system, the dynamism of which derives partly from its relation to the emergent hero who will win the hand of the king's daughter. This is, then, the quaternity (symbolic of wholeness) that may complement and resolve the duality of the king and the fool and the trinity of the king, his daughter, and the fool. According to that pattern, the old king keeps his nubile youngest or favorite daughter to himself until she has been won by the right man. Thus he may prescribe a series of tests for her suitors—in *The Tempest,* for example, the Duke Prospero requires Ferdinand to submit to such a test to win Miranda; and the king may make the tests so difficult that no suitor will manage to prove himself in them. In trying to hoard the daughter to himself, the old king is attesting to her value to himself and to the kingdom, but he is denying the reality of time, which brings the moment for a decisive alteration within the system. In his denial that this moment has come, the old king is, in fact, denying the value of his daughter, who is bound to the continuance of nature, and she is in a sense put in the position of the fool, the dispossessed plaything of the king. But in the life of the kingdom that moment must come: it is a necessity of nature and of spirit and of the kingdom in the never ceasing conflict between cosmos and chaos. In the play that moment came and went with no attention called to it as Lear offhandedly gave Cordelia away in his fury at what he took to be her ingratitude.

The practical problems with which Lear is faced in the whole course of the action may be reduced to these: What should he do about Cordelia? What should he do about the reality of evil and the ever present threat of chaotic powers? And what should he do about the folly in himself and in the world? Having failed to face the problem posed by Cordelia, he is confronted with that of evil; having failed to face that, he is reduced to a double of the Fool. In the company of the Fool, he is exposed to the evil that he had refused to see; and when it has spent its force, he is reunited with Cordelia. That is, he is brought back to the content of the original problem. When that problem first arose, Lear was blind to the character of Cordelia and the importance of the moment that had come; he was blind to the difference between the Duke of Burgundy, who was covetous of Cordelia's dowry, and the Duke of France, who was not; and he was blind to the difference between his two harpy daughters and Cordelia. What blinded Lear to the contrast was the prospect of a form of beatitude in which he and the kingdom, with himself at the center, would be held in a timeless moment. That beatitude is described by Jonathan Swift (in *A Digression Concerning the Original, the Use and Improvement of Madness in a Commonwealth*) as "the sublime and refined point of Felicity, called, *the Possession of being well deceived;* the Serene Peaceful State of being a Fool among Knaves." With the unrelatedness of a psychotic person performing magical acts to reinforce his delusional system against the threats of reality, the King offered himself up in a burlesque of religious faith to the lie of goodness in which he meant to retire, like a baby crawling onto its mother's lap. As the storm of his madness and of the universal disintegration passed, Lear arrived at a new form of vision that was also based on "seeming" and was also foolish, but it was foolish in a different sense. When he is reunited with Cordelia at the close of the action, it is not as the pettily tyrannical king who has banished her but as a fool who has himself been banished by such a king and who yet preserves the future of the kingdom in his enigmatic relationship to her.

Lear's behavior at the close of the play is in some ways similar to that of the Clown Bébé in a skit performed at the Cirque Medrano in Paris many years ago. Bébé comes into the arena sobbing and dragging a salted herring by a string. Other clowns try to find out what is wrong, but he can only compose himself to the point of blubbering, "My herring!" and then burst into tears again. Finally he manages to explain his grief: he had been taking his salted herring for a walk, and it had fallen into a puddle and drowned.

Bébé's gag touches upon ambiguities of seeming and upon the impulse to charity that are fundamental to *King Lear*. Bébé walks roughshod over our assumptions about reality: that a herring is a herring and not a dog, that a herring cannot drown, since its natural element is water, and that this herring is salted and therefore dead. The gag plays upon what we know of love and upon the curious irreality that death usually has for us, its quality as a mystery and our tendency to look for signs of life in it. The gag also touches upon the ambiguity between love and the kind of sentimentality that we find absurd. Though all of these ambiguities appeal to anxieties in us, we are saved from dealing seriously with them by the fact that Bébé is a clown. His delusion bewilders our intellect and causes us, in the way suggested by Plessner, to break out of the confusion through laughter. Yet we are touched, as we are by similarly tender absurdities of Grock and other fool actors.

By the end of the play Lear has in some ways reached the state of Bébé; these ways are consonant with the resolution of the tragic movement. The issue is no longer Lear's delusion, the poverty and exaggeration of his emotions, and his responsibility for their effects. The "thing itself" that Lear has become is to be accepted in all its irrationality.

Bébé grieves about a death that is for us a fiction, a death that occurred in a moment that can never have been. As we are touched by him, his herring becomes for us magical: if inanimate things are alive, they are so as receptacles of extraordinary power. (The fact that the dead thing, that is supposed to have been alive, is supposed in turn to have died suggests receding levels of illusion common in Shakespeare and the Baroque

224

theater. The effect upon us is simultaneously to make the herring wonderful and to make a joke of our wonder.) We are reminded of the moments in which the fact that anyone or anything is alive at all seems, when viewed against the background of chaos, death, and the unknown, a miracle. And we are also reminded of moments in which life in its fleetingness and arbitrariness seems an illusionary tapestry woven by a transcendent Prospero. Bébé's herring is an instance of the ever recurring point at which the meaningful world threatens to fall asunder and life to be swallowed up in death. But the herring is also an instance of the power that gives the world to us, that maintains its structure even when we have lost our grasp of it. And when Lear appears with the dead Cordelia in his arms and announces that she lives, we are brought by a king who is also a tragic clown to the same point of folly, an imagined breath that is a sign of connection with the hidden center that sustains us.

# 14  The Republic of Folly and the Holy Fool

A fool society called the Babinian Republic was founded in Poland in 1568.¹ The name, derived from "Baba," an old woman, was meant to characterize the run-down manor house in which the revels of the group were held. The society adopted a duplicate of the Polish Constitution and had offices of many kinds waiting to be filled by fools. If someone outside the society did something that was judged foolish by the members, he was invited to join it; if at first he did not, he was abused until he did. He was then given a license with a large seal and an office appropriate to his folly. If, for example, he had talked knowingly of things he did not understand, he was made an archbishop. The society grew so large that there was hardly an important person in any branch of church or government who did not hold an office in it. Finally the King of Poland, Sigismund August II, asked whether the Babinian Republic also had a king and was told that as long as he lived the society would not dream of electing another.

Like other saturnalian revels, those of the Babinian Republic violated the social order to dramatize the conceit that everyone, no matter what his social position, is basically foolish. However, though the conceit was applied to the King, and though he was assumed to be the king of the Babinian Republic as well as of Poland, he had a status different from that of other fools. Unlike them he did not have an overtly foolish identity inside the society and a nonfoolish one outside it: he was the king of fools and of nonfools, his office transcending the distinction between them. One reason for his special status is clear: if he had descended to the level of the other Babinian fools, he would, as simultaneously King and member of the Republic, have affirmed the state of the *Sovereign Fool* with which we have been concerned. He would have become the chief butt without having, on the level of symbolic forms, the power to call the play to a halt and to reassert his ascendancy. He would have lacked this power, because positions within the society were created and assigned by a burlesque but nonetheless potent decree. One of the members expressed this burlesque potency by claiming that the Republic was greater and more ancient than the realms of Alexander the Great or of the emperors of Babylon, Persia, or Rome. This joke implies not only that folly is more permanent than any kingdom but also that the reflection of the kingdom in folly might at any moment prove more substantial than the real kingdom—a variant of the fool problem summarized in Plate 20. By their allegiance to the make-believe Republic the Polish subjects in the fool society may have served the real state, since their folly was a form of the ritualized rebellion that demonstrates the strength of the established order. But if the King had accepted a fixed office in the society, he would, symbolically, have delivered the kingdom up to the foolish reflection of itself and to the powers that distorted the kingdom in that reflection. Ironically, however, to avoid this danger he resigned himself to occupying the indeterminate, half-and-half position—half inside the fellowship of fools and half outside it—that is characteristic of the royal jester.

This was the Polish King's prerogative; others with less right have had designs on the jester's position. Thus Lear's Fool was driven to complain, in G. L. Kittredge's interpretation of the speech, that he was unable to keep his folly to himself: "No, faith, lords and great men will not let me; if I had a monopoly out, they would have part on't. And ladies too—they will not let me have all the fool to myself; they'll be snatching" (I. iv. 151–54). In violating the fool's monopoly on folly, people of different ranks become equals. (The license of the court jester, which often allowed him to present the case for any party, was a form of freedom of speech in absolutistic circumstances, and festival foolery released individuals from their social positions, even if the social order remained implicit in it.) This democratization through folly means a quickening of both social life and individuality.[2] But, as the Polish King and the Babinian fool with whom he spoke realized, though the jester may not set limits to his folly, there is a point beyond which he cannot share his office with others except at the expense of the kingship. In his detached interest in the Babinian Republic, in keeping his dignity, yet letting himself be chaffed and thus in accepting with the proper reserve his parity with the Babinian fools, the Polish King showed an admirable understanding of one aspect of his office. He showed that he did not treat the symbolic center, of which the kingship was a manifestation, as a conscious content, something that he should be able to know fully and to control by will; he showed that he did not deny the unconscious and autonomous potency of that center. He did not need some of the lessons in imagination and civility that Lear had to learn in his madness.

The divinity of kings is paralleled in the royalty of gods, and the same motives that lead to the association between the king and jester lead to that between divinity and folly. Some gods laugh and even arrange jokes to enjoy; there are implications of folly in the story of Christ and in the attitude of the Christian believer, and in many times and places there have been holy fools.

Hermes in Greece, Loki in northern Europe, Maui in Polynesia, and Raven, Bluejay, Coyote, and Old Man in Indian North America are some of the many gods who have played pranks and caused laughter. Though their ethical sense is much weaker than their appetites, such tricksters often institute customs and bestow other blessings. Within the polytheistic societies in which these figures have arisen, their anticultural behavior and its culture-serving effects are accepted as a single whole. In monotheistic societies, on the other hand, the tendency that has made one god of many (or kept one god from dividing into many) rules out this kind of acceptance of the trickster, who is felt to raise problems of understanding, faith, and morals and usually assumes a diabolical form.

The association between divinity and folly that does occur in monotheism is the product of the same anthropomorphic imagination that attributes laughter to God. In general, laughter in the Bible is sometimes joyous but more often scornful of iniquity. God's laughter, more specifically, is a threat to the heathens and the enemies of Israel: "He that sitteth in the heavens shall laugh: the Lord shall have them in derision!" (Ps. 2:4. See also Pss. 37:13 and 59:8). He is pleased by the doing of justice and hence by the maintenance and furtherance of the principle of cosmos. But another conception of God's laughter, that it is good-natured, a kind of forgiveness, when the folly that is its object is not vicious, is implied by Erasmus; this view is amusedly tolerant of chaos in some of its

228

forms. In both conceptions God is the spectator rather than the agent of folly; and though the Christian God may love fools as well as sinners, he is usually thought to do so without being foolish himself.

Folly in the senses of dim-wittedness, madness, or trickiness has sometimes, however, been attributed to God by writers seeking a metaphor for what they take to be the absurdity of things. In this metaphorical usage folly is often colored by the meanness that one may sometimes feel when people are laughed to scorn in the Bible. The step from regarding God as a spectator of folly to regarding him as an agent of it is taken by a character in Iris Murdoch's *An Unofficial Rose:* " 'What do you think now?' 'I don't know. Perhaps that you are divinely stupid and God loves fools. Perhaps God is a fool.' " And, as an agent of folly, God has been regarded as a prank-playing jester. Thus in Melville's *Moby-Dick* Ishmael muses about certain moments

> when a man takes this whole universe for a vast practical joke, though the wit thereof he but dimly discerns, and more than suspects that the joke is at nobody's expense but his own. . . . And as for small difficulties and worryings, prospects of sudden disaster, peril of life and limb; all these, and death itself, seem to him only sly, good-natured hits, and jolly punches in the side bestowed by an unseen and un-accountable old joker.[3]

The same metaphor has been used by many others. In *Nostromo,* for example, Conrad speaks of "This life, whose dreary superficiality is covered by the glitter of universal blague, like the stupid clowning of a harlequin by the spangles of a motley costume. . . ." William Faulkner, too, wonders on behalf of one of the characters in *The Wild Palms* about the workings of "the cosmic joker," and the narrator of Graham Greene's *The Comedians* imagines the ship he is on as "driven by an authoritative practical joker towards the extreme point of comedy." In these remarks we hear echoes of Gloucester's outcry, "As flies to wanton boys are we to th' gods—/ They kill us for their sport" (IV. I. 37–38). But the comments on these writers of fiction are made in passing; they are not grand summations. They lack the force of Gloucester's speech.[4]

In fact, it is usually only in such troubled and querying remarks, and in jokes, that foolish qualities are attributed to the monotheistic God. To generalize the sentiment behind such remarks and to invest the generalization with feeling would be analogous to giving the king a fixed and permanent place among the clowns and revelers; it would be the supreme affirmation of the *Sovereign Fool*. Gloucester's speech circumvents this affirmation because the immediate reference is pagan and polytheistic, however Christian the play may be in its largest statement; and the speech is not isolated but makes connections of meaning with what is said by Lear's Fool, Lear, and Edgar. The novelists I have quoted were writing when the symbolism of the king and the fool carried less immediate conviction; lacking the intermediary term of the king between God and man, writers since Shakespeare have been at a disadvantage in dealing directly with the problem of God's possible folly. It has become easier to see ourselves in the flies than to see ourselves in Gloucester as he sees himself in the flies. An older tradition lives on: there are still, as there have been for centuries, especially in Catholic countries, jokes in which God is both the knave and the butt of his own silliness. However, such jokes are momentary concentrations of an attitude that is dispersed in the laughter at them.[5]

In Christian belief Jesus Christ is God and man, and his divinity is acclaimed in the imagery of kingship. Nonetheless, various details of his life and teachings correspond to motifs that have assumed other forms in the fool show. Jesus, for example, unlike the foxes and birds, "hath not where to lay his head" (Matt. 8:20); such homelessness is common both in the actual lives of fool actors and in the characters they portray. His teachings contain much that is foolish to the wise (I Cor. 1:27), and he made a spectacle of this folly. This spectacle reached its climax when he failed to refute Pontius Pilate's accusation that he took himself to be the King of the Jews. In this way Jesus branded himself a fool in the eyes of the Roman soldiers, who dressed him as a mock king and abused him (Matt. 27:11, 29). Mock kings are very often, though not always, fools; thus Philo of Alexandria, a contemporary of Jesus, reports that the anti-Jewish population of Alexandria expressed their contempt for Agrippa, King of Judea, by driving a naked idiot, Carabas, into the gymnasium, where they "set him up on high to be seen of all and put on his head a sheet of byblus spread out wide for a diadem, clothed the rest of his body with a rug for a royal robe, while someone who had noticed a

230

piece of the native papyrus thrown away in the road gave it to him for his sceptre." Then, "as in some theatrical farce," they hailed him as "lord." [6]

Though the mock king and the fool tend as types to converge in such a way, they do not do so directly in Jesus. It is one thing if the idiot Carabas serves as a mock king; it would be another if Jesus, who is wisdom (I Cor. 1:30), were to be a fool and not know it and be a mock king, thinking that he was king in reality. In this case, Jesus would be more richly funny and more worthy of contempt than a mock king who was merely idiotic. The Roman soldiers understood him to be enacting the *Sovereign Fool* in a way that was mad, sacrilegious, and yet dangerous only to him, since they took his divinely ordained kingship to be only a joke: to them he was not Christ. In not answering Pilate's accusation that he regarded himself as king, Jesus assumed an attitude that was formally similar to that of Sigismund August II, and his doing so may be regarded in something of the same light—though on a vastly different level—as the Polish King's refusal to protest against the joke at his expense.

Despite the solemnity and pathos of the Christian mystery, folly in Christ has found expression in jesting and clowning. Thus a fourteenth-century priest, imagining himself as a jester or comic actor, prayed in his epitaph, "Christe, tuum Mimum Salvum facias," and early in the seventeenth century Homagius styled himself "God's Court Fool." [7] And though Christ himself used the word "fool" in the basic Old Testament sense of the person condemned for imprudence, by threatening his followers with hell-fire if they used the word as a term of abuse (Matt. 5:22) he in effect opened the way to St. Paul's assertion that folly "for Christ's sake" is blessed (I Cor. 4:10). And this assertion, in turn, provided part of the rationale for the frolicking fools who much later pushed their way into the religious mysteries.[8] The medieval fool companies were like the Babinian Republic in maintaining their allegiance to the regal figures of pope and king whom they mocked and caricatured and to a religious truth beyond their play. But in that play they called upon the archaic feeling that idiots, madmen, and other grotesques are possessed by a power superior to reason. This feeling, too, could be made to awaken a sense of the rational unintelligibility and the numinosity of folly in Christ. Jesus' divinity was, then, imaginatively elaborated in terms deriving from kingship and from folly in various senses. Elements from both combine implicitly, not at the center of our attention but at a remove from it, to express the transcendence and totality of Christ as a content of our experience.

Folly of various kinds provides mimetic resources for those who wish to moralize or to express the nature of their personal religious experience. "Holy fools" are often satiric; their wit is basically that of the ironic mocking philosopher of Plato's dialogues. The Platonic ironist "is exactly like the busts of Silenus, which are set up in the statuaries' shops, holding pipes and flutes in their mouths; and they are made to open in the middle, and having images of the gods inside them . . . ; his outer mask is the carved head of the Silenus, but O my companions in drink, when he is opened, what temperance there is residing within!"[9] However, this sort of satiric folly must be regarded as a special development of the burlesque of the sacred with which we have been concerned. If a drunken lout impersonates the pope, the terms describing the ironic philosopher are reversed in the spectacle, but it may nonetheless be felt to have a religious implication (for the same reason that burlesque of the sacred is often itself a form of the sacred). In fact, though holy folly may castigate deviants from the religious path recognized by consciousness, more often it serves as a reminder that the most important truth is beyond consciousness and that the path is full of uncertainties; by jarring consciousness and awakening the imagination, folly makes our relationship to this "beyond" more immediate than it was. At the religious limits of discursive reason, then, the various kinds of fools discussed in these pages emerge in the symbolic expression of values beyond it. In Shakespeare and Dostoevski, for example, the simpleton is a figure of simplicity and purity of heart. And in twentieth-century fiction, that of Faulkner, Carson McCullers, and Flannery O'Connor, for example, deranged and idiotic grotesques raise problems of freedom and transcendence.

Some fool-saints of the Christian Church strike us as more prankish and grotesque than satirically moralistic. Among them are Jacopone da Todi (1230–1306) and Joseph of Cupertino (1603–63). Jacopone, who had abandoned the legal profession to pursue a life of religious devotion, once appeared at a village festival on all fours, naked except for a loincloth and the saddle of an ass on his back; he was bridled, with a bit in his mouth. On another occasion he smeared his body with something sticky, rolled in colored feathers, and then burst into a wedding feast. On still another he agreed to deliver to a man's home some chickens the man had bought and then put the chickens under the slab of the man's family grave.[10] The last of these bits of clowning was probably in part a *memento mori*, but in his foolish behavior as a whole the moralistic intention does not seem primary. Joseph was called *Boccaperta,* "the Gaper," because he was slack-jawed and for normal purposes exceptionally stupid. He gained renown by falling into mystical raptures, leaving the ground and flying considerable distances (and in the presence of people who must be taken seriously as witnesses).[11] Levitation has been reported of many holy people in various religions; it has been fairly common in the history of Christianity, but no other canonized saint has engaged in it so extensively. Joseph's ecstatic flights were not deliberately spectacular in the way Jacopone's doings were and unlike them were not regarded as funny. Still, those traits that are most impressive in Joseph—his stupidity and his miraculous flying—are often combined in "philobatic" fool actors. The grotesque and the miraculous assume various forms serving various functions and touch ambiguities of unconscious response; as a result the profoundest mystery and the most ephemeral joke may have similar contents.

"Fools for Christ's sake" are a special instance of a symbolism that is not confined to Christianity: they hearken back to primitive clowning (perhaps especially that of fools who have had their role thrust upon them by a supernatural vision), and there are analogous figures in at least some traditions of all the other world religions. In the Far East, especially in Zen Buddhism, concentration upon enlightenment often takes forms closer to pure clowning than does the holiness of most fools in Christ. The Zen monk Ryo-kwan, the "Great Fool" (1758–1831), for example, once found a bamboo growing up through the closet of his hut. He studied the progress of the bamboo till it reached the roof; then he took out a lighted candle and tried to burn a hole in the roof so that the plant could find its way to the sky and the sun, but he burned down the hut and the bamboo with it.[12] Like some of the foolish doings of Jacopone, this episode utilizes themes that are universally funny and could easily be made into a clown skit. Ultimate reality is not for the Zen monk a monotheistic God, and the attitude to which he aspires is one in which conscious views, especially those concerned with the nature of that reality, are denied. In this sense Ryo-kwan denies himself but causes folly to flourish. His attitude is one that calls to mind not so much the fool as jester, clowning to mime our relation to God, as it does the fool as "nothing," his self-abnegation in deference to the bamboo expressing a breakdown of the distinction between "I" and "not-I." Insofar as this "not-I" has religious value, it approximates the self, which is described in different terms in different religious traditions.

As we have seen, this breakdown of the boundaries of the ego recurs in various forms throughout the fool show. A fool story that, according to Doran, derives from ancient Indian sources, provides a model for the way in which the fool stands at the boundary of consciousness, even when it is concentrated in contemplation and leads us beyond it. The simpleton of the story is discovered standing with closed eyes before a mirror. When asked what he is doing, he replies that he is seeing what he looks like when he sleeps.[13] This fool suggests a quietude that is, at some furthest reach of things, on the verge of being broken by the stream of psychic life. We may easily place his folly in a religious context. He seems to contemplate his innermost nature in a parody of the way that God, also alone, consorts with his wisdom (Prov. 8:22–26). If we regard the mirror as that of St. Paul, the fool seems to circumvent the terms on which the Pauline simile was based. He does so in a way that suggests the problem of seeing one's original face before one was born, a topic of meditation in Zen since the time of the sixth patriarch, Hui-neng (or Wei-lang or Yeno, 683–713).[14] Hui-neng, too, used the simile of the mirror, not to describe how reality seems to us now but to describe how it seems when illusion has been dispelled:

> It is like a bright mirror. If no objects appear before it, nothing is to be seen in it. . . . When I talk about objects presented and their illumination, the fact is that this illumination is something eternal belonging to the nature of the mirror, and has no reference to the presence or absence of objects before it. . . . Seeing into nothingness—this is true seeing and eternal seeing.[15]

Though Zen reacted against the concepts it had inherited from India, there is a relation between Hui-neng's view and Indian speculations that

234

the phenomenal world is *līlā*—a kind of play for the delight of the Lord
or the Bodhisattva—or (as in Jainism) a quality of the illusion from
which we must be freed. The fool of the fool show often suggests this
cosmic play and its effect upon consciousness.

Enid Welsford writes about the stage clown detached from the play and
the court fool detached from social life:

> . . . in his capacity as detached commentator upon the action the fool
> exploits an inner contradiction; the incongruity due to that strange two-
> fold consciousness which makes each one of us realize only too well
> that he is a mere bubble of temporary existence threatened every moment
> with extinction, and yet be quite unable to shake off the sensation of
> being a stable entity existing eternal and invulnerable at the very
> centre of the flux of history, a kind of living *punctum indifferens,* or
> point of rest.[16]

In most nonfools this "twofold consciousness" is an anxious wavering. In
their real or pretended psychic dissociation, fools enact threats to the
stability of the ego; at the same time they are often enacting the
renunciation and self-forgetting, or self-remembering, that is in some
traditions felt to be demanded by the sense of cosmic play.

However, for most of us, fools and nonfools alike, life is largely action,
a play upon a stage, as it was for Hamlet. The "wooden 'O'" of the
theater is in one sense the "nothing" of the fool's nature; in another it is
more real than life as we live it. Whatever the nature of the theater or of
the action upon its stage, the day of the performance gives way to darkness.
There we are threatened with the meaningless cessation at which
Gloucester cried out. It is finally against this background that we must
understand the cock-cry of the fool on the Zurich tram. The cry of the
cock means deliverance from that cessation: the rebirth of imagination
and of consciousness. The fool among us is a perpetual link to the light
and the life in that darkness. The darkness in which light and life are a
hidden seed is so essential that it must share the value of whatever is most
important to us: if the king loves his scepter, he must love the fool who
may take it from him. Folly is thus one of our deepest necessities. The
fool actor makes of it the delight of his show.

# Notes

## Introduction

1. Desiderius Erasmus, *The Praise of Folly,* trans. Hoyt Hopewell Hudson (Princeton: Princeton University Press, 1941), p. 10.

2. *Maximen und Reflexionen,* No. 1113.

3. *Adversus haereses* II. 7. 5.

4. *The Structure and Dynamics of the Psyche,* trans. R. F. C. Hull, *Collected Works,* Vol. VIII (Bollingen Series XX) (New York: Pantheon, 1960), p. 214, par. 417.

5. The distinction is applied to esthetics by Wilhelm Worringer in his *Abstraktion und Einfühlung: Ein Beitrag zur Stilpsychologie* (Munich: R. Piper, 1911). It is explored more broadly by Jung in his *Psychological Types,* trans. H. G. Baynes (New York: Pantheon, 1923), especially in Chapter VII, pp. 358–71.

6. *Character and Motive in Shakespeare: Some Recent Appraisals* (New York: Longmans, Green, 1949), p. 42.

7. Enid Welsford, *The Fool: His Social and Literary History* (New York: Farrar & Rinehart, and London: Faber & Faber, 1935; reprinted in paperback, Garden City, N.Y.: Doubleday Anchor, 1961; reprinted in hardback, Gloucester, Mass.: P. Smith, 1966, and London: Faber & Faber, 1968) (cited hereafter as "Welsford, *The Fool,*" and references will be to the Doubleday-Anchor edition). This book is an excellent general history of fools and fool actors and their counterparts in imaginative literature, and it has a useful bibliography.

The documentation of the fool's past, presented in a way that tries accurately to set down what is known and to separate facts from the fiction of jests and fool stories may be said to have begun with Carl Friedrich Flögel's *Geschichte der Hofnarren* (Leipzig: Barth, 1789). And parts of the fool's history have been thoroughly explored in, for example, Barbara Swain, *Fools and Folly during the Middle Ages and the Renaissance* (New York: Columbia University Press, 1932), Irmgard Meiners, *Schelm und Dümmling in Erzählungen des deutschen Mittelalters* (Münchener Texte und Untersuchungen zur deutschen Literatur des Mittelalters, Vol. XX) (Munich: Beck, 1967), Olive Mary Busby, *Studies in the Development of the Fool in Elizabethan Drama* (New York: Oxford University Press, 1923), Allardyce Nicoll, *Masks, Mimes and Miracles* (New York: Harcourt, Brace, 1931), Erica Tietze-Conrat, *Dwarfs and Jesters in Art* (New York: Phaidon, 1957), Heinz

Wyss, *Der Narr im schweizerischen Drama des 16. Jahrhunderts* (Bern: Paul Haupt, 1959), Barbara Könneker, *Wesen und Wandlung der Narrenidee im Zeitalter des Humanismus: Brant–Murner–Erasmus* (Wiesbaden: Franz Steiner, 1966), C. L. Barber, *Shakespeare's Festive Comedy* (Princeton: Princeton University Press, 1959), Charles S. Felver, *Robert Armin, Shakespeare's Fool* (Kent, Ohio: Kent State University Bulletin [Research Series V], 1961), Robert H. Goldsmith, *Wise Fools in Shakespeare* (East Lansing: Michigan State University Press, 1955), and Walter Kaiser, *Praisers of Folly: Erasmus, Rabelais, Shakespeare* (Cambridge, Mass.: Harvard University Press, 1963).

But the problem remains of who and what the fool is behind and beyond his name, which is often loosely and arbitrarily bestowed as a term of judgment upon a variety of people, for example, by John Doran in his anecdotal *The History of Court Fools* (London: Richard Bentley, 1858; reprinted, Boston: Francis A. Niccolls, n.d., in an edition of 1,000 copies; references will be to the English edition). There are still questions to be raised about the forms and meaning of the phenomena available to us. Valuable suggestions concerning these questions may be found in M. Willson Disher, *Clowns and Pantomimes* (London: Constable, 1923; reprinted, New York: Benjamin Blom, 1968; references will be to the 1923 edition), and the essays by William Empson, "The Praise of Folly" and "Fool in Lear," in *The Structure of Complex Words* (New York: New Directions, 1951).

8. E. K. Chambers, *The Medieval Stage* (Oxford: Clarendon Press, 1903), I, 274–335. Much of this section is concerned with the long history, from about 1400, of attempts to control or put an end to the Feast of Fools. For puddings at the altar see *ibid.*, p. 294.

9. Barbara Könneker denies any strong relation between Erasmus and Shakespeare in their treatment of fools. Rather, she sees two largely distinct lines of development, one of Erasmus from Brant and, still earlier, the *Fastnacht* plays, the other of Shakespeare's fools from court jesters and such rogues as Till Eulenspiegel (who, in turn, derive from the *Fastnacht* fools). The Erasmian fool is for her the type of Everyman, whereas the Shakespearean fool is the outsider; the *Fastnacht* fool is completely delivered up to the power of instinctual drives, whereas the Shakespearean fool is wise. Erasmus' world is for her one in which folly is subordinate to reason and morality, whereas the Shakespearean world of *King Lear* is irrational and amoral (*Wesen und Wandlung der Narrenidee im Zeitalter des Humanismus*, Foreword and pp. 63, 249, 266, 326–27, 365, and 374).

Though there is some truth to this account, it neglects half-lights essential to an understanding of the historical facts. This may be seen in her use of the terms "Everyman," "outsider," and "wise fool." Everyman is, of course, normally not an outsider, but in representations of folly the two belong to a dynamic process that again and again breaks down the distinction between them. In fact, the very notion of the fool as Everyman implies a reduction of someone to no one, of the social to the asocial person. The Shakespearean fool sometimes shows traces of the same instinctuality that characterizes *Fastnacht* folly. And though *Fastnacht* made people into fools, their folly was still felt to belong to the "other side"; such fools were thus outsiders in ways that make them related to the court jester, the license of both being partly based on the same motives. We see, in effect, the easy convergence of Barbara Könneker's two types of folly in *Twelfth Night*. She further oversimplifies the picture of Shakespeare's folly by making a norm of the extreme case of Lear's Fool. We may grant her this, we may see Lear's Fool as very much the outsider, and we may appreciate how hellish the Lear world is; still, insofar as the play is universal, it is a version of the world of Everyman. And even if we accept the "wise fool" as a description of Lear's Fool, we must concede that it describes Polonius equally well; in this perspective "wise fool" becomes meaningless without a great deal of further definition.

## Chapter 1

1. A cock-crested fool appears in Lucian's *The Feast of the Lapithae*. For cock-crowing timekeepers see John Doran, *The History of Court Fools* (London: Richard Bentley, 1858), p. 228. According to Minsheu, *Guide into Tongues* (1625), "*naturall Idiots and Fooles have, and still doe accustome themselves to weare in their Cappes*, Cockes feathers or a hat with a necke and head of a cocke *on the top, and a bell thereon . . . and thinke themselves finely fitted and proudly attired therewith*" (cited in Leslie Hotson, *Shakespeare's Motley* [New York: Oxford University Press, 1952], p. 5). The Russian clown Popov has a sketch in which he comes into the arena with a suitcase from which a white cock escapes. As the cock walks along with him, they make the same movements, as though they were doubles. In Joseph von Sternberg's film, *The Blue Angel* (1929, with Emil Jannings and Marlene Dietrich), Professor Unrath is reduced to a cock-crowing clown-fool who gives his performance the authenticity of madness. (The cock spirit that possesses him is terrible. The benign, apotropaic power of the cock is apparent in *Hamlet*, I. i. 158–61, where the cock, singing all night long at Christmas, is said to keep evil spirits away.) Long before Professor Unrath, a connection was sensed between going mad and being transformed into a bird. Thus according to Irish legend, King Suibhne was driven out of his mind by a curse and "went, like any bird, in madness and imbecility," uttering lamentations; he felt as though feathers were growing from him (Welsford, *The Fool*, pp. 97–99).

2. The text of Shakespeare used throughout is the edition by Peter Alexander of *The Complete Works* (New York: Random House, 1952).

## Chapter 2

1. *The Structure of Complex Words* (New York: New Directions, 1951), p. 105.

2. Walter W. Skeat, *An Etymological Dictionary of the English Language* (Oxford: Clarendon Press, 1882), entry under "Fool."

3. *A Concise Etymological Dictionary of Modern English* (London: Secker & Warburg, 1952), entry under "Fool."

4. *Harlequin* (New York: G. Braziller, 1956), p. 18.

5. *Ibid.*, p. 19.

6. Francis Douce, *Illustrations of Shakespeare and of Ancient Manners* (London: Printed for T. Tegg, 1839), p. 509. There is even evidence to suggest that the English word "bauble" derives from a Greek word meaning "artificial phallus"; see Robert H. Goldsmith, *Wise Fools in Shakespeare* (East Lansing: Michigan State University Press, 1955), p. 105. The fool's "scepter" of the title of this study, incidentally, is a literal translation of the German *Narrenszepter*. It implies, as "bauble" does not, that the fool has powers in some way equivalent to those of the king.

7. *The Trickster: A Study in American Indian Mythology* (New York: Philosophical Library, 1956), p. 182.

8. John Cleland, *Memoirs of a Woman of Pleasure* (New York: G. P. Putnam, 1963), p. 261.

9. Eric Partridge, *Origins: A Short Etymological Dictionary of Modern English* (New York: Macmillan, 1966), entry under "Clown."

10. On the development of Clown see M. Willson Disher, *Clowns and Pantomimes* (London: Constable, 1923), pp. 86–88 and 185–202 ("Circus Clowns"), especially 188–89 and 196.

11. In this study "clown" and "fool" are used sometimes synonymously, sometimes not, in a compromise between current and earlier usage. The compromise is intended sometimes to suggest the singleness of the fool in diverse manifestations and sometimes the diversity within that singleness. "Fool" is the more general term; when it takes on a more specific meaning, it calls to mind the inadequacy or oddness of the silly person's point of view. The notion of the fool as sage is still alive; the word "clown" does not suggest wisdom. It suggests, rather, that a person makes a public display of his silliness for his own fun or that of others. "Clown" calls to mind a more bodily presence than that conveyed by "fool." Thus I sometimes use "clown" to make it clear that the person does not merely have an odd viewpoint and is not primarily a sage or holy man but deliberately makes a display of folly.

12. *Clowns and Pantomimes*, p. 33.

13. *Ibid.*, p. 34.

14. Ernest Weekley, *An Etymological Dictionary of Modern English* (New York: Dover Publications, 1967), entry under "Jest."

15. Sidney Tarachow, "Circuses and Clowns," in Geza Roheim (ed.), *Psychoanalysis and the Social Sciences* (New York: International Universities Press, 1951), III, 171. According to Erica Tietze-Conrat, "even in times when a jester really had to be 'fool' the word had a wider span: actors, minstrels, tumblers of all kinds; knaves, criminals, idiots; monsters and dwarfs, and innumerable variations of each kind—all fell under this heading" (*Dwarfs and Jesters in Art* [New York: Phaidon, 1957], p. 7).

16. *The Fool*, p. 55.

17. On the Egyptian jester see Tietze-Conrat, *Dwarfs and Jesters in Art*, p. 9, and

Welsford, *The Fool,* pp. 56–57. On Chinese dwarf jesters and pre-Columbian jesters see Tietze-Conrat, p. 86. John Doran asserts that Cortez sent two Aztec mountebanks to Rome to amuse Clement VII, the European household fool having already been imported into America (*The History of Court Fools* [London: Richard Bentley, 1858], pp. 79–80). On Roman cripples and freaks and Cardinal Vitelli's banquet see Tietze-Conrat, pp. 8 and 14, and on Greek chests for deforming children see *ibid.,* p. 7. On court dwarfs, artificial dwarfing, and the recipe mentioned, as well as on the organized stealing of children for mutilation and their employment as freaks, see John Boynton Kaiser, "The Comprachicos," *Journal of the American Institute of Criminal Law and Criminology,* IV, No. 2 (July, 1913), 247–64, and Edward J. Wood, *Giants and Dwarfs* (London: Richard Bentley, 1868), p. 261.

18. James G. Frazer, *The Golden Bough,* Part I: *The Magic Art and the Evolution of Kings* (New York: Macmillan, 1935), I, 279 f. Enid Welsford relates Winwood Reade's observation that in Africa albinos and dwarfs were *ipso facto* regarded as priests and magicians, and it is still widely believed in Europe that touching the hump of a hunchback brings good luck. Throughout the Greco-Roman world small bronze and terra-cotta figures were made to represent grotesques of various kinds: hunchbacks, pygmies, dwarfs, Negroes, and living skeletons; these figures included caricatures of normal people, the men usually represented as bald or idiotic or having an exaggerated phallus. It has been argued that they are portraits of mimic fool actors but also that they are mascots which served a magical purpose. According to Pollux, smiths fashioned "laughable things" called *Baskania* and placed them in front of their ovens to ward off the evil eye. Enid Welsford (*The Fool,* pp. 58 and 61), paraphrasing Phrynichus, describes these *Baskania* as "objects representing distorted human shapes which were hung outside workshops to prevent them from being bewitched. The possession of a hunchback, a bald head, or any striking deformity, is a good safeguard against this malignant influence, presumably because such misfortunes render one too wretched to excite either human or divine envy."

19. *The Fool,* p. 66.

20. Henslowe's Diary speaks of "a payer of gyents hose" for Kempe, the clown of Shakespeare's company. These trousers or "slops" are often mentioned by Shakespeare's contemporaries. A German description of the "English clown" dating from 1597 mentions his "shoes that don't much pinch his toes" and his breeches that "could hold two or more" (cited in Olive Mary Busby, *Studies in the Development of the Fool in Elizabethan Drama* [New York: Oxford University Press, 1923], p. 84).

21. Welsford, *The Fool,* pp. 78–79.

22. *Encyclopaedia Britannica* (1960), IX, 469, article "Fools, Feast of."

23. *Unspeakable Practices, Unnatural Acts* (New York: Farrar, Straus & Giroux, 1968), p. 69.

24. Cyril W. Beaumont, *The History of Harlequin* (London: C. W. Beaumont, 1926), p. 48.

25. *Clowns and Pantomimes,* p. 30.

26. Beaumont, *The History of Harlequin,* p. 48.

27. *The Fool,* p. 123, based on E. K. Chambers, *The Mediaeval Stage* (Oxford: Clarendon Press, 1923), I, 385–89. John Russell Brown remarks: "*Ram Alley* (1607–8) by Lording Barry has a clown who dresses as an ape to do lewd dances; Fletcher's *Mad Lover* has a dog-barking episode by a clown who had been in a masque of beasts. A tract called *This World's Folly: or a Warning-Piece discharged upon the Wickedness thereof* written by I. H. and published in 1615 . . . [in attacking the stage] singled out Greene of the Queen's Men for his 'stentor-throated bellowings, flash-choaking squibbles of absurd vanities' and his speciality of dancing as a baboon, metamorphosing human shape into bestial form" ("Laughter in the Last Plays," in *Later Shakespeare* [Stratford-upon-Avon Studies, No. 8] [London: Edward Arnold, 1966], pp. 109–10).

28. *Illustrations of Shakespeare,* pp. 508–9. Douce writes further (pp. 510–11): "The other dress, and which seems to have been more common in the time of Shakespeare, was the long petticoat. This originally appertained to the idiot or natural fool, and was obviously adopted for purposes of cleanliness and concealment. Why it came to be used for the allowed fool is not so apparent. It was, like the first, of various colours, the materials often costly, as of velvet, and guarded or fringed with yellow." On the dress of the fool in Shakespeare's time see also Welsford, *The Fool,* pp. 339–40, and Busby, *Studies in the Development of the Fool in Elizabethan Drama,* pp. 83–84. In *Shakespeare's Motley* (New York: Oxford University Press, 1952), Leslie Hotson argues ingeniously, but very improbably, that the Elizabethan stage fool wore a variant of the idiot's dress just described and that motley did not consist of patches but was a cloth of varicolored threads. E. W. Ives argues, to the contrary, that "if the essence of motley was a strongly contrasting pattern the difficulty of resolving 'motley,' 'pied' and 'parti-coloured' or similar expressions for the fool's coat disappears; 'pied' and 'parti-coloured' may indicate particular types of pattern but both lie within the generic 'motley.' . . . The essential thing was that the fool's coat should be patterned in an unusual fashion. Motley thus had no regular form; variations could be made to please each individual. Checked, striped, speckled, pied, patched, or parti-coloured coats were all admissible" (E. W. Ives, "Tom Skelton—A Seventeenth-Century Jester," *Shakespeare Survey 13* [Cambridge, Eng.: Cambridge University Press, 1960], p. 103). For medieval and antique antecedents of the Shakespearean fool's dress see Allardyce Nicoll, *Masks, Mimes and Miracles* (New York: Harcourt, Brace, 1931), pp. 160 f.

29. In his *History of Court Fools,* pp. 57–59, John Doran derives the European jester's bells from those worn by the Jewish high priests and by Eastern, especially Persian, kings, whereas other scholars derive them from Germanic cult, in which they were used to drive away demons; see Heinz Wyss, *Der Narr im schweizerischen Drama des 16. Jahrhunderts* (Bern: Paul Haupt, 1959), p. 15. It is in any case probable that the fool's bells originally had a sacral character (and that they are not simply a vestige of a medieval clothing style).

242

30. *The Fool,* p. 75. George Rosen writes about such phenomena: "Apparently in various human populations, perhaps in all, there are numbers of individuals who are capable of experiences such as possession and trance. These experiences, which may occur under a variety of circumstances, are characterized in current psychiatric terminology as dissociative states, that is, conditions where there is a division of consciousness with a segregation of mental processes and ideas to such an extent that they function as unitary wholes as if belonging to another person. These states and the experiences associated with them are not innately religous in character, but religious interpretations and values may be attributed to them, thus endowing them with special significance for a given group" (*Madness in Society* [Chicago: University of Chicago Press, 1968], p. 57). Rosen here calls attention to mental processes at work in revels and reflected in the clown doubles discussed in Chapter III and in the holy fools discussed in Chapter XIV.

31. *The Praise of Folly,* trans. Hoyt Hopewell Hudson (Princeton: Princeton University Press, 1941), p. 51.

32. *Ibid.,* pp. 51–52.

33. *Ibid.,* p. 52.

34. *Ibid.,* pp. 52–53.

35. Michael Balint, *Thrills and Regressions* (New York: International Universities Press, 1959), p. 125 (in chapter by Enid Balint, "Distance in Space and Time").

36. *Ibid.*

37. Chaplin's creation, Charlie, is more often than not understood as the "little man" battling for his, and our, individuality and freedom. Chaplin, too, sees Charlie in this way (but then Chaplin is often bathetic and silly in his assessment of himself and his work). Though there is clearly some truth in this opinion, to me the invincibility of Charlie's will is no more impressive than the fact that it is permeated with folly, so that, whatever he does or tries to do, he remains the vehicle of an autonomous power.

38. G. van der Leeuw, *Religion in Essence and Manifestation* (New York: Harper & Row [Harper Torchbooks], 1963), II, 432.

# Chapter 3

1. The first of these mottoes derives from Cicero, *Epistulae ad Familiares* IX. xxii, the second from Ecclesiastes 1:15 (Vulgate).

2. On the currency of the *Praise of Folly* in England in the sixteenth and seventeenth centuries see Walter Kaiser, *Praisers of Folly: Erasmus, Rabelais, Shakespeare* (Cambridge, Mass.: Harvard University Press, 1963), pp. 22–23.

3. *The Praise of Folly,* trans. Hoyt Hopewell Hudson (Princeton: Princeton University Press, 1941), p. 52. Erasmus had the story from Horace *Epistles* II. 2. 128–40.

4. Tristan Rémy, *Clownnummern* (Cologne: Kiepenheuer & Witsch, 1964), pp. 70–74.

5. For examples and discussion of "The Primordial Pair" see Alan Watts, *The Two Hands of God* (New York: G. Braziller, 1963), pp. 49–71, and Mircea Eliade, *Mephistopheles and the Androgyne or The Mystery of the Whole*, trans. J. M. Cohen (New York: Sheed & Ward, 1965), pp. 78–124. The Dromios are special in being identical twins, but Shakespeare employed many other fool pairs as well, among them Launce and Speed, Curtis and Grumio, Launcelot Gobbo and his father, Justice Shallow and Justice Silence, Dogberry and Verges, the two gravediggers, the clown and Autolycus, and Trinculo and Stephano.

6. William Empson, *The Structure of Complex Words* (New York: New Directions, 1951), pp. 107–8.

7. Hermann M. Flasdieck, "Harlekin: Germanischer Mythos in romanischer Wandlung," *Anglia: Zeitschrift für englische Philologie* (Halle [Saale]: Max Niemeyer Verlag, 1937), LXI (N.S. XLIX), 237.

8. M. Willson Disher, *Clowns and Pantomimes* (London: Constable, 1923), pp. 28–29.

9. *Ibid.*

10. *The Fool*, p. 316.

11. *Clowns and Pantomimes*, p. 44.

12. *The Fool*, p. xii.

13. *Ibid.*, p. 223.

14. *Shakespeare and the Popular Dramatic Tradition* (New York: King & Staples, 1948), p. 86. Although it is common to treat the passage as an interpolation, that editorial judgment is based on an interpretation of the role of Lear's Fool. However, as Bethell argues (p. 85), the passage not only is in keeping with the character of the fool as part of the Elizabethan "real world" but also has a good deal of relevance to the deeper themes of the play.

15. *Ibid.*, p. 86.

16. *The Folktale* (New York: Dryden Press, 1951), p. 192.

17. This play, called "L'Enlèvement d'Isabelle, Fille de Pantalon," is recorded in a series of engravings (by Joh. Balth. Probst, first published in Augsburg in 1729) reproduced between pp. 64–65 of Pierre-Louis Duchartre's *La Commedia dell' Arte*. (Paris: Editions d'Art et Industrie, 1955).

18. For Hanswurst's dream see Wolfgang Promies, "Träume der Poeten—'Songes Hanswurstiques,' " *Neue Zürcher Zeitung*, 5271–134 (December 6, 1964), Sheet 4. Valentin's duck-dream skit is described in Wilhelm Hausenstein, *Die Masken des Komikers Karl Valentin* (Freiburg i.B.: Herder, 1958), pp. 37–38.

# Chapter 4

1. Julian H. Steward, "The Ceremonial Buffoon of the American Indian," *Papers of the Michigan Academy of Science, Arts, and Letters*, XIV (Ann Arbor: University of Michigan, 1931), 190.

2. Welsford, *The Fool*, p. 233.

3. Ruth L. Bunzel, "Zuñi Katcinas," *Bureau of American Ethnology, Annual Report 47, 1929–1930* (Washington, D.C., 1932), p. 949.

# Chapter 5

1. For a balanced critical assessment of Lévy-Bruhl that attests to the value of his work see E. E. Evans-Pritchard, *Theories of Primitive Religion* (Oxford: Clarendon Press, 1965), pp. 78–99.

2. *Lehrbuch der Psychologie* (Vienna and Leipzig: Wilhelm Braumüller, 1912), pp. 90–91.

3. "The Ceremonial Buffoon of the American Indian," *Papers of the Michigan Academy of Science, Arts, and Letters,* XIV (Ann Arbor: University of Michigan, 1931), pp. 189–98.

4. In a school class in Luther's time "One scholar, called a *lupus* or wolf, was appointed to spy on the others and report lapses [from Latin] into German. The poorest scholar in the class every noon was given a donkey mask, hence called the *asinus,* which he wore until he caught another talking German" (Roland H. Bainton, *Here I Stand: A Life of Martin Luther* [New York: Abingdon Press, 1950], p. 25).

5. Steward, "The Ceremonial Buffoon of the American Indian," pp. 190–91.

6. *Fools and Folly during the Middle Ages and the Renaissance* (New York: Columbia University Press, 1932), p. 65.

7. Barbara Könneker, *Wesen und Wandlung der Narrenidee im Zeitalter des Humanismus: Brant–Murner–Erasmus* (Wiesbaden: Franz Steiner, 1966), pp. 59–60.

8. Violet Alford, *Introduction to English Folklore* (London: G. Bell, 1952), pp. 87–88.

9. *The Praise of Folly,* trans. Hoyt Hopewell Hudson (Princeton: Princeton University Press, 1941), p. 14.

10. *Ibid.*

11. *Ibid.,* pp. 14–15.

12. Felix Liebrecht, *Zur Volskunde* (Heilbronn: Gebr. Henninger, 1879), p. 407.

13. *Religion in Essence and Manifestation,* trans. J. E. Turner (New York and Evanston: Harper & Row [Harper Torchbooks], 1963), I, 202.

14. Francis Douce, *Illustrations of Shakespeare* (London: Printed for T. Tegg, 1839), pp. 305–6.

15. Steward, "The Ceremonial Buffoon of the American Indian," p. 195.

16. Iris Murdoch, *The Italian Girl* (New York: Viking Press, 1964), pp. 21–22.

17. Welsford, *The Fool,* pp. 138–39 and 151.

18. William Empson, *The Structure of Complex Words* (New York: New Directions, 1951), p. 109; Geoffrey Bush, *Shakespeare and the Natural Condition* (Cambridge, Mass.: Harvard University Press, 1956), pp. 100 and 113–15; W. H. Auden, *The Dyer's Hand and Other Essays* (New York: Random House, 1962), pp. 246–72.

19. Hermann W. Flasdieck, "Harlekin: Germanischer Mythos in romanischer Wandlung," *Anglia: Zeitschrift für englische Philologie* (Halle [Saale]: Max Niemeyer Verlag, 1937), LXI (N.S. XLIX), 329. According to the psychologist David C. McClelland, incidentally, demon lovers appear as manifestations of the "Harlequin Complex" in fantasies and dreams of women confronted with death; see his *The Roots of Consciousness* (New York: Van Nostrand–Insight, 1964), pp. 182–216.

20. Richard Weiss, *Volkskunde der Schweiz* (Erlenbach-Zurich: Eugen Rentsch Verlag, 1946), pp. 165–66.

21. James G. Frazer, *The Golden Bough,* Part IV: *Adonis, Attis, and Osiris* (New York: Macmillan, 1935), I, 273.

22. Fr. Nick, *Die Hof- und Volks-Narren* (Stuttgart: J. Scheible, 1861), pp. 474 ff. This collection presents an example of such an Easter tale. It is about a smith to whom Christ promises to fulfill four apparently foolish wishes as an expression of thanks for the smith's hospitality. The fulfillment of them allows him to outwit Death, the Devil, and even St. Peter, as the smith succeeds in pushing his way into Heaven.

23. John G. Bourke, *Compilation of Notes and Memoranda Bearing upon the Use of Human Ordure and Human Urine in Rites of a Religious or Semi-religious Character among Various Nations* (Washington, D.C., 1888), pp. 8–9.

24. *Ibid.*

# Chapter 6

1. *Tragedy and the Paradox of the Fortunate Fall* (East Lansing: Michigan State College Press, 1953), pp. 270–71.

2. *Ibid.*, p. 271.

3. Karl Valentin, *Gesammelte Werke* (Munich: R. Piper, 1961), pp. 359–71.

4. "Archaic Man" in *Civilization in Transition,* trans. R. F. C. Hull, *Collected Works,* Vol. X (Bollingen Series XX) (New York: Pantheon, 1964), p. 69, par. 140.

5. "The Marriage of Heaven and Hell," Plate 9, line 13, *The Complete Writings,* ed. Geoffrey Keynes (New York: Random House, 1957), p. 152.

6. *Paradise Lost,* II. 900. Merritt Y. Hughes, in his edition of the poem (New York: Odyssey, 1935), p. 70, derives the phrase from Ovid's "seeds of things" (*Metamorphoses* I. 9).

7. The gag is really a dramatization of an old and widespread proverbial expression (still current in Russia): someone "is so stupid that if you point at something he looks at your finger."

8. *Lachen und Weinen* (Bern: Francke, 1961), p. 191. (An English translation by James Spencer Churchill is to be published by Northwestern University Press in 1970.)

9. Edward Whitmont, "The Magical Dimension in Transference and Counter-Transference," in Gerhard Adler (ed.), *Current Trends in Analytical*

*Psychology* (London: Tavistock Publications, 1961), pp. 180–81. The analogy between ego-functioning and driving an automobile was suggested by Whitmont in a discussion.

10. *Ibid.,* pp. 183 and 180.

# Chapter 7

1. Welsford, *The Fool,* p. 278.

2. *Ibid.,* pp. 324–25.

3. Joan Riviere, summarizing Melanie Klein's development of Freudian ideas, writes: "The life of the emotions which is continuously active in us from birth to death is based on a simple pattern: fundamentally everything is either 'bad' or 'good,' nothing is neutral" (in Joan Riviere's chapter "The Unconscious Phantasy of an Inner World Reflected in Examples from Literature," in Melanie Klein, Paula Heimann, R. E. Money-Kyrle [eds.], *New Directions in Psycho-Analysis* [New York: Basic Books, 1956], p. 348).

4. *Religion in Essence and Manifestation,* trans. J. E. Turner (New York and Evanston: Harper & Row [Harper Torchbooks], 1963), I, 49.

5. *Aion,* trans. R. F. C. Hull, *Collected Works,* Vol. IX, Part ii (Bollingen Series XX) (New York: Pantheon, 1959), p. 198, par. 310.

6. *The Archetypes and the Collective Unconscious,* trans. R. F. C. Hull, *Collected Works,* Vol. IX, Part i (Bollingen Series XX) (New York: Pantheon, 1959), p. 164, par. 277.

7. Tristan Rémy, *Clownnummern* (Cologne: Kiepenheuer & Witsch, 1964), pp. 68–69 ("Der dressierte Floh"). Chaplin also presents a version of the skit in *Limelight.*

8. According to the Chandogya Upanishad (3. 14. 3), for example, "This soul of mine within the heart is smaller than a grain of rice, or a barleycorn, or a mustard-seed, or a grain of millet, or the kernel of a grain of millet; this soul of mine within the heart is greater than the earth, greater than the atmosphere, greater than the sky, greater than the worlds . . ." (*The Thirteen Principal Upanishads,* trans. R. E. Hume [London: Oxford University Press, 1934], p. 210).

9. A brief survey of problems concerning the Vice may be found in Welsford, *The Fool,* pp. 285–86. Questions have also been raised about the relations between the fool and the Devil in Continental drama; various arguments are conveniently summarized in Heinz Wyss, "Die teuflische Herkunft des Narren" in *Der Narr im schweizerischen Drama des 16. Jahrhunderts* (Bern: Paul Haupt, 1959), pp. 16–19. See also Maximilian Josef Rudwin, *Der Teufel in den deutschen geistlichen Spielen des Mittelalters und der Reformationszeit* (Göttingen: Vandenhoeck & Ruprecht, 1915), pp. 7–11.

10. The association between the Devil and the fool is still a topic of humor. In *Go West* (1925) Buster Keaton has let a thousand cattle loose in the city. Hoping to attract their attention and lead them to the stockyards, he puts on a red devil's

costume which he finds in a masquerade shop. In the final chase sequence he is running through the streets dressed as a devil, followed by the stampeding cattle; they are joined by the police and firemen. Keaton gets ahead of the police, who are pursued by the cattle. One policeman grabs his devil's tail, another policeman grabs the first one, still another grabs that one, until they form a furiously running chain behind the fool-devil. (This is also an example of the "Stickfast" or "tar baby" motif, discussed on p. 249, that so often appears in the fool show.)

11. The relationship of Christianity to pagan cults of fire and the sun provides a good example of how this division was effected and of the resistance to it. St. Eligius (588–659) decreed that the people of his diocese should not assemble like pagans on the days of the summer and winter solstices: "No one is to dance or jump around the fire or sing songs on St. John's Day [the summer solstice]. These songs are diabolical." The practices he was attacking were ancient—they are recorded in Ovid's *Fasti* IV—and continued to be so persistent that the Church tried to sublimate them. Thus a church song, printed in 1695, from the Swiss canton of Graubünden, includes a verse (freely translated): "Fire was once lit here when we threw the disks [representing the sun] at *Fastnacht* time. Mary, Light, Queen of Heaven, thou hast changed that; thou hast made this place holy so that thou mayest answer our petitions here." These once ritual games continued till recently, despite the Church's attempts at prohibition and assimilation. See Christian Caminada, *Die verzauberten Täler: Die urgeschichtlichen Kulte und Bräuche im alten Rätien* (Olten and Freiburg i.B.: Walter-Verlag, 1962), pp. 50, 94, and 96.

12. *The Complete Writings of William Blake,* ed. Geoffrey Keynes (New York: Random House, 1957), p. 155.

13. Paul Vercors, *Sylva,* trans. Rita Barisse (New York: G. P. Putnam, 1962), pp. 239–40.

14. Ruth L. Bunzel, "Zuñi Katcinas," *Bureau of American Ethnology, Annual Report 47, 1929–1930* (Washington, D.C., 1932), pp. 946–48.

# Chapter 8

1. Johan Huizinga, *Erasmus and the Age of Reformation,* trans. F. Hopman (New York: Harper, 1957), pp. 246–49 (a letter by Erasmus about the emblem).

2. *Ibid.,* p. 75.

3. G. van der Leeuw, *Religion in Essence and Manifestation,* trans. J. E. Turner (New York and Evanston: Harper & Row [Harper Torchbooks], 1963), II, 680.

4. Wilhelm Waetzoldt, *Hans Holbein der Jüngere: Werk und Welt* (Berlin: G. Grote'sche Verlagsbuchhandlung, 1938), p. 43.

5. Arnold van Gennep, *The Rites of Passage,* trans. Monika B. Vizedom and Gabrielle L. Caffee (Chicago: University of Chicago Press, 1960), p. 16.

6. As Mircea Eliade summarizes traditional ideas about these matters: "In archaic and traditional societies, the surrounding world is conceived as a microcosm. At the limits of this closed world begins the domain of the unknown, of the formless. On

this side there is ordered—because inhabited and organized—space; on the other, outside this familiar space, there is the unknown and dangerous region of the demons, the ghosts, the dead and of foreigners—in a word, chaos or death or night. . . . Because they attack and endanger the equilibrium and the very life of the city (or of any other inhabited and organized territory), enemies are assimilated to demonic powers, trying to reincorporate the microcosm into the state of chaos; that is, to suppress it. The destruction of an established order, the abolition of an archetypal image, was equivalent to a regression into chaos, into the pre-formal, undifferentiated state that preceded the cosmogony. . . . It is very probable that the defences of inhabited areas and cities began by being magical defences; for these defences—ditches, labyrinths, ramparts, etc.—were set up to prevent the incursions of evil spirits rather than attacks from human beings. Even fairly late in history, in the middle ages for instance, the walls of cities were ritually consecrated as a defence against the Devil, sickness and death. Moreover, the archaic symbolism finds no difficulty in assimilating the human enemy to the Devil or to Death. After all, the result of their attacks, whether demonic or military, is always the same: ruin, disintegration and death" (*Images and Symbols* [New York: Sheed & Ward, 1961], pp. 37–39).

7. Karl Kerényi, "The Trickster in Relation to Greek Mythology," in Paul Radin, *The Trickster: A Study in American Indian Mythology* (New York: Philosophical Library, 1956), p. 185.

8. Welsford, *The Fool,* pp. 160 and 346.

9. John Doran, *The History of Court Fools* (London: Richard Bentley, 1858), pp. 103–4.

10. In the Grimm story "The Golden Goose" only the fool-hero, who finally becomes king, can safely handle the bird; the many others who try to seize it stick to it or to one another. The "Stickfast" motif occurs frequently in the silent-film comedies. One silent-film fool, Carter De Haven, carries home a Christmas tree, which catches objects along the way; when he reaches home it is festooned with jewelry, a pocket watch on a chain, a small barking dog on a leash, and other oddments. Another silent-film fool, Billy Bevan, tracks tar into a church where he is to be best man at a wedding; the tar leads to many embarrassments—the best man and the bridegroom, for example, shake hands and get stuck together—and finally reduces the assembly to a sticky confusion, as everyone crawls on hands and knees through the tar in search of the lost wedding ring, which is also stuck in the tar. In still another silent film, *The Haunted House* (1921), Buster Keaton is a bank clerk who happens to dip his hands in glue and then tries to count a pile of bills; the result is a gluey mess of money that grows and spreads till it is stuck all over the counter and the floor. He smears it onto two men customers, who get their backsides stuck together; to free them, he cuts a hole in the trousers of one of them, and a woman then faints at the sight of the man's exposed underpants. Another employee tries to help Keaton but falls into the gluey mess; Keaton tries to free him with boiling water, an operation so painful that Keaton first must thoughtfully

anesthetize him by hitting him over the head with a hammer. Bank robbers try to stuff the gluey money into briefcases; they order Keaton to stick his hands up, but his fingers are glued inside his pockets. He falls into the mess on the floor; when he gets up, there is money stuck all over him.

11. *The Meaning of Shakespeare* (Chicago: University of Chicago Press, 1951), pp. 79–80.

12. C. G. Jung, *Psychology and Alchemy,* trans. R. F. C. Hull, *Collected Works,* Vol. XXII (Bollingen Series XX) (New York: Pantheon, 1953), p. 356, par. 459.

13. *Shakespeare Our Contemporary,* trans. Boleslaw Taborski (Garden City, N.Y.: Doubleday, 1964), p. 221.

14. *The Praise of Folly,* trans. Hoyt Hopewell Hudson (Princeton: Princeton University Press, 1941), p. 36.

15. "Alexander," XXVI. 4–6, in *Plutarch's Lives,* with an English translation by Bernadotte Perrin (Loeb Classical Library) (Cambridge, Mass.: Harvard University Press, 1958), VII, 300–301.

16. *Religion in Essence and Manifestation,* I, 115.

17. *Encyclopaedia Britannica* (1960), XV, 341, in article "Meteorites."

18. Skit performed by "Chicky [Altenburger] und Co.," Circus Knie (Switzerland), 1963.


# Chapter 9

1. A. M. Hocart, *Kingship* (London: Oxford University Press, 1927), p. 7.

2. J. G. Frazer, *The Golden Bough,* Part VII: *Balder the Beautiful* (New York: Macmillan, 1935), I, 1–2. John Weir Perry writes in a survey of literature about kingship: "In fact, in the entire gamut of cultures passing through that archaic era, king-killing is evidenced only in certain Indo-European cultures: In Magadha in eastern India among the founders of the Mauryan Dynasty, and in Sweden, and then only in the form of legends on the threshold of history; legend also speaks of it in Greece and perhaps in Ireland. The Africa that has been so much described as primordial is in fact a post-urban Africa with many signs of decadence of older forms of a high civilization resorbed into the jungle; therefore its king-killing could as well be a degeneration of erstwhile ritual death for renewal" ("Reflections on the Nature of the Kingship Archetype," *Journal of Analytical Psychology,* II, No. 2 [July, 1966], 155).

3. F. M. Cornford, *From Religion to Philosophy: A Study in the Origins of Western Speculation* (New York: Harper [Harper Torchbooks], 1957), pp. 105–6.

4. Herbert Weisinger, *Tragedy and the Paradox of the Fortunate Fall* (East Lansing: Michigan State College Press, 1953), p. 271.

5. *Ibid.,* p. 49.

6. G. van der Leeuw, *Religion in Essence and Manifestation,* trans. J. E. Turner (New York and Evanston: Harper & Row [Harper Torchbooks], 1963), I, 118–19.

7. Discussed in Anne Righter, "The Flawed Rule," *Shakespeare and the Idea of the Play* (New York: Barnes & Noble, 1963), pp. 121–38.

8. Welsford, *The Fool,* p. 57.

9. Michel de Ghelderode, *Escurial* [written in 1927], trans. Lionel Abel, in *The Modern Theatre,* ed. Eric Bentley (Garden City, N.Y.: Doubleday Anchor, 1957), V, 161–78.

10. The use of such rebellion in the service of the political and social *status quo* has been studied by various writers, among them Georg Simmel and Max Gluckman. For impressive examples see Gluckman's *Customs and Conflict in Africa* (Glencoe, Ill.: Free Press, 1955), pp. 123–26, and *Rituals of Rebellion in South-East Africa* (Manchester, Eng.: Manchester University Press, 1954), pp. 27–28.

11. *The Fool,* p. 74.

12. John Doran, *The History of Court Fools* (London: Richard Bentley, 1858), pp. 304–8; Welsford, *The Fool,* pp. 186–88.

13. *Gargantua and Pantagruel,* III. 37 (par. 4).

14. According to van der Leeuw, "Royal power . . . is world-power, but like that of the sun it is valid only for its own period. We date according to kings. In the imperial era their assumption of the government was regarded as the commencement of the world . . . ; the Egyptians likewise treated the accession as a constant parallel to the commencement of all things" (*Religion in Essence and Manifestation,* I, 122).

15. Doran, *The History of Court Fools,* p. 68.

16. For a vivid description of the Roman triumph see Robert Payne, *Hubris: A Study of Pride* (New York: Harper [Harper Torchbooks], 1960), pp. 41–44; for the quotation see *ibid.,* p. 42. The phallic, life-inducing character of primitive clowns and clowning—which complements the destructiveness of mocking satire—is expressed in the obscene jests; but it was sometimes also taken over in the person of the conqueror, who would "carry in his chariot, as a reminder of his common sexuality and also as a *fascinum* to avert the evil eye, a red-painted *phallus,* which he would show triumphantly to the people" (*ibid.,* p. 43).

17. For an example of a *quattrocento* painting of the Roman slave as an ass-eared jester see Erica Tietze-Conrat, *Dwarfs and Jesters in Art* (New York: Phaidon, 1957), p. 14. On the jester Faco see *ibid.,* p. 70.

18. Doran, *The History of Court Fools,* p. 83.

19. Robert Payne, *The Great God Pan: A Biography of the Tramp played by Charles Chaplin* (New York: Hermitage House, 1952), pp. 293–94.

20. "Alexander," LXXIII. 3—LXXIV. 1, in *Plutarch's Lives,* with an English translation by Bernadotte Perrin (Loeb Classical Library) (Cambridge, Mass.: Harvard University Press, 1958), VII, 428–29.

21. F. M. Cornford, *The Origin of Attic Comedy,* ed. Theodor H. Gaster (Garden City, N.Y.: Doubleday Anchor, 1961), p. 13.

22. *Die Gekrönten: Sinn und Sinnbilder des Königtums* (Stuttgart: Ernst Klett, 1958), p. 76.

23. *From Religion to Philosophy*, p. 108.

24. Wolff-Windegg, "Die mächtige Hand," in *Die Gekrönten*, pp. 197–201.

25. *Ibid.*, pp. 217–29. "Speer und Krone"; see also the article "Sceptre" in *Encyclopedia of Religion and Ethics*, ed. J. Hastings (New York: Scribner's, 1951), X, 635–36, which describes the "sceptre of Zeus," said to have been borne by Agamemnon in his capacity as a judge. Among the Chaeroneans this scepter was the object of a cult in which it was called "spear"; it has been assumed to be a conventionalized form of the oak of Zeus (article "Sceptre," p. 635).

26. John Cleland, *Memoirs of a Woman of Pleasure* (New York: G. P. Putnam, 1963), p. 261.

27. *Complex, Archetype, Symbol in the Psychology of C. G. Jung*, trans. Ralph Manheim (Princeton: Princeton University Press, 1959), pp. 111–12.

28. Alfred Plaut, "Hungry Patients: Reflections on Ego Structure," in Gerhard Adler (ed.), *Current Trends in Analytical Psychology* (London: Tavistock Publications, 1961), pp. 156–58.

29. See Michael Fordham, *New Developments in Analytical Psychology* (London: Routledge & Kegan Paul, 1957), pp. 134 and 156, and Eric Neumann, "Narzissmus, Automorphismus und Urbeziehung," in *Studien zur analytischen Psychologie C. G. Jungs*, Vol. I (Zurich: Rascher, 1955).

# Chapter 10

1. F. M. Cornford, *The Origin of Attic Comedy*, ed. Theodor H. Gaster (Garden City, N.Y.: Doubleday Anchor, 1961), p. 56.

2. *Shakespeare and the Natural Condition* (Cambridge, Mass.: Harvard University Press, 1956), p. 24.

3. *Ibid.*, p. 31.

4. Thomas Wright, *The Archaeological Album* (London: Chapman & Hall, 1845), p. 167. Several fool coins are reproduced and discussed on pp. 164–67. Others may be seen in [Jean Bénigne Lucotte] du Tilliot, *Mémoires pour sevir à l'histoire de la fête des foux* (Lausanne and Geneva: M.-M. Bousquet, 1751), title page and Plates 3, 11, and 12.

5. For the Harlequin playlet see Cyril W. Beaumont, *A History of Harlequin* (London: C. W. Beaumont, 1926), pp. 65–68. The "Mother of Fools," the head of the fool society at Dijon, was a man; see Carl Friedrich Flögel, *Die Geschichte des Groteskekomischen* (Liegnitz: Siegert, 1788), pp. 284–87. In various parts of England there was a festival of the "Fool Plough" which in the north of the country was accompanied by sword dancers, musicians, the fool, and the "Bessy," a man in grotesque woman's clothing. In eastern Yorkshire the plough was dragged by a group of youths headed by "Mab and his wife," a clown and a man in female garb; see *Funk and Wagnalls Standard Dictionary of Folklore, Mythology, and Legend*, ed. Maria Leach (New York: Funk & Wagnalls, 1949), I. 410, entry under "Fool Plough, Fond Plough, or Fond Pleeaf."

6. M. Willson Disher, *Clowns and Pantomimes* (London: Constable, 1923), p. 195.

7. Thelma Niklaus, *Harlequin* (New York: G. Braziller, 1956), pp. 49–51.

8. W. B. Yeats took up this familiar motif in an early poem, "The Cap and Bells," (*The Collected Poems* [New York: Macmillan, 1956], pp. 62 f.), which is based on a dream. The poem begins:

> The jester walked in the garden:
> The garden had fallen still;
> He bade his soul rise upward
> And stand on her window-sill.

> It rose in a straight blue garment,
> When owls began to call:
> It had grown wise-tongued by thinking
> Of a quiet and light footfall;

> But the young queen would not listen;
> She rose in her pale night-gown;
> She drew in the heavy casement
> And pushed the latches down.

The jester sends her his cap and bells and dies; his heart and soul then reach her (it is not clear how), and she accepts them as she could not accept the whole of himself as a living fool. On the dramatic level implied in Yeats's poem, the fool's pure yearning is for the woman already possessed by the hero or king or meant for one of them.

In Michel de Ghelderode's play, *Escurial*, the same kind of hopeless passion takes a less pure form, as the jester becomes the lover of the queen and is then killed by the cuckolded king (*The Modern Theatre*, ed. Eric Bentley [Garden City, N.Y.: Doubleday Anchor, 1957], V, 174–78).

9. Often the fool both does and does not "get the girl." He may remain committed at least as much to his folly and to the fool show as to her, though he approaches her, and even though his love for her is requited. In many of Buster Keaton's films, for example, Keaton earns the right to be near the desirable girl, as though he were moving toward marriage with her, while inwardly maintaining distance from her. At the close of *Go West* (1925) he asks, as a reward, for the cow he loves rather than for the cattle-rancher's daughter; they all drive off in an automobile, the old father and the girl in the front seat, Keaton and the cow in the rear. And at the close of *The General* (1926) Keaton, having been made an army officer, sits with his girl on the piston of his locomotive and kisses her as he returns the salutes of soldiers going to the washhouse. This combination of activities and his position at the side of the locomotive he loves (as he had loved the cow in *Go West*) express a momentary balance of divergent allegiances. If Keaton were to seclude

himself with the girl, he would narrow his contact with unstructured potentialities and she would cease to be the catalyst leading him to heights of accomplishment. His openness to the world, his "poly-adjustment," as J.-P. Lebel has called it (*Buster Keaton* [London: A. Zwemmer, 1967], p. 101), and his transcendence of the normal are essential to his comic character and are at the same time the perfect expression of his love. This transcendence is achieved through an increase in concentration, a more precise delineation of character; and though the girl may be *femme inspiratrice,* she is finally subservient to the gag in which he makes a show of his foolish nature.

10. Among these critics are Alois L. Brandl, Arthur Thomas Quiller-Couch, and Edith Sitwell. The point is discussed in the Arden *King Lear,* ed. Kenneth Muir (Cambridge, Mass.: Harvard University Press, 1959), in a note on p. 217.

## Chapter 11

1. Samuel Taylor Coleridge, in *Coleridge's Shakespearean Criticism,* ed. T. M. Raysor (Cambridge, Mass.: Harvard University Press, 1931), II, 212; Francis Fergusson, *The Idea of a Theater* (Garden City, N.Y.: Doubleday Anchor, 1953); Geoffrey Bush, *Shakespeare and the Natural Condition* (Cambridge, Mass.: Harvard University Press, 1956); L. G. Salingar, "The Elizabethan Literary Renaissance," in Boris Ford (ed.), *The Age of Shakespeare* (Harmondsworth: Penguin Books, 1955), pp. 88–89; Harry Levin, *The Question of Hamlet* (New York: Oxford, 1959), pp. 121–28.

2. Bush, *Shakespeare and the Natural Condition,* p. 100.

3. *The Idea of a Theater,* p. 112.

4. *Ibid.,* p. 125.

5. *Ibid.,* p. 134.

6. Sigmund Freud, "The Motives of Jokes—Jokes as a Social Process," in *Jokes and Their Relation to the Unconscious,* trans. James Strachey, *Complete Psychological Works* (London: Hogarth Press and the Institute of Psycho-Analysis, 1960), VIII, 140–58.

7. *The Idea of a Theater,* p. 126.

8. *Ibid.,* p. 127.

9. Erica Tietze-Conrat, *Dwarfs and Jesters in Art* (New York: Phaidon, 1957), pp. 50 and 105. On the ambiguous interplay between death and the fool in literature before Shakespeare see Barbara Swain, *Fools and Folly* (New York: Columbia University Press, 1932), pp. 42 ff. Salingar sees Death as the "supreme 'antic'" in *Hamlet (The Age of Shakespeare,* pp. 88–89). William Empson turns his attention briefly to "the business of the macabre, where you make a clown out of death." He observes that "Death in the Holbein Dance of Death, a skeleton still skinny, is often an elegant and charming small figure whose wasp waist gives him a certain mixed-sex quality, and though we are to think otherwise he conceives himself as poking fun; he is seen at his best when piping to an idiot clown and leading him

on, presumably to some precipice, treating this great coy figure with so gay and sympathetic an admiration that the picture stays in one's mind chiefly as a love scene" (*Some Versions of Pastoral* [Norfolk, Conn.: New Directions, 1950], p. 14).

10. *Shakespeare's Royal Self* (New York: G. P. Putnam, 1966), p. 174.

## Chapter 13

1. Arden *King Lear,* ed. Kenneth Muir (Cambridge, Mass.: Harvard University Press, 1959), p. 9.

2. Charles H. Long, "Creation from Nothing," *Alpha: The Myths of Creation* (New York: G. Braziller, 1963), pp. 146 ff.

3. Gérard van Rijnberk, *Le Tarot: Histoire, iconographie, ésotérisme* (Lyon: Paul Derain, 1947), p. 262.

4. Charles Williams, *The Greater Trumps* (New York: Pellegrini & Cudahy, 1950), p. 227.

5. James Kirsch says rightly about Lear's "Nothing will come of nothing": "The opposite of course is true. Everything comes of nothing once it is taken in a non-rational, non-qualitative sense ('nothing' being identical with the unconscious in the modern sense)" (*Shakespeare's Royal Self* [New York: G. P. Putnam, 1966], p. 192). Kirsch relates this "nothing" to the Cabbalistic concept of *En Sof,* to "the origin of everything," in S. Friedlaender's *Schöpferische Indifferenz* (Munich: E. Reinhardt, 1926), and to Hegel's "the quality of utter indistinguishableness."

6. John F. Danby, "The Fool and Handy-Dandy," *Shakespeare's Doctrine of Nature* (London: Faber & Faber, 1961), pp. 102–13.

7. Welsford, *The Fool,* p. 265.

8. *Shakespeare Our Contemporary,* trans. Boleslaw Taborski (Garden City, N.Y.: Doubleday, 1964), pp. 100 f.

9. *The Meaning of Shakespeare* (Chicago: University of Chicago Press, 1951), p. 548.

## Chapter 14

1. Carl Friedrich Flögel, *Geschichte des Groteskekomischen* (Liegnitz: Siegert, 1788), pp. 350–52. (Flögel gives, as his source, Stanislaus Sarnicius, "Annales Polonici," appended to Joannes Dlugossius, *Historia Polonica,* Vol. II.)

2. The quickening of social life consists partly of the *participation mentale* that results when nonsense lowers the level of consciousness and causes us to laugh; a person's individuality is shown partly in how he laughs, what he laughs at, and what he does to make others laugh. Laughter thus reflects the ambiguity between collective and personal elements of behavior. This ambiguity is also reflected in various ways in the fool show. The appearance and behavior of a fool actor may include highly collective traits, and his character may, nonetheless, be highly individual. The makeup of a circus clown is, for example, stylized, and though the

species "clown" is more striking in the over-all effect of his appearance than is his personality, each clown's makeup is his alone, his ownership of it being guaranteed by an unwritten patent respected among circus performers.

3. In Chapter XLIX ("The Hyena"), Herman Melville, *Moby-Dick,* ed. Charles Feidelson, Jr. (Indianapolis: Bobbs-Merrill, 1964), p. 302.

4. Similar ideas have been taken up by writers concerned primarily with theological problems. Raymond J. Nogar, for example, speaks of the "divine madness of the revelation" and claims that "Christ reveals Himself as the eccentric" (rather than as the principle of Teilhard de Chardin's concentric "Christophere") (*The Lord of the Absurd* [New York: Herder & Herder, 1966], pp. 151 and 124). In opposing the tendency to attribute too much orderliness to the world, Nogar writes, "No one can contemplate the beak of the Brazilian caw-caw . . . without concluding that the Creator is a clown" (*ibid.,* p. 143). Nogar's main purpose is to contend that God is not so much order as being, which maintains the world with all its messiness and senselessness. In the interests of this purpose he alludes to God's folly, but he does so without really giving more weight to the metaphor than do the fiction-writers I have mentioned. The theologian Harvey Cox also employed this conceit in a lecture on "Christ the Harlequin" (delivered in March, 1968, at Harvard University as one of the William Belden Noble Lectures).

5. In Chapter XXXIII of *A Passage to India* (New York: Harcourt, Brace, 1924), p. 289, E. M. Forster remarks, for the moment adopting the Indian point of view, that "There is fun in heaven. God can play practical jokes upon Himself, draw chairs away from beneath His own posteriors, set His own turbans on fire, and steal His own petticoats when He bathes. By sacrificing good taste, this worship achieved what Christianity has shirked: the inclusion of merriment. All spirit as well as all matter must participate in salvation, and if practical jokes are banned, the circle is incomplete."

6. "Flaccus" ("In Flaccum"), 37–39, in *Philo,* with an English translation by F. H. Colson (Loeb Classical Library) (Cambridge, Mass.: Harvard University Press, 1960), IX, 322–23.

7. John Doran, *The History of Court Fools* (London: Richard Bentley, 1858), pp. 54–55.

8. See Robert Curtius, "Jest and Earnest in Medieval Literature," *European Literature and the Latin Middle Ages* (New York and Evanston: Harper & Row [Harper Torchbooks], 1963), pp. 417–35, and V. A. Kolve, "Religious Laughter," *The Play Called Corpus Christi* (Stanford, Calif.: Stanford University Press, 1966), pp. 124–44. Christianity inherited the classical notion that only what is serious is dignified; St. Paul forbade "foolish talking" and "jesting" (Eph. 5:4), and St. John Chrysostom argued that Christ never laughed. Still, Petrus Cantor defended laughter by saying that it belonged to human nature, which was created by God, and the official position of the Church concerning laughter remained open. Medieval buffoonery in religius contexts was nurtured by traditions that held the Fall to be the result of clownlike stupidity, and laughter at it was felt to express sanity and

even holiness. This attitude was, of course, thought to be justified by Scripture. A case in point is the long-standing use, mentioned in Chapter 3, of Eccles. 1:15 (Vulgate), *Et Stultorum infinitus est numerus,* "The number of fools is infinite," for burlesque and the glorification of folly.

9. Robert H. Goldsmith, *Wise Fools in Shakespeare* (East Lansing: Michigan State University Press, 1955), pp. 11–12. (Erasmus develops the Platonic conceit at length in "Sileni Alcibiadis.") The conceit is basic to Goldsmith's interpretation of folly in Shakespeare's plays. Lear's Fool is always an interesting case in point in any view of folly; for Goldsmith "He is the supremely wise fool who expresses in his heartfelt devotion to Cordelia and to his king the Christian virtues of patience, humility and love" (p. 67). The same intellectual and moralistic emphasis is made by Enid Welsford, to whom Lear's Fool is "the sage-fool who sees the truth . . . whose role has even more *intellectual* than emotional significance . . . , [who is] the disinterested truth-teller, the 'punctum indifferens' of the play" (*The Fool,* pp. 256 and 258).

10. Walter Nigg, *Der christliche Narr* (Zurich and Stuttgart: Artemis, 1956), pp. 76–77.

11. Herbert Thurston and Donald Attwater (eds.), *Butler's Lives of the Saints* (New York: J. P. Kenedy, 1956), III, 587–91.

12. Daisetz T. Suzuki, *Zen and Japanese Culture* (New York: Pantheon, 1959), p. 369.

13. Doran, *The History of Court Fools,* p. 71.

14. Suzuki, *Essays in Zen Buddhism, First Series* (New York: Rider, 1949), p. 208.

15. Suzuki, *The Zen Doctrine of No-Mind* (New York: Rider, 1949), pp. 29–30.

16. *The Fool,* pp. 324–25.

# Index

For dramatic and fictional characters see titles of the works in which they appear.

# Index

# Index

# Index

# Index

# Index

# Index

The text of this book was composed in eleven-point Granjon, two points leaded. The Granjon face was designed for the linotype by G. W. Jones and was named for Robert Granjon, a great French type founder and printer of the sixteenth century. Actually, however, it bears no relation to any face that Granjon cut, being based chiefly on a group of faces that can safely be attributed to Claude Garamond, the most notable type designer of his time, who died in Paris in 1561. Granjon bears a greater resemblance to Garamond's own types than do any of the various faces that are now given the name of Garamond.

The book was composed and printed by Kingsport Press, Inc., of Kingsport, Tennessee. The paper is Warren Olde Style, manufactured by the S. D. Warren Company, of Boston. Typography and binding design are by Paul Randall Mize.